Interaction in the Language Curriculum

APPLIED LINGUISTICS AND LANGUAGE STUDY

General Editor
Professor Christopher N. Candlin, Macquarie University

For a complete list of books in this series see pages ix–x.

Interaction in the Language Curriculum

Awareness, autonomy and authenticity

Leo van Lier

LONGMAN

London and New York

Addison Wesley Longman Limited
Edinburgh Gate, Harlow,
Essex CM20 2JE, England
and Associated Companies throughout the world.

*Published in the United States of America
by Addison Wesley Longman Inc., New York.*

First published 1996
Second impression 1997

ISBN 0 582 248795 PPR

British Library Cataloguing-in-Publication Data

A catalogue record for this book is
available from the British Library

Library of Congress Cataloging-in-Publication Data

Van Lier, Leo.
    Interaction in the language curriculum : awareness, autonomy, and
    authenticity / Leo van Lier.
        p.   cm. — (Applied linguistics and language study)
    Includes bibliographical references and index.
    ISBN 0–582–24879–5
    1. Language and languages—Study and teaching.   I. Title.
    II. Series.
P51.V36   1996
418'.007—dc20   95–39097
                                                            CIP

Set by 8 in 10/12 pt Ehrhardt
Produced through Longman Malaysia, PA

Contents

Author's Preface

This is a book for language educators. It is the report of an ongoing project which has been evolving for the past half dozen years or so, and to which I am continually making changes. The reader should not see it as a finished product, therefore, but rather as a snapshot of work in progress, an illustration of an open-ended process that can and should have no closure.

The book is intended as a philosophical approach to the language curriculum, as an attempt to resolve dichotomies such as knowledge and values, theory and practice, research and teaching, and an illustration of what happens when we think consistently in process rather than product terms. At the same time I have not taken any of the common meanings of terms such as theory, practice, research, curriculum, and learning as given, but tried to find new meanings for them that fit new ways of thinking, and achieve terminological integrity throughout. I have not gone far enough in all these matters, but I hope I have made some useful notes in the margin of our ideals.

I hope that the reader will find the book practical as well as theoretical, down-to-earth as well as philosophical, in fact, I hope that it will not fit in any of the usual pigeon holes. Most of all I hope that it will encourage readers to think for themselves and to construct their own lifelong project of language education. Although I have done my best to be as clear and non-technical as possible, there are places where I have felt it necessary to provide some more theoretical backup, and these sections have been set off from the main body of the text by indentation, spacing and a vertical line in the left margin. The reader is of course free to skip such passages, though I feel they are important for the argument they support.

As always, a number of people have assisted in the development of this book, first of all Chris Candlin, whose support and vision have been crucial, and secondly several generations of students at the Monterey Institute of International Studies, who must at times have wished that the AAA was out of the way and done with. Well, it is out of the way now, though I hope it is not quite yet done with. Even so, several of them generously read parts of earlier incarnations and made useful comments. I would particularly like to thank Kim Marie Cole, Eve Connell (who also transcribed some of the classroom data), Paul Magnuson, Stephanie Stauffer, Troy Titterington, and Carol Woods.

Conversations with several colleagues, especially Kathi Bailey, Josep María Cots, Rod Ellis, Celia Roberts, and Ruth Larimer, have also helped to clarify many points, though I may have failed to profit fully from all their suggestions.

Aída, Jan and Marcus will be almost as pleased as I am that the book is finally finished. My thanks to them for their support and patience.

Was der Leser auch kann, das überlass dem Leser. (What the reader can do, leave that to the reader.)

(Ludwig Wittgenstein, 1980b:77, *Vermischte Bemerkungen*. Frankfurt: Suhrkamp)

APPLIED LINGUISTICS AND LANGUAGE STUDY

General Editor
Professor Christopher N. Candlin, Macquarie University

Error Analysis
Perspectives on second
language acquisition
JACK C. RICHARDS (ED.)

Stylistics and the Teaching of
Literature
HENRY WIDDOWSON

Language Tests at School
A pragmatic approach
JOHN W. OLLER JNR
Contrastive Analysis
CARL JAMES

Language and Communication
JACK R. RICHARDS AND
RICHARD W. SCHMIDT (EDS)

Learning to Write: First Language/
Second Language
AVIVA FREDMAN, IAN PRINGLE
AND JANIC YALDEN (EDS)

Strategies in Interlanguage
Communication
CLAUS FAERCH AND
GABRIELE KASPER (EDS)

Reading in a Foreign Language
J. CHARLES ALDERSON AND
A.H. URQUHART (EDS)

An Introduction to Discourse Analysis
New edition
MALCOLM COULTHARD

Computers in English Language
Teaching and Research
GEOFFREY LEECH AND
CHRISTOPHER N. CANDLIN
(EDS)

Language Awareness in the
Classroom
CARL JAMES AND
PETER GARRETT

Bilingualism in Education
Aspects of theory, research and practice
JIM CUMMINS AND
MERRILL SWAIN

Second Language Grammar:
Learning and Teaching
WILLIAM E. RUTHERFORD

The Classroom and the Language
Learner
Ethnography and second-language
classroom research
LEO VAN LIER

Vocabulanly and Language Teaching
RONALD CARTER AND MICHAEL
McCARTHY (EDS)

Observation in the Language Classroom
DICK ALLWRIGHT

Listening to Spoken English
Second Edition
GILLIAN BROWN

Listening in Language Learning
MICHAEL ROST

An Introduction to Second Language
Acquisition Research
DIANE LARSEN-FREEMAN AND
MICHAEL H. LONG

Language and Discrimination
A study of communication in
multi-ethnic workplaces
CELIA ROBERTS, TOM JUPP AND
EVELYN DAVIES

Translation and Translating:
Theory and Practice
ROGER T. BELL

Process and Experience in the
Language Classroom
MICHAEL LEGUTKE AND
HOWARD THOMAS

Rediscovering Interlanguage
LARRY SELINKER

Language as Discourse:
Perspectives for Language Teaching
MICHAEL McCARTHY
AND RONALD CARTER

Second Language Learning:
Theoretical Foundations
M.A. SHARWOOD SMITH

Analysing Genre:
Language Use in Professional Settings
V.K. BHATIA

From Testing to Assessment:
*English as an International
Language*
CLIFFORD HILL AND
KATE PARRY (EDS)

Interaction in the Language
Curriculum
*Awareness, Autonomy and
Authenticity*
LEO VAN LIER

Transcription conventions:

T	Teacher (unless otherwise noted)
L, L1, L2, etc.	Individual learners, unless name is given
LL	Several learners together
...	A pause of roughly one second; different numbers of dots indicate shorter or longer pauses
?	rising intonation on the preceding segment
so:::	colons indicate lengthening of the preceding sound
(who)	single brackets indicate unclear or probable item
((laughter))	double brackets indicate comment on transcript or context
[hm ..	superscripted square bracket indicates onset of overlap or back channel
[si:m]	square brackets indicate phonetic transcription or approximation
=	indicates a turn which continues below, at the next = symbol; usually the intervening line contains brief back channels or comments.

1 The AAA curriculum

Introduction

The curriculum outlined in this book grew out of an action research project I conducted a few years ago. The project started when, after having taught linguistics and second language acquisition to graduate students for a number of years, a nagging concern could no longer be put aside. This concern is probably quite familiar to most fellow-teacher educators, since it relates to a central problem in graduate programs: the relationship (or lack thereof) between theoretical course content and the practical issues and exigencies of everyday language teaching. Teachers often ask: 'How does this relate to classroom teaching?' and: 'What's the use of all this theory?' Sometimes an answer may be available, other times we may have to reply with an evasive: 'Theoretical knowledge is part of being a professional teacher.' The latter sounds a bit like 'We know what's good for you,' an admonition which, in my experience as a parent, is not terribly effective.

The action research project consisted of teaching a beginning ESL grammar class[1] in order to investigate the following question:

Standing with both feet firmly planted on the classroom floor, what are the theoretical issues in linguistics, education, and other fields, that are relevant, here and now, to the teaching job and the learning job?

Since I was also teaching introductory linguistics and second language acquisition at that time, I consciously tried to investigate the issue of relevance in both directions:

(a) What part of the academic content matter is relevant to the ESL class?
(b) What part of the ESL class is relevant to the academic content matter?

In some ways the research was a failure. I found that, in the midst of the complex demands of classroom practice, I had little time to worry about, say, universal grammar, parameter setting, or the interface hypothesis. In that sense, SLA researchers and other theoreticians are surely correct when they say that much of their work may not have direct pedagogical implications or applications. Does that mean that such kinds of research and theories can be ignored by language teaching practitioners? I would, most emphatically, reject such a conclusion as being extremely short-sighted. I agree with Halliday, when he says:

> . . . we should beware of thinking that every subject exists simply to serve the needs of education. There is a tendency for educators to demand an immediate pay-off: if we can't apply these ideas directly here and now in our teaching, then we don't want anything to do with them. This attitude passes for a healthy pragmatism: we're practical people with a job to do, no time for the frills. In fact it is simply mental laziness – a refusal to inquire into things that may not have any immediate and obvious applications, but which for this very reason may have a deeper significance in the long run. Most of linguistics is not classroom stuff; but it is there behind the lines, underlying our classroom practices, and our ideas about children, and about learning and reality. (Halliday 1982: 15)

Teachers who hope, in these pages, to find advocacy for omitting various theories of SLA, linguistics, or education (among others) from graduate programs or inservice courses, will be disappointed. There are many important ways in which theoretical knowledge can be useful other than those dictated by immediate applicability. I cannot specify these ways in a general sense, since I believe that every professional must labor to dis-cover such relevance. My action research did not yield any direct clues, but that does not mean much. Intangibles are often more influential than tangibles. If you can't see it, that doesn't mean it isn't there. If you can't count it, that doesn't mean it doesn't count.

However, there are some ways in which my action research did turn up fruitful results. Several avenues of research became prominent that had hitherto rather taken a back seat in my teacher development activ-ities, as I expect they have in the work of others as well. These avenues, pointing to such concepts as awareness, attention, intrinsic motivation, self-regulation, and pedagogical (inter)action, gradually suggested the outlines of a way of theorizing, from the perspective of the language classroom, that deserved to be brought into focus as a guiding metaphor for practicing teachers. Once in focus, and in progress, this way of theor-izing itself may lead to a need to become familiar with less immediately applicable theories in cognitive science, linguistics, and other areas. What the work presented here aims to do, in other words, is to put the horse of professional awareness before the cart of theoretical subject matter.

The ideas put forward in this book are not intended as a theory, in the sense of an organized body of knowledge, or a depository of research findings and hypotheses. Rather, the book treats theory, research, and practice as an essential unity in the process of doing curriculum (there should be a verb associated with curriculum: 'curriculizing,' perhaps).

Theorizing, researching, and practicing are thus inseparable ingredients in the professional conduct of a language educator. Rather than speaking of a new theory, or a new approach or method, I will use the term *language education curriculum*, defining curriculum in a *holistic* and *process* sense. It is holistic in the sense that every part and every action must be motivated by and understood in relation to all other parts and actions, in an integrative way; it is process-oriented in the sense that pedagogical interaction is motivated by our understanding of learning rather than by a list of desired competencies, test scores, or other products. The setting of goals and objectives, and the construction and assessment of achievement, are themselves integral parts of the curriculum process, rather than pre-established constraints that are imposed on it from the outside.

Lawrence Stenhouse once said that the curriculum has to be brought into the room 'on a porter's barrow' (Rudduck & Hopkins 1985: 67). A curriculum, in this view, is a systematic collection of accumulated knowledge and experience, from a multitude of sources, that guides classroom practice. Stenhouse envisaged that the porter's barrow contained boxes of books, collections of charts and pictures, films and tapes, and so on.

The language curriculum that I will conceptualize in this book is, like Stenhouse's example, drawn from a variety of disciplines and classroom worlds. This does not mean that it is a collection of objects to be delivered to educational recipients, but rather a process of assisting learning informed by a background of knowledge and experience which I try to make as rich and varied as I can. Let me just briefly sketch the main ingredients (without going into detail just yet), so that the reader will know where we are going.[2] In the pages that follow I will address the following points, which will be elaborated in detail in subsequent chapters:

1. three foundational principles
2. relationships between theory, research, and practice
3. theory of learning
4. theory of curriculum and instruction
5. the centrality of interaction

The curriculum is based on a triad of foundational principles or 'constants' which themselves cannot be further reduced or grounded, since they constitute what I consider essential properties of the educational enterprise. These principles, *awareness*, *autonomy*, and *authenticity*, or AAA for short, are amalgams of knowledge and values, or in other words, they are a unity of epistemological and axiological beliefs. Although I would not wish to claim that they are universal, valid for everyone in any cultural or temporal context, they represent, I suggest, a fair consensus of our current intellectual knowledge and moral aspirations as language educators. However, rather than suggesting that all readers adopt my principles as a canon for the construction of their own curriculum, I suggest that they be used as merely an example for the construction of one's own set of foundational principles. The first and most crucial step of developing a curriculum is the articulation of the knowledge and values upon which it is founded. And in order to avoid the seductive comfort of fads and bandwagons, it is preferable to articulate one's own principles than to take over someone else's uncritically.

I have modeled my foundational principles on the Peircean concepts of firstness, secondness, and thirdness, together forming what he called a *genuine triad*, in which each member can only be explained in relation to the other two. These connections will be discussed in a number of places in the book. Since they are based not only on what we know – or think we know – about the nature of language learning, but also on the ethical basis, the *purpose* of our work, the AAA curriculum cannot be the application of rational or utilitarian strategies or techniques to achieve predetermined outcomes or objectives. Instead, it has to grow from an understanding of our learners and what they want to achieve.

Next, the concepts of theory, practice, and research, and their dynamic interrelationships, are reexamined, redefined, and reconstructed to allow for the development of an *educational theory of practice*, taking guidance from the work of Bourdieu, Freire, Foucault, inter alia. Notions such as action research, teacher research, and pedagogical thoughtfulness, familiar to many educators from the work of Lawrence Stenhouse, Stephen Kemmis, Ken Zeichner, Max van Manen, and many others, are anchored in and motivated by this theory of practice, and are therefore integral to the language curriculum and to teacher development for the language curriculum.

As mentioned above, any curriculum must be based on our knowledge of the learning process and the learning context, as well as on our values and purposes (including those of the teacher, student, parent, and any other stakeholder). The key to responsible (and effective) pedagogical interaction is *understanding the learner* (which includes understanding learning), and a theory of learning is therefore needed to underpin the development of strategies for pedagogical interaction. The theory of learning which informs the AAA curriculum is based on the developmental psychology of Vygotsky, in which social interaction is seen as the key to learning, and in which language and cognition are interdependent processes. Vygotsky's central notion of the zone of proximal development (ZPD) can be profitably related to Bruner's process of scaffolding, as well as to Piaget's 'grasp of consciousness,' and the growth of self-determination underlying work on intrinsic motivation by Deci and colleagues, on achievement motivation by Heckhausen and others, and autotelic learning as described by Csikszentmihalyi.

Finally, the importance of interaction in language education cannot just be taken for granted, but the interaction itself must be meticulously described and understood. For one thing, there are many ways of interacting, and it is safe to assume that some will be more beneficial to learning than others. Furthermore, the relations between wider social processes and conditions (such as power and control) and social interaction for learning need to be investigated. Thirdly, interpersonal language use must work in tandem with innately constrained processes of language development which, though they are as yet ill understood, undoubtedly exert a strong influence on all social and academic development.

For these reasons, as well as for others which will undoubtedly come to light, interaction is the most important element of the curriculum, and this is manifested in several different ways. First of all, the study of interaction is a major focus of teacher research, as well as a key element in teacher development. That is, improvements and innovations in professional practices require a close monitoring of interactional work and systematic attempts at changing it in desired directions. For this research, conversation analysis and the microsociological work of Goffman provide crucial tools and insights. Secondly, learning tasks must be designed so as to promote the types of interaction which our research identifies as providing optimal opportunities for learning. Thirdly, and perhaps most importantly, the concept of interaction itself – in all its manifestations – must be illuminated so as to avoid a narrow definition leading to superficial communication or even pseudo-communication.

The three foundational principles: *Awareness, Autonomy,* and *Authenticity,* or AAA for short,[3] allow language education to unfold in a regulated yet creative manner, within a framework of individual and social *constraints* and *resources.* Unlike most curricula and learning theories, the AAA curriculum is explicitly grounded not only in knowledge but in human values as well. The general curricular framework that is drawn up on this basis can, like any other, be realized in a wide variety of practical *syllabuses,* by which I mean flexible specifications and provisions of means for instructional action. Although this book is concerned with the curriculum rather than any specific syllabus, practical examples of and suggestions for classroom work will be given throughout the book. Indeed, this is inevitable since I set out to construct a language curriculum *based on classroom experience,* although bearing in mind the many relations that exist between the classroom and the wider social and political context.

The AAA curriculum presented in this book is relevant to all branches of language education, native language (e.g. literacy, grammar composition), second language, and foreign language. In addition, it makes specific proposals for a language policy *across the curriculum.* However, given my own interests and experiences as an educational linguist and a teacher educator, most classroom illustrations are taken from second and foreign language classrooms, and classrooms with language minority students. In spite of that explicit bias, I try to ensure that it will be possible for language educators in other areas to see the relevance of all the points under discussion. My aim is to draw together what all language educators share in terms of professional concerns and options, regardless of the many differences which make every setting, classroom, and pedagogical encounter unique.

It will not take the reader long to realize that most, if not all, of the ideas put forward in the coming chapters are familiar to the professional educator in one form or another. I do not pretend to have discovered any new educational or pedagogical facts or concepts. What I plan to do is to go on a new journey through a well-known and well-traveled landscape, plotting my own map as I travel, while consulting all the other maps that already exist. The journey will show language education in a new light, even though its components, if inspected one by one, may reveal things we have always known.

The purpose of a curriculum is to guide the processes of teaching and learning. It can do this in quite explicit, controlling ways, or in more subtle, flexible ways. In the former case, external control may cause curriculum and pedagogical needs to drift apart, and a situation similar to Peddiwell's 'saber-tooth curriculum' (1939) arises. In this satirical tale of Paleolithic times, the curriculum consisted of 'tiger-scaring, fish-grabbing, and horse-clubbing,' skills that were essential for survival in those days. However, Paleolithic pedagogues continued to teach these skills even when, due to various environmental changes, there were no more tigers to scare, no fish to grab, and no woolly horses to club. In that changed situation, when a radical suggested that antelope-snaring should replace the now obsolete horse-clubbing, the wise old men said, smiling most kindly:

> We don't teach horse-clubbing to club horses; we teach it to develop a
> generalized strength in the learner which he can never get from so prosaic and
> specialized a thing as antelope-snare-setting. (Peddiwell 1939: 43)

This argument, of course, reminds us of such present-day conundrums as the wisdom or folly of allowing calculators in math lessons, spelling and grammar checkers on computers, or the utility of grammar diagrams in English lessons (though, so far as I know, sentence-diagramming has never been quite as essential for survival as fish-grabbing may once have been). More especially, the 'saber-tooth' example should warn against the current fashion of competency-based curricula, in which techniques equal capacity.

The curriculum proposed in this book will, I hope, fare better than the 'saber-tooth' curriculum, because it addresses basic human principles of language education that remain constant however much the practical demands of language use may change. This is so because they are not simply based on particular pieces of content, but rather on what, to the best of our current knowledge, we know about learning, and even more importantly, what we (and I hope I am right in assuming a high degree of consensus here!) agree are basic human values we wish to strive for.

The book is planned in the following way. First, in the remainder of this chapter, I define the basic concepts that recur as underlying themes throughout the book, terms such as *principle*, *choice*, *curriculum*, *constraints*, and *resources*. In the second chapter I look at the relationships between theory, research and practice, and propose a new way of theorizing: the *theory of practice*, based on the work of the French sociologist Pierre Bourdieu. Chapters 3–6 address the *learning theory* that supports the AAA curriculum. Particularly important notions that will be explored are language awareness, motivation and authenticity. In the next section of the book, in chapters 7 and 8, the interaction in classrooms will be examined in detail. The constructs of *contingency* and *scaffolding* form the basic phenomenological core of the AAA curriculum, since they open up the processes of learning as they occur between teachers and students in the classroom. Finally, chapter 9 suggests how teacher research and professional development that is compatible with the AAA curriculum can be carried out.

Strategies and prescriptions

According to Widdowson (1990: 7), 'language teaching can be seen as a principled problem-solving activity: a kind of operational research which works out solutions to its own local problems.' The primary researchers in this endeavor are, it seems reasonable to propose, the teachers. Since they do not work in a vacuum, teachers are in different ways assisted in their operational research of finding solutions to problems. In some cases, this assistance is voluntarily chosen or secured by the teacher him or herself. In other cases, however, the assistance is provided – or imposed – by agencies (political, institutional, social, commercial, etc.) that have a stake in the teaching/learning process, and therefore may exert some form of control. This control may be manifested in a number of different ways, some overt and visible, others tacit and invisible.

We should note that in the above paragraph I used the words *assistance* and *control*, suggesting that there is perhaps some connection between these two terms, even though in some ways they would seem to be contradictory. The reader may reflect on this, and consider how in certain circumstances, in fact in many different ways, *helping* and *controlling* might be one and the same thing. Let us elaborate a little on this idea.

It is clear that a teacher's job is made easier by such auxiliary packages as curricular frameworks produced by education agencies, textbook series, and resource books of strategies and techniques. At the same time, however, these auxiliary packages exert influence over what is actually done in the classroom, sometimes so much so that they appear to be obstacles rather than facilitators. It is useful to keep in mind the intricate interplay between controlling and helping or, to use Giddens' (1984) terminology, between *constraints* and *resources*, since it is a theme that will recur frequently in this book. We might compare the dynamism of constraints and resources with the rules of a game: the rules of chess say that you can only move a knight in such and such a way, and a bishop in other specific ways. This certainly constrains you as a player, it means that you cannot do what you want, at least not if you want to remain inside the game. However, this very rigidity in the rules allows the game to take place at all, so that we must draw the conclusion that constraints and resources depend on each other, and the game depends on both of them in equal measure.

Just like the chess game, the educational 'game' must also be a dynamic interplay between constraints and resources. If there is excessive control, and we are told exactly what to do and when to do it, then education ceases to be education. If, on the other hand, we reject all constraints, then education will likewise be impossible, since it will degenerate into chaos. A key issue for teacher research is to distinguish between constraints intrinsic to the teaching/learning setting, and artificial constraints which a particular system or institution enforces on the teaching/learning setting. The former are true constraints which, in Giddens's sense, *direct* activities, and are empowering, the latter merely *control*, and are disempowering. An excess of artificial constraints may make teachers feel that their authority is being eroded.

The process curriculum consists of exploring, articulating, examining, and developing the constraints and resources in the educational setting, from the perspective of clear principles which guide the search, or rather, the research. This moves the process curriculum one step beyond Widdowson's problem-solving research. We are not just interested in finding our problems and then finding ways of solving them one after the other, rather, we move beyond problem-solving to problem-*posing*, in the sense advocated by Paulo Freire and other critical educators. We critically examine our educational reality and, keeping our principles firmly in mind, we determine what constraints and resources exist in the setting, and are then able to develop strategies for action.[4]

The teacher does not enter the classroom with an empty head and an empty bag. Teaching and learning materials are necessary, and planning lessons is an indispensable aspect of the teacher's craft (although learners can share in the responsibility of both the collection of materials and the planning of lessons, as I shall illustrate in later chapters). As true professionals, teachers articulate their principles so that they can make *principled choices* in their lessons. In addition, *reflection* on the classroom problems and processes that they encounter every day allow them to develop *pedagogical tact* (van Manen 1991) in dealing with the constant unpredictable challenges of teaching. If, as I shall argue later in this book, successful teaching is a blend of planning and improvization, teachers must develop the ability to make principled decisions and choices in a wide range of pedagogical activities, ranging from the choice of materials to the conduct of activities in lessons. By the same token, they must be held *responsible* and *accountable* for those choices, and this has wide-ranging implications for teacher education.

The AAA curriculum wants to open up the choices for teachers and students by explicitly formulating educational principles (the *sine qua non* being that the AAA principles are universally acceptable), and proposing strategies for putting those principles into practice. It rejects narrowing down the options by prescribing techniques or specifying solutions. The curriculum is designed to be a *liberating* force, encouraging every teacher to create his or her own theory of practice. I have tried to keep the book readable and relatively jargon-free, although the reader may encounter passages that are dense and complex. At such times I have found it necessary to establish solid theoretical foundations and cross-disciplinary connections to avoid possible charges of scientific tourism. The reader is of course free to skip such passages.

I now turn to a preliminary discussion of the basic constructs underlying the AAA curriculum, beginning with the basic pedagogical values expressed in the three principles I have proposed.

Principles

Where do principles come from? In the imperfect world in which we live, they may come from many quarters, and they are not always the sorts of principles that can provide lasting guidance for our actions. In the first place, surrogate principles may be derived from packaged solutions offered in inservice courses and workshops: the standardized lesson format, the golden rules neatly laid out and listed, the handbook which claims to hold all the solutions, the fail-safe and foolproof recipes, in short, all the one-size-fits-all gimmicks and fads promoted by often well-meaning educationists and writers. There is much advice around that is not useful, though we may not find today the kind of convenient culprit H.L. Mencken found in Teachers College Columbia, which in 1940 he accused of having 'done more harm in the United States than any other educational agency, save maybe the public schools.' He continued:

> It has been dominated by quacks since the beginning, and their quackeries are
> now in full blast everywhere. They have not only seized the public schools,
> but nearly all the private schools. The man primarily responsible is probably
> John Dewey, though he doesn't go the whole way with the rest of the
> brethren. (quoted in Westbrook 1991: 501)

It appears that dissatisfaction with educational policies is nothing new!

A second source of principles is institutionalized demands, embodied in tests and quantified levels, generalized hierarchies of success, ladders of achievement, profiles of outcomes and lists of competencies, do-as-you're-told measurements of professional adequacy and in general the bureaucratic accountability which always threatens to take over when true principles are in decline. Thirdly, principles may be extrapolated from research and theories in the making: promising but unconfirmed directions suggested by unfinished but hastily applied fragments of scientific work (the latest fashion), or untested transfers from one world to another, such as skills from industry to education.

What alternatives do teachers have to such suspect sources of principles to guide their professional conduct? To find an answer, or to at least find the beginnings of a new direction, I propose to link the basic *epistemological* questions of language learning (the knowledge base of our field) to the axiological or ethical issues which I believe concern most dedicated teachers (our *values*). This joint consideration of knowledge and values in the profession of language learning leads me to propose three foundational principles to form the basis of the language curriculum I will explore in this book. These principles are as follows:

- Awareness
- Autonomy
- Authenticity

For preliminary guidance I present these three principles with some of their epistemological and axiological arguments (or maxims) in the form of a grid (see Figure 1), with the understanding that subsequent chapters will elaborate on these and related aspects of language learning and teaching.

These principles and their maxims will form the basis of the curriculum discussed in this book. To provide an overview I will now briefly discuss each principle in turn, reminding the reader that they will be discussed again in depth in chapters 4–6. From the start I want to emphasize that the principles, though they are here examined one at a time, only make sense as a unity. Each one can only be understood in relation to the other two.

Awareness

It is an ancient principle of learning that all new learning will be impossible unless it can be related to existing knowledge (some of it innate, probably) and experience. To illustrate this, here is a story that I

	Epistemology	Axiology
Awareness	• focusing attention • role of perception	• know what you are doing, and why • conscious engagement • reflection
Autonomy	• self-regulation • motivation • depth of processing	• responsibility • accountability • free choice • democratic education
Authenticity	• language use in life • relevance • communication	• commitment to learning • integrity • respect

Figure 1   Principles of the curriculum

remember from my first psychology course many years ago, and which is perhaps apocryphal.

A stone-age man from New Guinea was taken to a big city by anthropologists who wished to study his reactions to modern civilization. All day they drove him around in a taxi, showing skyscrapers, big stores, busy streets, buses, railways, bridges, and so on. At the end of the day they asked him to tell them what he had seen. He replied that he had been amazed by the strength of a skinny old mule he had seen pulling a cart piled high with all sorts of junk. They asked him what else he had seen. Nothing. The skinny old mule was the only thing he had seen, he simply could not comment on anything else.

To learn something new one must first notice it. This noticing is an awareness of its existence, obtained and enhanced by paying attention to it. Paying attention is focusing one's consciousness, or pointing one's perceptual powers in the right direction, and making mental 'energy' available for processing. Processing involves linking something that is perceived in the outside world to structures (patterns of connections) that exist in the mind. Our 'savage' could not notice things that were totally unfamiliar, because he had no knowledge or experience which could help him to point his attention in the right direction.

We don't know exactly what it is we have to notice in order to learn language. It is likely that there are many different kinds of learning involved. For example, learning the meaning of a word may be an entirely different learning process than learning its pronunciation, or its syntactic properties (see Levelt 1989, particularly chapter 6, on the structure of lexical items). We therefore have to attend to different kinds of things and in different ways, depending on the precise job of learning before us. Slobin's *operating principles* address various aspects of the child's awareness in acquiring the first language, such as the tendency to pay attention to the ends of words (Slobin 1985). Such principles of awareness and attention, and in general the reciprocal relations between an individual and the language-using world, can be fruitfully studied from the ecological perspective of J.J. Gibson (1979; see also E.J. Gibson 1991; Forrester 1992). What is generally known now by the mechanistic information-processing term *input*, becomes *affordance*, that which is offered by the linguistic environment and perceived by the learner, thus emphasizing complementarity and promising a resolution of the object/subject dichotomy (E.J. Gibson 1991: 559). The kinds of things that may guide – or encourage – appropriate attention-paying, in other words the cultivation of affordances, in second language learning and in language learning in general, form part of the topic of this book.

Language awareness, whether deliberate or spontaneous, is thus a crucial aspect of language learning, both first and subsequent. In addition, educational settings require awareness of learning strategies and processes, social awareness of classroom structures, awareness of learning and teaching styles, and so on. These various aspects of awareness will be discussed in more detail in later chapters.

Autonomy

It is a truism that learning has to be done by the learner. This means that teaching cannot cause or force learning, at best it can *encourage* and *guide* learning. The impetus for learning must come from the learner, who must *want* to learn, either because of a natural human propensity to do so, or because of an interest in the material. It is interesting to consider a comment on this by Chomsky (who does not normally venture into pedagogical territory), in response to a question on the utility of recent findings in linguistics for language teaching:

> The truth of the matter is that about 99 percent of teaching is making the students feel interested in the material. Then the other 1 percent has to do with your methods. And that's not just true of languages. It's true of every subject. (Chomsky 1988: 181)

Two features are central to autonomy: *choice* and *responsibility*. If the learner is merely a passive recipient of instruction, the attention-paying mentioned above will be weak and unfocused. Moreover, most learning, especially complex learning, requires high and sustained cognitive effort, 'the investment of deliberately initiated thought' (Sullivan & Conway 1989), and this is determined by the degree of positive affect assigned to the activity. And positive affect derives partly from feelings of control, ownership, and competence (aspects of the 'autotelic,' or self-regulating personality described in Csikszentmihalyi 1990; cf. also the importance of self-regulation in the study of metacognition, e.g. Weinert & Kluwe 1987, and most of all, of course, in the work of Vygotsky 1978).

The autonomous learner must be able to make significant decisions about what is to be learned, as well as how and when to do it. Further, the autonomous learner is responsible for learning as well as lack of learning, so long as adequate opportunities are available in the setting. There is now a significant body of research literature about autonomy in learning and other social activities, starting with the work of Vygotsky, Piaget and Bruner, and continuing with Deci and Ryan's intrinsic motivation and causality orientations (1985), and so on. This work will be reviewed in subsequent chapters, especially chapter 5.

Authenticity

The third member of the AAA principles is *authenticity*. In the language learning literature this usually refers to the materials that are used (the *texts*). Texts (including pictures, realia, etc.) are authentic when they are not especially written or prepared for the language learner, but rather taken from the world at large. Newspaper articles, novels, poems, TV soap opera episodes, commercials, paintings by van Gogh, and so on, are all authentic in this definition, whereas dialogs, exercises, reading texts, illustrations, and so on, written to be included in language textbooks, are not.

In this book, however, authenticity is approached from a different angle. I take as my starting point the existentialist definition of *authentic*: an action is authentic when it realizes a free choice and is an expression of what a person genuinely feels and believes. An authentic action is *intrinsically motivated*. Inauthentic actions, on the other hand, are undertaken because everyone else is doing them, they 'ought' to be done, or in general they are motivated by external forces.

Authenticity, in this all-encompassing sense, is very closely related both to awareness and to autonomy. It is at the same time the *result* and the *origin* of awareness and autonomy. How is such a seemingly contradictory relationship possible? To understand this, we need to go all the way back to Kant's categories, in which the third category in a class 'arises from the combination of the second with the first' (Kant 1934: 82) and to Peirce's transformation of these in his notions of 'firstness, secondness, and thirdness,' roughly equivalent to *object* (e.g. the language itself), *action* (or engagement with the language, e.g. through interaction), and *interpretation* (success and understanding).[5] The AAA principles thus form a genuine Peircean triad, in which each member cannot be conceptualized without the other two. To take the notion of authenticity from such philosophical underpinnings to the practical applications in language classrooms, is the topic of chapter 6.

. . . and Achievement

I have used the AAA as guiding principles in my own work for a number of years now, and from time to time people suggest perfectly reasonable candidates for further principles, or 'a fourth A.' These have included such notions as accountability, assessment, and achievement (note the uncanny coincidence that they all start with A as well!). I continue to resist such additions, and my stubborn decision to stick to the triad as a basic unifying construct may strike some as a rather peculiar numerological (or even pseudo-religious!) fixation on the number three. However, I would like to advance a less esoteric reason, namely that I wish to guard against proliferation of categories by preserving the notion of the triad as a structuring system.

On the other hand, the basic triad of the AAA is of little use unless it is structurally and functionally connected to other phenomena in learners' education and social life. In this sense suggestions to add other principles indicate an existing problem and therefore need to be taken into account. The way I propose to do this is briefly outlined in this section.

The three principles of awareness, autonomy, and authenticity refer basically to personal (or, to be precise, *intra*personal) properties relating to a person's motivations, aspirations, actions, and development. While I regard these as appropriately central, it is clear that personal development is intricately bound up with interpersonal issues. Indeed, the dynamic intertwining of the intrapersonal and the interpersonal is one of the focal concerns of Vygotskyan developmental psychology, and in later chapters this dynamism will be explored in a variety of directions. For now, I propose a formal link between the foundational principles outlined above, or the *primary* AAA, as we might call them, and a *secondary*, or subsidiary triad, which links the former to the social, interpersonal world.

The second triad consists of the three concepts of *achievement*, *assessment*, and *accountability*, or *knowledge* of success (and for success read also progress, competence, proficiency, etc.), *demonstration* of success, and *justification* of pedagogical action. What 'counts as' success is determined by a host of factors, historical, social, cultural, genetic, and so on, which I cannot go into now. What 'counts as' appropriate documentation of success, and adequate demonstration and justification, is mostly an institutional, and sometimes a bureaucratic, affair as perennial debates about testing and certification amply show.

In this book I will primarily discuss the first A of this secondary triad: *achievement*, since a full discussion of assessment and accountability falls outside the scope of the book (even so, all these concepts are of course interrelated in many ways, and I will indicate connections wherever appropriate). Achievement refers to improvement and accomplishment, as seen against both an earlier point of development, and a goal or objective that provides a target and a direction. It is the answer to the question 'How am I doing?,' and it will be provided partly by the learner (feeling of knowing), and partly by information (feedback) coming from various sources in the environment.

Sometimes it will be easy for people to provide the information themselves, as in the case of a physical skill the performance of which is itself a demonstration of success. When a child can ride a bicycle for the first time without training wheels and without swerving off the path, the achievement is obvious, both to the rider and the proud parent. At other times, particularly in areas of more complex mental activities and academic skills and knowledge, feedback from external sources will be required, though gradually, with increasing self-determination, personal knowledge of one's own achievements is likely to play a greater role. For many significant accomplishments in life, society has established a series of signposts that signal progress along the way. For example, in a swimming program, children might progress from Tadpole to Minnow, and from Minnow to Dolphin. In school, if they stay long enough, they may progress from secondary school (the *Abitur* in Germany, A Levels or GCSEs in the UK, and so on) to BA, then to MA, and finally to Ph.D. In these and many other ways society canonizes and institutionalizes achievement in the areas it values.

In linking the primary triad to the secondary triad, as shown in Figure 2, I relate *autonomy* to *achievement*, primarily through the notion of *motivation*. In motivation, internal and external factors (called ideocentric and sociocentric in the diagram) meet and contribute ingredients which together determine the educational experience. The learner's growing self-regulation fosters feelings of knowing, which, by combining self-knowledge with sociocultural knowledge, become knowledge of success. How these are to be *demonstrated* (and for whose benefit), and how educational activities are *justified* (and to whom), are matters which, as I mentioned above, fall outside the scope of this book (they are part of educational policy and politics).

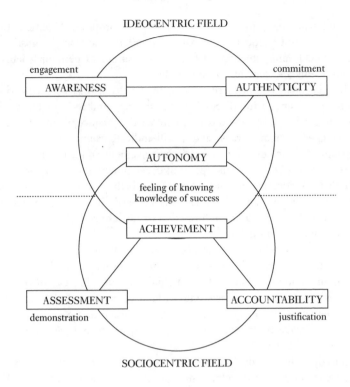

IDEOCENTRIC FIELD

engagement   commitment

AWARENESS ——————— AUTHENTICITY

AUTONOMY

feeling of knowing
knowledge of success

ACHIEVEMENT

ASSESSMENT ——————— ACCOUNTABILITY

demonstration   justification

SOCIOCENTRIC FIELD

Figure 2   Linking primary and secondary triads

Issues relating to achievement will be discussed when appropriate in
different chapters, though they are primarily relevant in chapter 5. In
general terms, from the perspective of the foundational principles underlying the AAA curriculum, personal considerations should take
precedence over political and institutional ones, self-knowledge over
evaluations by others, intrinsic over extrinsic motivation, self-assessment
over institutional assessment, and so on.

The curriculum

Having introduced the three principles underlying language education, I
now turn to the curriculum to indicate how it might embody these principles.

In many educational institutions the educational material (the 'to-be-
learned') is divided into subjects: language, physics, mathematics, and so
on. Students must 'take' a given number of subjects for a given number

of hours per week, and in some cases they may also choose some electives. The hours are spread out over the school days in a certain fashion, repeated identically week after week or, in some cases (most American high schools), even day after day. This grid of institutionalized educational slots, the rigidity of which is clearly more administratively convenient than pedagogically sound, is one way of defining the curriculum. It yields the 'fifth grade curriculum', or the 'high school curriculum.' In addition, the progression and content of each subject may also be spelled out in greater or lesser detail by educational authorities, whether at the school, district, provincial, or ministerial level. This yields the 'fifth grade mathematics curriculum', and so on. It tells the teachers what has to be 'covered' during a particular period of time (e.g. school year).

A third type of curriculum is an *approach* to teaching a certain subject in a certain way, e.g. the communicative approach, the whole-language approach, phonics, and so on. This notion comes very close to what is often called 'method', though it does not need to be as fully packaged as a method usually is.

Another way to look at the curriculum is to use Hawkins' distinction between a *horizontal* and a *vertical* curriculum (1987a: 2). The horizontal curriculum is synchronic, a timetable of subjects and slots, planned by the principal (or the director of curriculum, etc.) and hung on the wall (the first curriculum described above). You look at it and you know where to go and when, for what. The vertical curriculum is diachronic, and consists of the cumulative experiences and learning processes of the students as they progress in their scholastic careers. This is in a sense the students' subjective curriculum. We thus have a distinction between breadth and depth, or between attention to language as spread over the various classrooms (Bullock's '*across* the curriculum,' [DES 1975]), and as embedded inside the students' learning experiences.

Although this distinction is of necessity somewhat imprecise, it is very useful if we want to avoid a narrow role – or worse, no articulated role at all – for language education. Such a narrow role would be the inevitable result of an emphasis (perhaps driven by bureaucratic concerns) on the horizontal curriculum, and a concurrent lack of attention to the depth of students' language experiences.

The distinction between a horizontal and a vertical curriculum, or between breadth and depth, presents four basic curricular options to help us to decide what it is we want to do and what we want to avoid. We want to avoid limiting language education to haphazard and piecemeal activities in a single subject 'language lesson.' We should also avoid similar unfocused work across the curriculum, that is, dealing with language in the different subject areas just when it occurs to us or to the textbook writer, and constantly running the danger of talking at cross-purposes. Next, we do not want to restrict language education to a designated 'language' or 'English' lesson, without systematic connections to other academic work. What we want to promote is a systematic in-depth approach to language education across the child's entire educational career, emphasizing the central instructional and social role of language all over the school (in the classroom, the corridor, the office, and the playground), and the role of language (and dialect, minority language, and so on) in society.

The most satisfactory solution to language education will be a combination of breadth and depth, with well-explicated links between the language lesson and other lessons, including of course the foreign language lesson. This is a long-term objective in need of much pioneering work, but a logical consequence of the view of language education expressed in this book. I would like to mention two aspects of such cross-subject links that would lend themselves to immediate action research (I realize that a prerequisite for success – or a result of success! – would be a breakdown of the compartmentalization which is the rule in most of today's schools).

First, an interesting experiment would be to have a 'Language Awareness Specialist' in a school, and to monitor and document his or her activities carefully. Tasks for such a specialist would include observing classes to identify common language problems, forging links between language arts, ESL, foreign language, and subject classes, exploring possibilities for writing/reading across the curriculum, and so on. Such a 'language broker' or 'language ombudsman' might facilitate language growth and language awareness, while at the same time averting language-based disasters for these students. After all, many schools have the services of educational psychologists available, and it does not seem too far-fetched to see an equally viable role for an *educational linguist*.

A second potential link would be between the L1 and the L2 lesson. It is often said by L2 learners that there is no better way to raise awareness of one's own language than by learning a second language.[6] Yet, in foreign language lessons the native language is usually either banned (in accordance with the tenets of the direct method or audiolingualism) or only grudgingly tolerated as a last resort (in most communicative courses). Conversely, in the native language lesson a discussion of foreign language concepts and experiences is not considered relevant. This artificial separation is partly due to a very stubborn but entirely unfounded popular belief that two languages necessarily compete with each other in a learner's mind, and partly to a lack of contact and collaboration between mother tongue and foreign language teachers. In actual fact there is an enormous potential for cross-fertilization between native language and foreign language(s) which is insufficiently exploited in the schools (though see Duff 1989, and Harris & Savitsky 1988, for two different approaches to using students' language resources), and which could be an important vehicle in the development of higher cognitive skills and critical thinking. I believe that this cross-fertilization is what Rudolf Flesch had in mind when he remarked that, for the sake of clear thinking, 'the important thing is not the learning of foreign languages, but the activity of translation' (1951: 49).

A strong note of caution is in order, however, before we leave this topic for the time being. I do not wish to suggest that the L1 should be used in any L2 lesson whenever learners and teachers might find it convenient, or that random code-switching is advisable in bilingual classes. Instead, I suggest that innovative ways can be found of playing L1 and L2 off against one another productively (see Butzkamm 1980, Jacobson 1990, for examples in different contexts).

To summarize, the curriculum advocated here expands the role of language along two dimensions: *horizontally* by forging links between different subjects, exploring cross-curricular themes, and dealing with global linguistic problems and issues; *vertically* by providing deep and rich language experiences throughout the child's academic career, and building usable and lasting language skills, both oral and written.

To achieve this expansion (in some respects, transformation) of the language curriculum, the AAA principles provide a crucial sense of direction. Students are encouraged to develop their language *awareness* (and other kinds of awareness that are intricately bound up with language: learning, cognitive, social), to become *autonomous* (i.e. have choices and responsibilities, and develop their own sense of direction), to strive for *authenticity* in their learning experiences in general and their language experiences in particular (this authenticity includes consistency, integrity, and respect, in addition to rich and varied sources and resources), and to recognize – and be recognized for – their *achievements*. Most of this book will expand on the consequences implied in the directions laid out in this paragraph.

We now turn to the most practical level of our discussion, the expression of the curriculum in the shape of syllabuses.

The syllabus as 'Triptik'

The principles underlying the language curriculum share the abbreviation AAA with the American Automobile Association ('the Triple A').

Without wishing to suggest that the curriculum is merely a service dispensing road maps (then it would not be a process curriculum; within the travel metaphor, the curriculum is rather like the journey), I would like to pursue the analogy a little by visualizing a syllabus as a 'Triptik.' This is a spiral-bound collection of maps tracing the route a member has requested for a specific trip. On these maps, which you flip over as you travel along, there is a wealth of information about the places you pass through: gas stations, interesting sights, parks, hotels, as well as smaller-scale maps of larger areas of interest, large-scale town plans, side roads worthy of exploration, and so on. The Triptik is thus a useful metaphor for an ideal syllabus: a collection of maps with information and options, a guide, but one which leaves the students the freedom to stop where they want to, to travel alone for a while or in groups, to go off on some tangent if it seems interesting, but always coming back to the main road, and keeping the destination in mind. The syllabus – as Triptik – does not tell you where (and how far, how fast) you want to go, it gives you the advice and assistance that you ask for. Neither does it evaluate the trip or comment on the traveler's (or travelers') experiences along the way. The syllabus, like the Triptik, is neutral, indifferent, though designed for a specific occasion. It lays out the options and points to the landscape. I think it was Korzybski who said that the map is not the territory. In a similar way, the syllabus is not the journey. Experience, appreciation, criticism, and so on, are not laid down in the syllabus, they are merely made available by it, and brought to it by the learners.

As I have said, such a syllabus is an ideal, and ideals are usually not attainable. However, ideals are always useful and sometimes necessary as models, even if in practice compromises have to be made. An ideal syllabus as suggested by the Triptik is only relevant if it is based on the three principles of *awareness* (know where you are going, what you are doing, and why), *autonomy* (have the freedom of choice, exploration, personal preferences, but also the responsibility for your own and your companions' journey), and *authenticity* (commitment and interest, relevant and real-life experiences). In other words, the syllabus is a set of tools (a set of maps, a travel kit) that allows the curriculum to unfold, as a process; it is a mediating concept between curriculum and classroom action. This brings us back to the starting point of this chapter: using basic principles derived from knowledge and values as a guide for language education.

Constraints and resources

On p. 8 I described the curriculum as a dynamic interplay between constraints and resources. Following Giddens, social structure is 'always both enabling and constraining, in virtue of the inherent relation between structure and agency (and agency and power)' (1984: 169). Compare this view of structure to a piece of music which is constrained by tonal scales and chords, but not limited by them. The musician (or composer) may use a conventional musical code (or may ignore it, of course!), but nevertheless creates original musical structures. Since we are concerned with the curriculum as process, we look at structure not as a given shape, as a music score we see in front of us, but rather as a movement in time which we are constructing from within, according to our own ideas of what it should look or sound like, along with all past, present and future advice from everyone who plays a role.[7]

The language curriculum and any syllabus enabling it provides *structure* to the students' learning world. This structure, like the game of chess mentioned above (p. 8), has two sides to it, with one side enabling the other. On the one hand the structure *limits* or *constrains* the kinds of things that can be done, and on the other hand it provides *opportunities* and *resources* for doing things.[8] Most human groups and activities are similarly structured, whether we talk about the family, political parties, and religious ceremonies, or about baseball, paintings, and barbecues. There are always constraints (including rules and regulations) on what to do and what not to do, and there are always resources available for carrying out the actions associated with the setting or the activity.

We can then see the curriculum as a journey to a particular destination (more or less clearly defined at the outset), and the syllabus as guide (a sketch, map, or manual) sensitive to the constraints and resources of one particular set of human activities: learning in educational institutions. The three principles on which the language curriculum is based give guidance for practical actions, but more importantly, they frame the constraints and the resources appropriate to the setting, which are then illuminated and elaborated in the syllabus.

Conclusion

In this chapter I have provided the basic ground rules for constructing a curriculum based on our *knowledge* of language learning and education, and on our *values* of language use in society. I wanted to begin with a clear and sharp focus, so that we can pose our contemporary problems and possibilities efficiently, and set out on the path of educational language development with a clear sense of direction .

Recall my earlier statement from Stenhouse, that the curriculum has to be brought into the room on a 'porter's barrow' (p. 3), since it includes all the teacher knows and has experienced, and everything that influences his or her philosophy and practical actions. Useful though Stenhouse's picture of the curriculum is (perhaps a *database* would be a more appropriate image now), his description is not the whole curriculum, but just the *baggage* for a journey, whereas the actual *journey* itself is the real curriculum (since it is a *process* curriculum).

The baggage, all the influences and experiences we carry with us, has to be organized somehow, and I have suggested that the basic organizing criteria are derived from knowledge (both professional and common sense) and values (moral, including beliefs and attitudes).

It is assumed that the resulting three foundational principles of awareness, autonomy, and authenticity find broad agreement among today's practitioners, although the interpretation and application of them might vary in practice. More importantly, however, all practitioners, as part of their own curriculum, must articulate their own set of principles, and be prepared to defend them and live and work by them.

Further, the curriculum is structured in terms of constraints and resources, ideally resulting in a harmonious balance of directions and opportunities.

Whereas the curriculum is vast and bulky, if we follow Stenhouse's image, and certainly it is a momentous and somewhat unpredictable undertaking if seen as a process or journey, the syllabus should be compact and lean (I am tempted to say that we must travel light, though I may be stretching the metaphor). Prabhu (1987) makes a distinction between *simple* and *sophisticated* syllabuses. The latter may in fact by their very completeness and wealth of detail limit creative language use and varied exposure in the classroom, whereas the simple syllabus leaves room for the introduction of contextually appropriate texts and spontaneous language use, as well as for language-related issues brought up by the students themselves. Further, like the AAA Triptik, the syllabus should provide options and panoramas which suggest exploration and areas for further study, rather than material which has to be 'covered.'

Notes

1 Although the immediate context illustrated here is that of ESL (English as a second language) and SLA (second language acquisition), the resulting curriculum is intended to be applicable to all of language education, and indeed, to the role of language in education in general.

2 In order not to clutter the text with a multitude of references at this point, I will merely mention the relevant names here and advise the reader to consult the index and references for further details. As mentioned in the preface, I have set apart certain parenthetical and theoretical remarks by indentation and a vertical line in the margin.

3 Many other formulations are possible. For example, in an airplane magazine I read about a psychologist who formulated the principles respect, responsibility, and resourcefulness (I unfortunately omitted to write down the exact reference). To a certain extent, we all have to articulate our own principles, but I would expect there to be an underlying universality shining through the variety.

4 cf. Breen & Candlin 1980, which also recommends this approach.

5 The triadic structure will be further elaborated in a number of places in the book, since it cannot be fully treated here. The interested reader is invited to consult the index. See also Oller 1990.

6 This does not apply, unfortunately, to situations of subtractive bilingualism, where young children are taught L2 before L1 has been firmly established. In such cases special steps need to be taken to ensure that L1 is not lost, with often dire consequences for the child's family life and cultural equilibrium.

7 See chapter 2, where this idea is further developed along the lines of Davidson's *passing theory*.

8 As I have indicated, I have taken the notion of constraints and resources from the work of Anthony Giddens (e.g. 1984). Interestingly, in a recent book Howard Gardner (1991) elaborates a very similar structure, though without drawing on Giddens.

2 The curriculum as a theory of practice

It is not enough that teachers' work should be studied: they need to study it themselves.

Stenhouse 1975: 143

Introduction

In the first chapter I used the terms *curriculum* and *theory* almost interchangeably, and there are several reasons for this. One of the reasons is that the work proposed here is meant as a clearly defined professional outlook on the educational process, rather than as the development of a theory in the traditional sense. Another reason is that the curriculum breaks down the barriers between theory, research, and practice, in order to construct new, dynamic relationships between these interrelated aspects of scientific activity. A third is that it transcends the traditional boundaries that have been set up between different branches of science, and consciously seeks information, whatever the source, to move the pedagogical process forward.

In this chapter I will sketch the AAA curriculum as a theory of practice (as exemplified in the work of Pierre Bourdieu, e.g. Bourdieu and Passeron 1977) that does the above things: it represents pedagogical work as a process of practicing, theorizing, and researching. Our growing understanding of this process determines the relevance of information from different sources and disciplines. The theory of practice is thus a mode of professional conduct which in some respects differs from traditional ways of doing theory, research, or practice. In other respects, however, it is no different than any other thoughtful approach to work, whether that work be the splicing of genes or the nurturing of a vegetable patch in your back yard. We need to first demystify the concepts theory, research and practice, then reorient our practical activities through perception, action, and reflection, towards theorizing, mediated by research. The result of this theorizing is useless if it is not ploughed back into practice. This is what I meant when, above, I said that the curriculum is a *professional outlook*, a practical philosophy of education in a sense. Theory, research and practice, as dynamic ingredients of the theory of practice, are part and parcel of this professional outlook. Let us now begin to explore how a theory of practice might be brought about.

The teacher as researcher

There is currently a great deal of talk about redefining the roles of the people involved in the educational enterprise, particularly the role of the teacher. At the most direct level of classroom roles, this is expressed in terms of recommendations such as the currently popular one that the teacher should be 'a guide on the side' rather than 'a sage on the stage.' At the broader level of curricular innovation, a number of terms reflect how educational theorists see the role of the teacher:

- reflective practitioner (Schön 1983)
- thoughtful teacher (Zeichner 1983)
- action researcher (Kemmis & McTaggert 1982)
- teacher as researcher (Stenhouse 1975)

Despite differences of detail among the many recommendations, they all share an interest in encouraging teachers to become more autonomous agents in their professional activities, and to understand and harness various marketplace forces, notably administrative and academic ones. Reflecting this intent, the word *empowerment* has become extremely popular, so much so that at times it seems hard to find out what it means. The entire movement towards empowerment must be seen as part of a general sociopolitical conjuncture in *Western* society, which seeks to define the actor as free agent, which examines the nature of democracy, and which is in general suspicious of the power of official institutions and bureaucracies, while at the same time feeling increasingly controlled by these external forces. At a theoretical level, we may also relate it to the decline of positivism and its most visible educational outgrowths, such as rote learning and psychometric testing. This decline has, as one of its results, brought about a questioning of quantitative research and academic grand theory.

The democratization of research and the mistrust of theory can have both beneficial and harmful consequences. While it may not heal the rift that exists between academic theories and educational practices, teacher research can, by creating its own theory, escape the blind opportunism or routinization of theory-less practice.[1] On the other hand, this same democratization and disaffection with theory can also lead to this very theory-less practice if it is *not* accompanied by some form of teacher research. Having thus suggested the need for some kind of theory of practice, the next step is to work out guidelines for scientifically responsible conduct and criteria for the control of the quality of research. Since this kind of research is likely to be rather heterogeneous (since it is context-dependent), and may in any case turn out quite different from the accepted patterns of academic research which tend to be (quite loosely, to be sure) based on the example of the physical sciences, different criteria and mechanisms for quality control must be found, or it will be difficult to distinguish good research from bad research.

Research is another word for scientific investigation. Webster's Collegiate Dictionary describes it as 'investigation or experimentation aimed at the discovery and interpretation of facts, revision of accepted theories or laws in the light of new facts, or practical application of such new or revised theories or laws.' Quite a heterogeneous group of activities, even in so short a space as a dictionary definition, and this should warn us not to take too narrow a view of the activity of researching. Note, especially, that researching can be done in the service of practice as well as theory. I will return to this issue in the next section below.

Language education is inevitably based on theory, whether it be an *explicit*, articulated one, thought through and thought about, crafted by the teacher on the basis of pedagogical practice, with the help of relevant curricular and extra-curricular resources, or an *implicit* one, grown from unexamined practice and unreflective experience. If the theory is explicit, the teacher is potentially *in control* of his or her own professional life and progress, even though institutional and other constraints may contest that control. If the theory is implicit, it is highly unlikely for the teacher to be in control, regardless of the amount of institutional freedom available.

Since all teachers have a theory of teaching, at least an implicit one, the first task of curricular renewal is to invite interested teachers to examine their own theory, making it explicit if it has hitherto remained implicit, and determine options for pedagogical action on its basis. In making their theory explicit and developing it, teachers give meaning to their pedagogical actions and *empower themselves*[2] and may engage in *pedagogic research* (Widdowson 1990: 55–70), thus becoming *teacher researchers* or *extended professionals* in Stenhouse's sense:

> The critical characteristics of that extended professionalism which is essential for well-founded curriculum research and development seem to me to be:
>
> The commitment to systematic questioning of one's own teaching as a basis for development;
> The commitment and the skills to study one's own teaching;
> The concern to question and to test theory in practice by the use of those skills.
>
> To these may be added as highly desirable, though perhaps not essential, a readiness to allow other teachers to observe one's work – directly or through recordings – and to discuss it with them on an open and honest basis.

> In short, the outstanding characteristics of the extended professional is [sic]
> a capacity for autonomous professional self-development through systematic
> self-study, through the study of the work of other teachers and through the
> testing of ideas by classroom research procedures. (Stenhouse 1975: 144)

The theory of educational practice which is the foundation of a new language curriculum is fundamentally different from the theories which predominate in academic discussions. That this is necessarily so, is illustrated by the following observations:

1. Apart from work in the Vygotskyan tradition (e.g. Moll 1990, Lantolf & Appel 1994), and the collaboration of Howard Gardner and Robert Sternberg on practical intelligence (Sternberg, Okagaki, & Jackson, 1990), theories in relevant fields, such as cognitive science, linguistics, and second language acquisition (SLA), do not generally address language-pedagogical issues, neither at a theoretical nor at a practical level. Indeed, some SLA researchers explicitly distance themselves from pedagogy, perhaps in order to bolster their theoretical stature (see van Lier 1991c, 1994, for examples as well as critiques of such a stance). Such theories, and the research conducted in their support, cannot be the driving force behind pedagogical practice, however crucial they may otherwise be.

2. Teachers have to conduct their own research, in support of their own theories. To use Widdowson's terms, teacher research is *insider research*, which is contrasted with *outsider research* conducted by external researchers, 'with teachers as part of the data or the object of inquiry' (Widdowson 1990: 59). An interesting third possibility is *collaborative research*, in which external and internal researchers collaborate; whether such research can break the barriers between insider and outsider research is itself a useful research topic.

3. In addition to classroom research, teacher research includes critical research on other aspects of the profession that influence teaching and learning, such as community–school relations, communication with administrators, the relationship between funding and quality of education, effective and authentic (but non-bureaucratic) forms of assessment and accountability, and many more. In other words, teacher research goes well beyond the classroom, since empowered teachers can no longer be told to keep their innovative activities confined to the space within the four classroom walls.

4. The teacher's pedagogical theory needs input not only from professional experience, but also from relevant fields of scientific activity, whether or not they directly address issues of learning. In some cases it is easier to see the relevance of theoretical discussions than in others. Vygotsky's zone of proximal development (ZPD, for a definition see

p. 46) appeals directly to the thoughtful teacher, but the applicability of computer models of neural networks may be less clear-cut. However, the teacher's theory of practice should be sufficiently *open* to assess the importance of information even if it is not immediately and directly applicable in the form of some teaching activity.[3]

5. Most importantly, the theory of practice, which addresses the full complexity of decisions and influences shaping practitioners' work inside and outside classrooms, dissolves the oppositions and rigid distinctions between theory, research, and practice that are implied in much scientific work. It also neutralizes the separation between *object* and *subject*, or *scientific fact*s and *moral values*. In the present framework this is done by explicitly building both knowledge and values into the basic AAA principles, as I explained in the last chapter.

To require such theorizing and researching from teachers may appear unrealistic in view of the reality in which most teachers live nowadays. In many countries this reality includes larger class sizes, more hetero-geneous students (in terms of both linguistic and cultural backgrounds), and a diminished status in the community. As one veteran high school teacher said, lamenting the 'erosion of the teacher's authority,'

> Thirty years ago, the teacher controlled the classroom. The teacher was like the captain of the ship . . . All that has changed. Teachers today are like peons. They don't have clout any longer . . . They've taken away the feeling of professionalism that you ought to have. (Maeroff 1994: 18–19)

No doubt many teachers look back wistfully to a time when they had more 'clout' and when things appeared to be simpler and more harmoni-ous. There is little doubt that we now live in a more complex world, and old educational structures can no longer handle all that is required of educators. We may note that current views of the teacher's role reject much of the 'authority' that made these earlier times attractive. This was an authority that society bestowed (and still does bestow, in some cul-tures) on the classroom context, but it now no longer does so in many cases. One may regret and lament this, but there is no alternative to seek-ing a new definition of professionalism, one which is not based on authority and control, but on other factors. This book is partly an attempt to find and describe some of those factors. Seeing the cur-riculum as a theory of practice, and incorporating a dimension of research in one's teaching, is one way to transform the notion of profes-sionalism from an authority-based one into a research-based one. That this can be a profitable direction is corroborated by statements such as the following, from a survey of teacher researchers:

> Experienced teacher–researchers stated that their research brought them many personal and professional benefits, including increased collegiality, a

sense of empowerment, and increased self-esteem. Teacher–researchers viewed themselves as being more open to change, more reflective, and better informed than they had been when they began their research. They now saw themselves as experts in their field who were better problem solvers and more effective teachers with fresher attitudes toward education. They also saw strong connections between theory and practice. (Bennett 1993: 69)

When teachers work in this way they cannot work in isolation, but need to communicate with one another, exchange ideas, and report their work. Teacher organizations, interest groups, and networks, are thus essential to a teaching profession which is developing a theory of practice, especially since such work cannot be limited to a one teacher–one classroom research context. In the following section I will look at the relationship between practice, research, and theory in more detail.

Theory, research, practice

> *It would be erroneous . . . to perceive practical psychology as an application of previously established theories. The relationship should be reversed, with practice selecting its own psychological principles and ultimately creating its own psychology.* (Kozulin 1990: 101)

Before I continue I would like to invite the reader to think of the terms *theory*, *practice*, and *research* as a series in which one of the terms must be marked as the odd-one-out, rather like some lists in vocabulary exercises or intelligence tests. As an example, if we had the series *potato*, *onion*, and *noodle*, then *noodle* would be the odd-one-out (the other two are vegetables). Doing the same with the series *theory*, *practice*, and *research*, which one would you mark as the odd-one-out?

I have regularly given a test with the words *theory*, *practice*, and *research* embedded in it to teachers, academics, and graduate students, and the overwhelming majority have consistently marked *practice* as the odd-one-out, at a ratio of more than 9 out of 10. The defense that some of my guinea pigs offer for their choice is of great interest, and it goes something like this: 'I know that these three terms go together, but you forced me to choose and I had to circle one of them; it's an artificial separation.' This is precisely the point. While many researchers may argue that the three terms are intimately related, when they are put on the spot they will invariable relate research to theory, *rather than* to practice. What this shows is that, for most people, the link between theory and research is stronger than that between either of these two terms and practice. A crucial feature of the theory of practice is to deny this *hierarchical assumption*. Further, the assumed *sequence* or *order* of scientific activity, which usually runs in either of the following two directions, is also questioned:

theory → research (→) practice   (= 'theory-first')
research → theory (→) practice   (= 'research-first')

In Figure 3, three possible views of the relationships between theory, research, and practice are sketched. The prevailing situation in our field seems to be I, where research is seen as a service to theory, and there may be some sporadic information flowing from theory towards practice, probably sought by practitioners rather than offered by theorists (the dashed arrow), but hardly any flow of information from practice to theory or research. Option II represents a more dogmatic or top-down situation in which theorists (fueled by research) dictate to practitioners what they 'ought to' know and what they ought to be doing, learning, or unlearning. What I want to advocate in this book is option III, in which all three aspects of the field are in balance, with free-flowing channels of communication between them. Such a situation is in my view the only way the qualifier 'mature' can be appropriately applied to the various professions involved in language education.[4]

The balanced view expressed in option III would be the result of a harmonious working together of academics, teachers, and all others engaged in education. From the teacher's perspective, however, *practice* provides the chief impetus for the development of a theory of practice. The teacher as researcher therefore works with a model that may look more like a continuing spiral, where practice, research, and theory continually reinforce one another.

Traditionally, teacher research is envisaged primarily as action research on classroom issues, since the classroom is the domain in which the teacher is professionally active. It is appropriate that classroom pedagogy will remain the central focus for the theory of practice but, as I indicated on p. 27 above, the critical stance and the contextual analysis

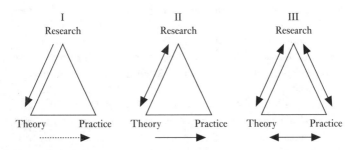

Figure 3   Relationships between theory, research, and practice

that are part and parcel of this work will inevitably mean that the teacher researcher will broaden the focus of enquiry to include the multitude of forces that impinge on classroom processes from the outside: the social context, the institutional structures, the political climate, and so on. This broadening of focus means that the knowledge base of the teacher researcher is correspondingly widened, even though relevant knowledge will necessarily be refracted via the lens of the classroom. Indeed, to borrow the words of Alex Kozulin, the classroom itself is turned from a field of activity into a subject of inquiry (1990: 18). So, we are justified in starting out on the path of the theory of practice by way of an examination of classroom research, and this will be the focus of the next section. This will be followed by a preliminary discussion of action research (to be taken up again in the final chapter of the book), and after that we will broaden the contextual focus of teacher research in two directions: the interdisciplinary connections of a theory of practice, and the wider contextual world of the teacher's scope of activity.

Classroom research and action research

On an earlier occasion (van Lier 1988) I defined the central question of classroom research as follows:

> How to identify, describe and relate, in intersubjective terms, actions and contributions of participants in the . . . classroom, in such a way that their significance for . . . learning can be understood. (van Lier 1988: 47)

The classroom is both the easiest and the most difficult place for the teacher to do research. It is the easiest place because it is the main place of work, because whatever happens there can have the most impact on learning, because the 'subjects' of research – teacher, students, aides, and perhaps occasional others – are naturally gathered there, and, most importantly perhaps, because it is the one place where the teacher appears to have a reasonable degree of power, autonomy, and the opportunity to make meaningful changes.

It is also the most difficult place to do research, because the teacher is so busy there that there hardly seems time or opportunity to focus simultaneously on teaching *and* on the complex demands of research. Secondly, the intense involvement in the classroom, and the constant urgency of moment-to-moment decision-making, militate against the objective stance, the stepping back to take a detached look, that research activity demands. Thirdly, the teacher may be so preoccupied with improvement that the careful descriptive and analytical work required by research, slow and steady rather than fast and furious, always seems to take more time than can be reasonably allotted to it.

Quite apart from all these considerations, there are a considerable number of academics who strongly feel that it is not the business of the teacher to do research at all (except, possibly, under the tutelage of an experienced researcher), since it would take time and effort away from teaching, and it is a specialized activity best left to specialists (Jarvis 1981).

For these reasons it is clear that classroom research is not a simple and uncontroversial affair that the teacher can just walk into without further ado. A cautious approach, careful planning, and as much collaboration as possible are required. As regards suitable topics, there surely can be no shortage of them in any setting. Rather, the problem most commonly is where to start. However, to begin with a list and a question such as 'These are the problems in my classroom, which one shall I start with?' may well start the teacher researcher off on the wrong foot and encourage a fragmentary problem-solving approach. Not that there is anything wrong with identifying problems in one's work and attempting to solve them, but *problem-solving* must be sharply distinguished from *research*. In the theory of practice, as elaborated above, research forms an essential link between practice and theory, whereas problem-solving is merely a part of practice *per se*, without necessarily implying a theoretical dimension.

The centerpiece of any classroom research is *observation*. As anyone who has observed classes knows, this is not simply a matter of sitting in the back of the room and looking at what is going on. Nor even looking carefully and taking notes, since what we see and what we write down will be highly selective, based in part on our prior ideas about teaching and classrooms, on what impresses us at the moment, on what we think is most important, and so on. To observe with research in mind, we need to find a way to make our observations systematic, without however biasing or skewing what is going on. This is no easy task, as a perusal of the multitude of observation instruments, coding sheets, and checklists will tell us (see van Lier 1988, Allwright 1988, Allwright & Bailey 1991).

The task of observation is further complicated if the classroom in question is the teacher's own. You cannot teach and observe yourself teach at the same time: it is necessary to step back and look in a detached manner. How can this be accomplished? There are basically two ways in which observation on one's own classroom can be done. First, the teacher can find a colleague and make a peer-coaching arrangement involving reciprocal observations: you observe my classroom and I'll observe yours. In this way, not only is someone able to observe lessons in a detached, more or less neutral sort of way, it is also possible to progressively focus on researchable issues, through conversations about the observations. The result may be a rewarding collaborative investigation.

A second possibility is to record the lessons on audio or video tape and to play these back. This becomes particularly fruitful if the lessons, or significant chunks of them, are transcribed carefully. The transcription process tends to shed a different and fresh light on the interaction process and the dynamics of the classroom (van Lier 1988). For example, if we come across a small segment such as the following:

A   . . . and he was also or- or- organist ((meaning: organist in a church))
B   yes the- he organized it . . . uhum

we notice that the teacher (B) misinterprets the student's utterance, seemingly a rather trivial little incident. However, it may indicate a general pattern of unequal discourse in the classroom, where the student's voice perhaps does not carry a great deal of weight, and is routinely reinterpreted or reformulated in accordance with the dictates of the teacher's agenda. If that is the case, further inspection of transcribed data should reveal other instances. If so, reflection on this matter may indicate that such interaction is not conducive to conversational development, and an action research experiment could be undertaken to try and find different ways of interacting.

The most commonly recommended form of classroom research is *action research*. In the words of Kemmis and McTaggart (1982: 5), 'action research provides a way of working which links theory and practice into the one whole: ideas-in-action.' Cohen and Manion define action research as 'small-scale intervention in the functioning of the real world and a close examination of such intervention' (1985: 174). Action research links theoretical and pedagogical concerns by identifying for treatment classroom problems or practices selected by the teacher through self-monitoring, or by the teacher and a peer in a peer-coaching format (see further, chapter 9). Through the various stages of action research (for a brief summary, see van Lier 1988: 68) the issue is defined, literature is consulted, and expertise sought when appropriate, a treatment is planned and executed, the results are monitored and evaluated, and so on.

All these actions, and the purposes for which they are undertaken, beg large questions which are likely to take action research in critical directions, particularly if the teacher researcher moves from the problem-solving (as mentioned above) to a more problem-posing approach, which looks at the classroom as a historically evolving and culturally embedded system. Thus, Candlin (1993) distinguishes between 'weak' and 'strong' versions of action research, and in a similar vein, I make a distinction between *technical* and *critical* research (see chapter 9; see also Crookes 1993).

Some uses of action research in teacher education will be explored in chapter 9. Here it is worth pointing out that it rarely works out the way it is planned. At the TESOL convention in San Antonio, 1988, David Nunan reported on some Australian pilot projects on action research, and expressed disappointment at noting the almost total failure of the attempt. I remember suggesting in personal communication that this failure may have been due in part to the fact that the projects were attempted by individual teachers on their own, and that collaborative projects might have a better chance of succeeding. From my own experiences since then (see p. 1) I would like to add now that the *cyclical* nature of action research is rarely straightforward. A colleague might ask me 'What cycle are you on right now, observation, reflection, or what?', and I could not give an answer. This might suggest that my project was a mess, and I was not following proper action research procedures. I might have answered, 'A little bit of everything, I guess,' and this would have been close to the truth. The steps and cycles do not happen in sequential, successive fashion, I think, but rather they are simultaneous strands that are braided together as one goes along. I might think about planning while observing, reflect while planning, revise my plan while acting, and so on.

A further comment worth noting at this point is that the crucial but ill-defined step of *reflection*[5] cannot be slotted in and bracketed as a time-bounded, manipulatable activity ('I'll reflect from six to seven this evening'). In my case I found that most of the reflecting was done *after* the project was over and I had had a chance to study the transcripts, review large amounts of relevant literature, and make sense of my notes and reactions. These activities are still continuing, and are continually fueled by further observation of others teaching and analysis of classroom interaction recorded by students in regular classes. It is therefore true when Kemmis and McTaggart (1982) say that action research is 'a way of working' (see above), rather than a research project with a beginning and an end.

Interdisciplinary connections

I mentioned in the introduction to chapter 1 that one of the purposes of my action research was the search for theoretical issues that showed themselves to be relevant from the classroom floor. I looked particularly for issues that are not normally regarded as part of the 'core curriculum' of graduate language teaching programs. This broader perspective led to examination of issues such as *intrinsic motivation*, *pedagogical scaffolding*, and *awareness raising*, all of which will be discussed in subsequent chapters, and some of which suggested activities and pedagogical actions that I have since tried out and which will be described in detail later on.

More important than the actual changes made during the course, has been the growing realization that current programs for language teachers do not adequately address the required knowledge base and strategic development of an aware, autonomous, and authentic teacher. And, of course, the AAA curriculum depends for its success on such a teacher.

The teacher's main task is to *understand* the students, particularly insofar as their learning activities in the classroom are concerned. This is necessary and sufficient (in most circumstances) to ensure a successful class, since it will naturally lead to instructional actions that are optimal *vis-à-vis* the students' learning processes. For such an understanding to develop, the two key terms, *language* and *learning*, need to be examined closely. In addition, the *cognitive* and *social* aspects of language learning need to be studied and related. In the classroom, *interaction* is the most visible manifestation of learning processes at work, although *inner speech* may well be equally crucial.

To these ingredients of the instructional process we need to add, from the learner's perspective, *motivation* for learning and the related notions of *self-determination* and *achievement*. From the teacher's perspective we need to add a search for the best ways of assisting learning, for example through working within Vygotsky's *zone of proximal development* or Bruner's related notion of *scaffolding* (see chapter 8).[6] In this perspective, assisting learning means *facilitating access* to language, knowledge, and skills, rather than *simplifying tasks*. I might quote the worthy slogan from content-based language teaching, 'Amplify, don't simplify!'

Looking ahead to subsequent chapters, a particularly useful concept to add to this view of the teaching/learning process is Csikszentmihalyi's *flow* or 'optimal experience.' These are special experiences (Maslow called them *peak experiences*) in which attention can be both relaxed and intensely focused on the task, in which intrinsic motivation emerges and flourishes, and learning becomes an organic experience (though not necessarily an effortless one, as we shall see). As Csikszentmihayli describes it (1990), during flow experiences, time appears to be irrelevant, effort is unnoticed, and skills are in perfect balance with challenges.

Finally, language use and language learning are part of the social world in which learners live. This social world has institutionalized structures in which language learning is supposed to take place. Therefore, whatever is done in the classroom, and whatever is regarded as appropriate behavior, and success, cannot be understood apart from the setting and the various influences that make it into what it is, and that includes, of course, the actions and expectations themselves. An element of cultural psychology (Cole 1990, Shweder 1990) or educational anthropology is therefore indispensable. Vygotsky's view that intellectual development is determined to a significant extent by social processes and relations, is particularly well suited to incorporate a wider cultural perspective.[7]

Viewing learning psychology as cultural psychology naturally leads us to an ecological perspective on the context of learning (cultural psychology can in many ways be seen as an 'ecological psychology,' cf. Cole 1990). Currently, two different ecological perspectives are influential in developmental psychology: the Batesonian perspective, which regards *mind* as a social construct, and which holds that 'the mental characteristics of the system are immanent, not in some part, but in the system as a whole' (Bateson 1972: 483; see Bowers & Flinders 1990: 234); and secondly, the Gibsonian ecological approach to visual perception (I mentioned this earlier, on p. 12), with its central notion of *affordance*, which emphasizes the interdependence of learner and environment (J.J. Gibson 1979; Forrester 1992). Applied to language education, the ecological perspective emphasizes social interaction, which makes linguistic affordances available to the developing child, and the cultural context in which language learning takes place. Incorporating the Batesonian emphasis on culture with the Gibsonian notion of affordance, though this has so far not happened, could lead to a particularly fruitful framework for investigating the sociocognitive processes involved in language learning.

I have here traced these various connections in bird's-eye fashion, to give the reader a global look at the argument before going into a detailed discussion of the theory of practice. In the following chapters I aim to integrate these and various other ingredients into a unified theory of classroom learning, which is itself one component of the theory of practice.

The scope of a theory of practice

From the classroom perspective, a theory of practice needs to encompass both the mental, or *intrapersonal* side of the learning process and its social, interactive, or *interpersonal* side. It is particularly crucial to relate the two if we believe, with Vygotsky, that much of learning resides in the interaction between these two sides. We can just *assume* that this is so, because it seems reasonable, but that would not yield a very useful theory. We need to *understand* the mechanisms whereby social interaction fuels cognitive growth, particularly in the case of language, where the complexity of hypothesized rules might suggest that most of the structure must be innate and therefore the role of learning must be limited. However, the question of innateness, of 'nature versus nurture,' though a very important and interesting one, plays only a minor role in the theory of practice. The business of learning is so multifaceted and complex that, regardless of how the nature/nurture issue turns out,[8] the educator's work will be undiminished, and the same problems and questions will remain to be addressed. An examination of the sociocognitive interface of learning will be attempted in chapter 7, under the heading of *contingency*.

Our understanding of learning and of interaction allows us to construct a theory of teaching and curriculum which is based firmly on evidence from classrooms. The theory of practice will thus consist of three distinct but interrelated tiers:

1. a theory of learning
2. a theory of pedagogical interaction
3. a theory of instruction

The theory of practice studies a reality in which we are *involved*. This involvement is the prime object of our study. As such, empirical data include the words and actions of the participants and their contexts, results on tests, interviews and questionnaires, and the usual array of data-gathering tools. In addition, however, less tangible phenomena need to be investigated: processes of decision-making, the constraints on and resources for pedagogical action, perceptions of quality and success, the nature of commitment, in short, the entire process of *professionalization* in the sense intended by the AAA curriculum.

Looked at holistically, as an evolving process, the theory of practice is our *project* for professionalization. Since the project is based on the epistemology and axiology of the AAA principles, increasing knowledge, and an increasing awareness of ethical values, form the core of professionalization, and this leads to an understanding of where we are going, and why. More important than an understanding of our reality is the next step that this understanding allows us to take: the investigation of the direction of our efforts. As Oliver Wendell Holmes said, 'I find the great thing in this world is not so much where we stand as in what direction we are moving' (quoted in Ryff 1985: 55).

Conclusion

A theory of second language learning which derives from and is built out of the daily practices, activities, and reflections of the people involved in language learning, of necessity turns on their head many of the assumptions and research-methodological prescriptions which currently are taken for granted by most researchers. It may, for example, be anathema to some 'hard-nosed' proponents of scientific method that ethical considerations (e.g. the values underlying the three principles discussed in the previous chapter, in other words, an explicit ideology) should play a decisive part in theory construction. Further, a suggestion that learning, interaction, and teaching cannot profitably be discussed without taking into account institutional (socioeconomic and political) constraints and resources, or without discussing at the same time the purposes of learning, from the perspective of society as well as the individual, may strike some as mixing scientific and extra-scientific concerns.

A theory of practice will by definition maintain that a separation of 'scientific' and 'practical' issues is artificial and detrimental to any particular field of study, but particularly so to a social field such as language learning. The social practices of teaching and learning can only be understood by showing how they are structured from a historical perspective[9] (as shown by, e.g., the feeling of loss of authority expressed by the teacher quoted on p. 28), as well as a contemporary sociocultural perspective.

In this book I will focus more on the *micro* than on the *macro* aspects of the context of language learning, on the classroom rather than on the institution or the state. The reason for this is not that I regard the local issues as more important than the global issues, but rather that I feel that I can best contribute to the theory of practice from my own perspective: that of the classroom floor.[10] In addition, it is useful to regard the classroom as a complex adaptive system (or CAS, to use terminology from complexity theory; see Lewin 1993, Abraham 1994) in which, to quote Stephen Jay Gould, 'details are all that matters' (1993), and it is fruitless to search for simple causal relations.

I will thus begin with the *learner*, as the entity most intimately involved in the learning process (the *theory of learning*). Next, I will discuss the learner in *conversation*, or *interaction*, in the classroom, with peers and others (the *theory of interaction*). Finally, I will conclude in the same place that I began, the *curriculum* (the *theory of curriculum and teaching*), with some suggestions for teacher development, and a brief discussion of implications for educational and social policy.

Notes

1 No practice can ever be completely theory-less, but in extreme cases teaching can be carried out by agents who act like puppets, unaware of the theoretical strings that control their motions.

2 Turning *empower* into a reflexive – as opposed to passive – verb suggests that power must be taken or created, not just passively received from some invisible agency.

3 See the quote from Michael Halliday on p. 2.

4 The meaning of 'mature science' is not defined in Kuhn (1970). Newmeyer and Weinberger suggest that maturity means a separation of the functions of science, applied science, and engineering (1988: 41).

5 'Reflection' is a multipurpose word like 'thinking,' and we need to specify what it involves and especially what it is we need to reflect *about*, and for what *purposes*. It is questionable if uncritical reflection, like navel-gazing or gentle rumination, is of major value from a research perspective. Within the AAA perspective, scrutiny of both *knowledge* and *values* are central to reflection.

6 Vygotsky's ZPD refers to the difference between being able to do an activity on one's own, and being able to do it with the help of someone else. Bruner's notion of scaffolding addresses the specific ways in which assistance can be provided (see further, p. 46).

7 See, e.g., Gallimore & Tharp 1990 for an elaboration of this view; see also Bourdieu's reproduction theory (Bourdieu & Passeron 1977), and Paul Willis's educational ethnography (1981).

8 We may like to remember Peter Medawar's quip that both nature and nurture contribute 100 percent to development (Bruner 1986: 135).

9 The historical basis of complex institutional structures such as schools is clearly visible in Foucault's approach to the 'archeology of knowledge' (1972).

10 I also do not want to end up like the person of whom Wittgenstein once said: 'He wants to sit on six stools at once, but he has only got one arse' (Monk 1990).

3　The growth of proficiency

Introduction

This chapter addresses the first of the three tiers of the AAA curriculum laid out in the preceding chapter: the theory of learning, particularly the *intrapersonal* side of it. As guidance for this chapter I will not use the sorts of experimental evidence that are customary in psychological theories of learning, though I shall refer to the work of developmental psychology when I consider it relevant.

My guidance in proposing the view put forward here comes, first and foremost, from my classroom experiences as a student, a teacher, and an observer in a variety of roles. These experiences provide fuel for reflection on what goes on in people who are engaged in some 'official' (that is, purposeful, deliberate, and overtly acknowledged) business of language learning. My aim is to present a plausible and practical account of language learning, not to make causal claims or make statistical predictions. I set myself the task, as a teacher, of understanding my students, and the results of that pursuit are presented here.

In the second place I am guided by the foundational principles of *awareness*, *autonomy*, and *authenticity*, and the secondary triad of *achievement*, *assessment*, and *accountability*, which provides the links with the educational context. My theory of learning is therefore determined by my values and beliefs about what sort of activities human learning and language development are, and should be, within a specific social and insitutional context.[1]

The third source of information is the psychological work mentioned above, and particularly that which is consonant with the AAA curriculum, notably work in the Vygotskyan and Piagetian traditions, as well as insights from a variety of other sources. In elaborating my views and casting them in a curriculum-theoretical mold I have been extremely encouraged to find that all three sources mentioned here:

(a)　practical classroom experiences and understanding
(b)　principles and values regarding language use and language education
(c)　psychological and social-psychological research on learning

have produced remarkably converging input to the work. To some extent, of course, one tends to finds what one wants to find, but the consistent pattern of reinforcements from multiple sources that I have found gives me strong hopes that the exposition of language education presented here is the best that can be presented given our current state of knowledge and societal aspirations. As usual, time will of course tell how justified my optimism is.

Overview

Figure 4 is provided as a 'road map' for this chapter. It is also a map of the road traveled by the learners in their learning careers, from their first exposure to the language, to full proficiency or however far they happen to get. In this (unfortunately two-dimensional) representation there are a

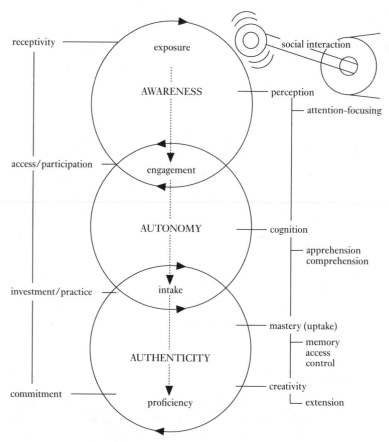

Figure 4 The growth of proficiency

number of *movements* or *cycles*, indicating that language learning is a gradual and cumulative process, or the result of a number of processes working simultaneously and successively, rather like a team of people building a house. These are *exposure – engagement – intake – proficiency*. On the left side are some *conditions* which I consider necessary: *receptivity – access/participation – investment/practice – commitment*; and on the right are various *outcomes* or results: *perception – cognition – mastery (uptake) – creativity*. These conditions and outcomes should not be seen as sucessive in a linear fashion, but rather partly parallel and partly cyclical, determining one another in a reciprocal fashion. The learning process moves along in a metamorphic fashion (as suggested, e.g., by Rutherford 1987), determined by the conditions, fueled or propelled by the dynamism of the AAA principles in concert with social interaction, and resulting in the various outcomes. The end result is the language proficiency that the student reaches, most likely being forever a proficiency-in-progress.

The diagram shows (in a highly metaphorical way, of course) the central importance of *social interaction*, which moves all the elements of the process, in the form of an 'engine' (with apologies to the painter Paul Klee) that gets the learning wheels of awareness, autonomy and authenticity turning and thus produces learning like a CD player produces sound (the true substance, music, like language and meaning, must of course be supplied from elsewhere). Below I shall go through the various parts of the diagram step by step, describing the view of language learning I have constructed on the basis of a study of praxis. In this sequential description a number of issues of crucial, more global, importance will necessarily receive insufficient attention. I will discuss them in separate chapters following the present one. These global issues are:

- language/learning awareness   ch. 4
- intrinsic motivation (autonomy)   ch. 5
- authenticity   ch. 6
- contingency (social interaction)   ch. 7
- assistance (the curriculum in practice, e.g. scaffolding)   ch. 8
- teacher development (e.g. action research)   ch. 9

Exposure

As a language teacher one cannot escape the feeling that language lessons in and of themselves are not sufficient to bring language learning about and to lead to eventual proficiency. If the lessons – whether they are once a week, once a day, or more frequent than that – are the only occasions on which the students are engaged with the language, progress will either not occur or be exceedingly slow. The students' minds must occupy themselves with the language *between* lessons as well as *in* lessons, if improvements are to happen. I do not only or primarily mean homework – though it can no doubt be of great assistance – but rather a process of inner speech, being mentally 'busy' with the language, reflecting on language-related phenomena, and noticing things that are relevant to progress. The more lessons I observe, the more I become convinced that language development occurs *between* lessons rather than *during* lessons, and I do not mean this as an indication that the lessons I observe are inefficient or bad. Rather, I feel that language learning is the cumulative result of sustained effort and engagement over time, with continuity being central. The lessons can give raw food (or ingredients) for learning, as it were, and if they are done well they can give the student a healthy appetite, but the cooking, consumption, and digestion of the food occur spread out over a long, institutionally uncontrollable time period (i.e. the school or classroom cannot determine how, when, where, and at what pace learning is going to happen). Traditional syllabuses may offer the linguistic food in pre-cooked or even pre-chewed manner, in the hope that the entire process can thus occur inside the classroom, under the watchful controlling eye of the mandated supervisor (the teacher), but technology cannot, not even in league with bureaucracy, circumvent digestion.

Eric Hawkins has compared the teaching of French in British schools to 'gardening in a gale' (1987b: 97). On this view, after the teacher has succeeded in planting a few 'tender seedlings' of the target language in the students' minds, the bell rings and the students go out into the corridor, the playground, other lessons, and other places where a relentless gale of English blows these tender seedlings away again. The next time the French teacher sees the students again, the ground is just as barren as it was before. This, it must be said, is a rather gloomy portrayal of foreign language lessons (and presumably other lessons as well), and one can only hope that things are not quite that bad in most cases. However, it points to a real problem of all foreign language learning, and to a lesser extent also the learning of academic and formal registers of the native language. If the gap between what is done in the classroom, and what is done outside the classroom, is too great, then the possibilities of learning anything at all are very seriously impaired. This gap does not only, or even primarily, refer to differences in activities, topics, and interaction, but most forcefully to a gap in values and aspirations. The 'gale' does therefore not only blow in a foreign language learning setting in which the target language is not perceived as a particularly valuable commodity, but also in native language and second language settings where classroom and society send messages which, to the student, appear to contradict one another.

To give an example, I have heard adult learners of English in California (migrant workers, illegal immigrants working in the gardening business, etc.) report regularly that they really want to learn English, they are aware of its importance, they are willing to plough through any number of worksheets and vocabulary exercises, but they simply cannot make their mouth say 'those things' the way native speakers do: a friendly greeting is no longer a friendly greeting once it has been recast in the strange language. This psychosocial (or cultural, perhaps) gap may account for difficulties with group work and various kinds of communicative activities with many such students.

A gap can also occur when students feel that the classroom does not give adequate help in facing tasks outside that classroom which appear insurmountable. To give an example, in an ESL grammar class I taught some time ago I noticed that students appeared to be unable to listen systematically and obtain useful input outside the classroom. I therefore asked them to bring an 'entry ticket' to class every lesson. This was a 3×5 card on which they had written down, without worrying about the spelling, something they had heard in their daily pursuits. I hoped that these entry tickets would encourage the students to open their ears and start being aware of the real language around them.

However easy this may seem to the native speaker, this turns out to be a very difficult task for beginning ESL students. So far I am not entirely clear about why exactly this should be so difficult, though I regard it as an important task to investigate this question. No doubt shyness about eavesdropping and self-consciousness about scribbling on cards in public places is part of the problem for some students, but there is undoubtedly far more to *linguistic access* than that.

The *access* which is at stake here is access to *exposure*, i.e. the language which surounds the learner. Clearly, exposure is necessary to learn language. The main question that arises, however, is how the learner gains access to this exposure-language. The accessibility of exposure depends primarily on three sets of factors:

(a) characteristics of the exposure-language
(b) characteristics of the learner
(c) characteristics of the setting in which the learner encounters the exposure-language

It is not clear what the ideal characteristics of exposure-language are. If one reads most of the literature, or if one listens to arguments against bilingual education, one gets the impression that *quantity* of exposure is crucial. In other words, the more language you surround the learner with, the better. However, we must also consider the *quality* of the exposure-language. The language must be *usable*, one way or another. If the learner cannot or will not use it, for whatever reason, then shoving more language down the learner's throat is likely to make matters worse rather than better. Exposure-language is usable when the learner can make sense of it, is receptive to it, and makes an effort to process it. It is possible to imagine circumstances and environments in which any amount of exposure might be useless, and other situations in which small amounts of exposure might be sufficient. I therefore regard quality as far more significant than quantity. But what do we mean by quality? Minimally, I suggest, quality is that which facilitates access and usability (we must therefore not confuse quality of the *exposure* with quality of the *language*, an obscure yet crucial distinction we will return to in chapter 6, when we discuss authenticity). One of the things that definitely facilitates access and usability is *comprehension*, in fact it is the one characteristic stressed by Krashen and his followers, when they speak of comprehensible input as being the only causal factor in language acquisition (1985). I will return to the problematic notion of comprehension below, but its importance can be illustrated with the following anecdote.

Many years ago I had the opportunity to travel regularly to Finland. Having had considerable success in 'picking up' languages before, I somehow felt that I should be able to learn Finnish, to 'crack the code,' as it were, if I just turned on the radio in my hotel room and listened to the news, interviews, songs, and whatever, for a sufficient number of hours. It did not take me too long to realize that I was making no headway whatsoever, since I could not understand a word, indeed, I had no way of identifying when one word stopped and another began, since Finnish, not even being an Indo-European language, was so fundamentally different from any language that I knew, that I simply could not find any place to start. I provided myself with lots of exposure, but I could not do anything with it.

Another way in which access to exposure can be improved or, in other words, another aspect of the quality of exposure-language, is the availability of *assistance* of one form or another. One form of assistance is *contextual information* (public signs, standard greetings, and so on, the kinds of things Klein [1985] has called *embedding*), another form is help from other people, through interaction. As far as such help from people is concerned, we can draw on Vygotsky's *zone of proximal development* (ZDP) as a useful construct for language learning. It can be defined as follows:

It is the distance between the actual developmental level as determined by
independent problem solving and the level of potential development as
determined through problem solving under adult guidance or in collaboration
with more capable peers. (Vygotsky 1978: 86)

Elsewhere Vygostky simply states that 'what a child can do with assistance today, she will be able to do by herself tomorrow' (1978: 87). We
will have more to say about various forms of assistance, especially those
that can be applied in the language classroom setting, using for example
Bruner's accounts of *scaffolding* (especially in chapter 8), which is closely
related to Vygotsky's ZPD.

We now turn to the ways in which the usability of exposure-language
may depend on the *learner*. Researchers often appear to assume that by
looking at the exposure-language itself one can find the characteristics
that make it either useful or useless. Thus for example, Krashen's notion
of input at 'i + 1' would appear to be a property of the language rather
than the person exposed to the language. In actual fact, however,
whether or how the exposure-language is used (and is comprehended)
depends first and foremost on the learner, and his or her prior knowledge, attitudes, interests, analytical abilities, communicative dexterity,
and so on (barring, of course, such excessive gaps as the one illustrated in
my Finnish example).

Further, comprehensibility appears to be regarded as a monolithic[2]
property of the language, which is either present, or absent. That is,
either I comprehend, or I do not comprehend. But in life we rarely ever
understand anything either completely or not at all: we usually understand things more or less, or we begin by understanding them a little,
and gradually our understanding grows, though we rarely reach full (100
per cent) understanding of something, especially in the case of language
(cf. Rost 1990). How much do we need to comprehend in order to profit
from exposure-language? 'Just enough,' might be the only reasonable
answer that can be given, and it is probably of little interest to seek for
more precision than that (see further the comments on familiarity
below).

The third factor that influences the accessibility of exposure-language
is the setting or set of circumstances surrounding the language learning
process. Recent immigrants and refugees who need to work extremely
hard to survive and who seek support from one another often learn little
or nothing of the host language. The following case is not atypical.

A Latin-American immigrant who has lived for a number of years in
the USA (female, unmarried) works long hours in a small textile factory
in New Jersey, every day traveling an hour-and-a-half each way from
Astoria, Queens, to work. During the day she is exposed to a consider-

able amount of English, but it is doubtful that she attends to much of it. She speaks no English beyond a few stock phrases and understands little beyond the standard expressions and instructions at work. At home, where she lives in the same house as her younger sister and the latter's family, all interaction is in Spanish. She relies on her savvier sister and her Latino boyfriend for complex dealings with the English world. She has considerable exposure to English, but uses little of it, and she has arranged her life in such a way as to be able to cope without learning English.

Among first-generation immigrants, such a scenario is quite common. Even many couples with children do not learn the host language although they see their children acquiring it while at the same time losing their native language, the family's only means of internal communication (for a famous example, see Richard Rodriguez' autobiographical *Hunger of memory*, 1982). There are thus countless families in which, to a greater or lesser degree, communication between parents and children has ceased. In many cases the parents are resigned to sacrifice themselves for the sake of their children, though tragically, the lack of communication may result in the breakdown of the family, which in turn may result in school dropout, gang activity, and estrangement from home even in those cases where a child, against all odds, has succeeded in the mainstream world.

When considering exposure-language and its accessibility for language learning, such sociocultural circumstances clearly play an important, often decisive role. Massive preoccupation with matters of survival, or other complex demands, can make it difficult to use exposure-language efficiently, or at all. The same can be said of a sociocultural environment which appears excessively bewildering, threatening, or unwelcoming. The culture shock that many immigrants experience may be accompanied by *language shock*, and when the culture shock wears off, the language shock may persist. In addition, native language support structures may have been created that make the learning of the host language less vital, especially when compared with the multitude of other pressing matters faced by the immigrant.

To sum up, exposure to language is clearly not sufficient for language development (except, perhaps, for native language development during the first years of life, though even here I believe the conditions described hold to some degree). When all other factors remain constant, increasing the amount of exposure will have little or no effect on language development. Far more important are various characteristics which we may collectively call the *quality of exposure*. Roughly speaking, this quality is determined by characteristics of the *language* (contextuality, accessibility), of the *interaction* (particularly various forms of assistance that may be available), and of the *sociocultural setting*. All in all, if we were to put the quality in one word, it would have to be something like 'participatability.' This is characterized by *engagement*, rather than Krashen's comprehensibility, which is only one, perhaps not always crucial, aspect of it; instead of *comprehensible input* it is therefore better to speak of *language engagement*.[3]

This completes our discussion of exposure, the raw material in the learning process. Once we have ensured the possibility of access to the exposure-language available to the learner, we can see how the learner can profit from exposure. We will therefore now proceed to discuss how exposure can become usable.

From exposure to engagement

In order to profit from exposure to language the learner needs to be *receptive* to the exposure-language. Receptivity is a concept well known from psychology (where it can be found under a variety of names, including openness, readiness, etc.), and particularly from the work of Abraham Maslow. In second language work the concept of receptivity has received most attention in Allwright & Bailey 1991. They define it as 'a state of mind, whether permanent or temporary, that is open to the experience of becoming a speaker of another language' (p. 157). Receptivity can also be related to *exploration*, *manipulation*, and *play*, notions which are closely linked to learning. Harlow's experiments (1950, described in Deci & Ryan 1985: 13) showed that 'monkeys learned to solve a puzzle apparatus for no other reward than the enjoyment of doing it,' and he used the term *intrinsic motivation* to refer to this phenomenon. Similarly, Deci and Ryan report studies which found that rats spontaneously explored novel places, and persisted in doing so even when this involved experiencing hunger and pain. Such curiosity-related behaviors are thus powerful stimuli for learning.

Receptivity, particularly when it is related to curiosity and the other phenomena mentioned, is clearly an important element in language learning. But it would be a mistake to regard it as simply a passive state of openness rather than a spirit of exploration. It is often remarked that children have this curiosity and spirit of exploration when they first get to school, or to their first foreign language lesson, but that it is gradually killed off there. Maslow said that 'the present school system is an extremely effective instrument for crushing peak experiences and forbidding their possibility' (1971: 195). If we want language learning to be a success, we must clearly ensure that receptivity and curiosity are maintained. Csikszentmihalyi's notion of flow (1990) is a useful guide in this respect, and we will elaborate on this in later chapters (see also chapter 2).

A person who is receptive to exposure-language will *pay attention* to that language. This paying attention[4] is an *active* response, although it may not be conscious and deliberate in the usual sense. In one sense, consciousness is 'awareness of the activity of the mind' (Vygotsky 1986: 170), and conscious attention would therefore involve being aware of attending (a common term for this level of consciousness is *meta-consciousness*, see further chapter 4). But a person can attend to something with or without being aware of attending. Though at times conscious attending may assist in a more efficient *selecting* or *directing* of the attention (focusing, see below), in general I can find no evidence that the quality of perception is directly affected, one way or another, by the attending being done consciously or non-consciously (in the above sense). One can be intensely aware of the object one is perceiving, without being conscious of that awareness.[5]

Figure 5 shows the relationships of the various processes involved in perceiving an object (including a linguistic utterance), and also implies a continuum from less to more engagement. Consciousness is seen as a separate superordinate mental activity which may or may not accompany any of the states, or instigate any of the actions mentioned.

Some writers, e.g. Krashen (1990) and Smith (1986), claim that the most useful learning is *incidental* (that is, not done 'on purpose'). However, they confuse wanting to learn with being forced to learn (including forcing oneself to learn because of certain pressures), creating a false dichotomy between deliberate learning and incidental learning. Clearly, I can want to learn something, and consciously apply my various mental powers to the task. How this can be regarded as being inferior to

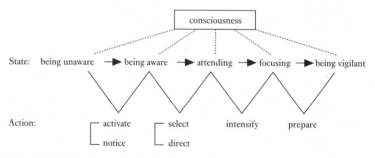

Figure 5   Varieties of attention involved in perceiving an object

learning by chance (while doing something for whatever purpose), is incomprehensible. The important thing is to get the perceptual processes going in as efficient a manner as possible, and our consciousness (as well as guidance from other people) can help us to check that this is being done. Although certain mental processes may not be open to inspection (Pylyshyn 1984 calls them *cognitively impenetrable*), and not all learning is necessarily conscious, 'the acquisition and restructuring of knowledge generally requires the conscious participation of the subject,' as Gombert concludes in his comprehensive overview of metalinguistic development (1992: 195).

I now return to the ways in which we can describe the various factors that provide access to exposure, using a practical example as illustration.

> Some readers may note that, in contrast with earlier work in this area (van Lier 1991a), I have decided to drop the word *input* from my discussion of language learning. This may seem curious, given that it has become one of the most intensively studied elements in language acquisition in the last decade or so (Gass & Madden 1985, Krashen 1985). There are two reasons for this. First, many accounts do not systematically distinguish between exposure and input, and there is a danger that the active role of the learner, in terms of choices and strategies, is neglected, and *quantity* (in terms of both volume of language and time of exposure) threatens to take precedence over *quality*. More importantly, however, I feel that we need to move away from viewing language learning (or any learning, for that matter) in terms of the input/output metaphor (or, more generally, from an information-processing perspective; cf. Forrester 1992). In this metaphor, input flows from an external source (perhaps a teacher, or another learner) to the learner, who mentally processes it and then has it available to produce output. This transmission process can, in one variant of the input view, be facilitated (i.e the input can be made more comprehensible) by interaction, since participants can negotiate their comprehension by requesting and producing modifications (Long 1985, Pica, Young, & Doughty 1987). Since it focuses on dialogical rather than on monological transmission, this work is a step in the right direction. However, it still adheres to the input/output view of learning, where items in the input, whether put there on purpose or not, have a causal (perhaps triggering) effect on acquisition processes in the learner. A similar view leads innatists such as Steven Pinker (1994: 278) to reduce the requirements of speech input to children to a focus on the 'here and now,' and certain other characteristics of 'motherese,' such as typical intonation patterns, slower rate of delivery, and a high proportion of questions and directives. This is once again a causal, and rather mechanistic, perspective on learning in which the establishment of intersubjectivity and reciprocity, and the social nature of language and cognition, are ignored. It is this linear cause–effect view that needs to be replaced by a more complex view in which cognition, language, learning, and consciousness are in themselves dialogical constructs (Marcus & Zajonc 1985, Graumann 1990). This will be the tenor of my discussion of contingency in chapter 7.

One of the 'entry tickets' in the activity mentioned above had the words 'BIG DEAL!' written on it. It may be useful to look at this example in the light of the perceptual processes discussed here. The student who handed the card in had obviously been aware of this piece of language (possibly as a result of the learning task I had set as a teacher), and had selected it from among other pieces of language for closer attention. Note here that one can pay attention to an utterance (or any sound, of course) some time *after* that utterance has occurred. We might say that our attention is *drawn* to the utterance, for some reason. Our memory can hold the utterance for subsequent inspection. In the case of our student, his attention had been drawn to 'BIG DEAL!' because the utterance puzzled him, not being sure what it meant (even though he might know what the words *big* and *deal* meant, individually). A more intensive focusing on the utterance, *in situ*, would not likely have helped in this case since, as it turned out, the student had not attended to (at least not sufficiently to remember it) the utterance to which 'BIG DEAL!' was a response. The 'entry ticket,' and my subsequent comments and contextual illustrations of the idiom, functioned as a sort of pedagogical or 'surrogate' focusing, hopefully with the result that, next time the student hears the expression, he knows what it means and can figure out why it was said. Eventually he may be bold enough to use 'BIG DEAL!' himself if he feels the appropriate occasion arises (he might say to himself or a friend: 'I've been dying to try this out for a long time').

If perception is as important as I am suggesting, what is the appropriate level of engagement, and how do we obtain it? Returning to my Finnish example above, I was clearly aware of the language on the radio, I was paying attention to it (to *all* of it, and therein lay much of the problem), I was even trying to focus hard on whatever I could, except that I had no idea what to focus on. I did get impressions of the sound patterns, the rhythm, and the stress and intonation patterns of Finnish, and these impressions may have been useful in some intangible way in my subsequent more systematic efforts at learning Finnish. But I could clearly do no productive focusing, since I had nothing to *guide* such focusing.

Focusing is a term which suggests an orientation of the subject towards an object. The metaphor of a camera lens comes to mind. Further, it might even mean, for a teacher, focusing the student in a transitive sense, in the way that a photographer focuses a camera. I suggest that this transitive sense is not useful to us. However, the subject → object focusing is only half the story. Equally important is the *activation* of cognitive networks of the subject. In the case of my Finnish exposure there was nothing, beyond sounds, rhythms and tones, that could possibly be activated, and therefore I could make no headway. In the case of my student, activation may have been possible because the words *big* and *deal* were familiar, or perhaps because the conversational structure was familiar. If someone had just said 'impenetrability,' the student might not have attended at all (it would have been just one among a myriad of incomprehensible things drifting by constantly). The point, then, is that perceptual effort of a certain strength must be matched or backed up by the activation of mental networks (schemata, perhaps), and this can only happen if there is a link between what is perceived and what is in the mind. Familiarity, or recognition, is an important part of this process, and this suggests that an exposure → input conversion cannot be externally driven, e.g. by a transmission-oriented teacher or curriculum, but rather, engagement with language occurs when the learner's internal knowledge system, including the language knowledge-to-date, interacts ('resonates,' to use an ecological metaphor from J.J.Gibson 1979) with the environment. Under such conditions, exposure-language offers *affordances*, to use J.J. Gibson's term (see E.J. Gibson 1991: 558), which are learning opportunities for the learner.

In L1 acquisition, focusing on language is to a large extent (initially, at least) genetically driven, and is probably activated most significantly by social interaction with meaningful others (particularly the mother, see Murray & Trevarthen 1985, Trevarthen & Marwick 1986) in the environment. This focusing is often intense, all-absorbing, and accompanied by a readiness to act and take risks since, as Trevarthen & Marwick put it, 'all infants over 3 months enjoy . . . a risky but partly successful engagement of action and emotion with a recognized and trusted partner' (1986: 293). Very often there is thus a heightened state of awareness which has been called *vigilance* (Price 1969, Piaget 1976). In this state of heightened awareness the child is ready to act on partly predictable, partly novel stimuli. Price gives the example of a cat eyeing a mouse:

> The cat as he crouches ready to spring . . . is prepared for any one of many possible mouse-movements. We have seen that this preparedness for alternatives is one of the characteristic features of animal (and human) vigilance. But this is not all. The cat is prepared to jump in the appropriate direction, whichever of these alternatives is realized . . . Practical reason, rather than theoretical, is Pussy's strong point. (Price 1969: 127, 129)

In L2 learning, as well as in academic L1 study in schools (including literacy), this social-biological vigilance can no longer be taken for granted, so that attention and focusing (and vigilance, on rarer occasions) must be fostered by other means – including making things interesting and comprehensible, setting high expectations, promoting intrinsic motivation, and many other time-honored pedagogical ideals.

One of the means advocated in this book is the development of language awareness and learning awareness or, in more general terms, *language learning awareness,* so as to facilitate both the engagement with exposure-language, and the simultaneous activation of cognitive structures (see chapter 4).

I have suggested that in instructional settings, attention-focusing needs to be fostered (see also Gass 1991). But this does not mean that we can or should predict what it is that will be focused on. In the 'BIG DEAL!' example above, the use of 'entry tickets' was a way to promote focusing, but what was actually focused on was determined by the student. Some teaching methods appear to assume that it can be decided beforehand, for every student, what is to be focused on, how, and when, and this is, I think, a very wasteful procedure. The emphasis should rather be on providing a rich variety of exposure-language, and to let the students pick what they need. It is not necessary to worry about the things that are not picked. To use Neisser's analogy: 'To pick one apple from a tree you need not filter out all the others; you just don't pick them' (1976: 84–5). However, we must make sure that there are apples within the reach of all students (this is where *access*, in the form of comprehensibility, familiarity , assistance, and so on, comes in). This view of exposure as the provision of opportunities for engaging with language is, as I have suggested before, an *ecological* approach (as elaborated for visual perception by J.J. Gibson 1979), in which interactional contexts offer or provide affordances that the learner or child may perceive and act on.

To sum up, exposure-language provides material for learning if the student is receptive and attends to (parts of) the exposure-language, and if there are sufficient means of access (e.g. comprehension, familiarity, assistance) for the perceived material to activate cognitive networks, thus creating the possibility for linking interaction and cognition. Engagement can thus take place when language is attended to, perceived, and made available for sociocognitive processing.

From engagement to intake

When a learner engages with language, perceives, notices, and focuses on language items or phenomena (affordances), a variety of cognitive, emotional, or physical responses can take place. I have decided to retain the term *intake* to refer to language that is responded to by the learner, in other words, processed in various ways. The processing of language requires an *investment* of effort on the part of the learner. This investment can be cognitive, emotional, or physical (or a bit of all three). The basic environment for the processing of language is social interaction, particularly conversation. In fact, the distinction between *social processes* and *cognitive processes* is unclear, and as a result one now fairly commonly encounters the term social-cognitive processes (Forrester 1992). How these social-cognitive processes work will be discussed in a separate chapter under the heading of *contingency*, i.e. the ways in which utterances are *tied* to the world (including other utterances), and at the same time *project* into the unknown.

Investment of effort leads to two kinds of understanding: *apprehension*, a kind of intuitive, unverbalized (or unverbalizable) knowing, and *comprehension*, which includes the more familiar types of expressable and analyzed knowledge. This distinction, though it has been widely discussed for centuries in philosophy and psychology, has received remarkably little attention in language learning theory.[6] The two terms, as I use them here, follow closely the definitions and descriptions in Kolb (1984). Equivalent distinctions are made by Arnold (1960), who calls the two processes *intuitive appraisal* and *reflective judgment*, respectively, and by Bruner (1963), who uses the terms *intuitive* and *analytical thinking*.

These two modes of knowing are intimately interconnected. Indeed, rather than assuming two separate kinds of understanding it might be better to think of a continuum which would have such notions as intuitive, unanalyzed, tacit, feel, and so on, on one side, and such notions as explicit, communicable, analyzed, rational, and so on, on the other. It might be tempting to think of the apprehension end of that continuum as representing more primitive, less mature, incipient forms of thinking, and of comprehension as embodying 'higher-order' thought processes. I think that would be a serious mistake, for several reasons. In the first place, much of our knowing is of the apprehension kind since the subject matter which it is about simply makes it unsuitable for rational, analytical, or reflective mental operations. Wittgenstein gives the following examples to illustrate an important distinction between *knowing* and *saying*:

> how many feet high Mont Blanc is–
> how the word 'game' is used–
> how a clarinet sounds.

> If you are surprised that one can know something and not be able to say it, you are perhaps thinking of a case like the first. Certainly not of one like the third. (Wittgenstein 1958: 36)

The same is true for the phenomenon Bourdieu calls 'feel for the game' (1990: 66). Many parents will be familiar with this if they have ever enrolled a child in, say, a soccer program and watched the practice sessions. At first the children just kick the ball around, in whatever direction, all of them running after it like a swarm of bees. At some point, one or more of the children begin to show a 'feel for the game,' and the way they play is transformed completely, almost from one moment to the next. It may well be that this 'feel for the game' cannot be expressed or explained in so many words: you know it when you have it, and you know it when you see it. If something similar exists in language development, and I see every reason to assume that it does, the interesting question is how a language learner develops such a feel. A provisional answer is, by participating and working hard.

A second important consideration is the primacy of intuition in the advancement of human knowledge, documented by many scientists and thinkers. Thus, Mach has said: 'Intuition is the basis of all knowledge' (Feyerabend 1987: 199); and Bergson has said: 'From intuition one can pass to analysis, but not from analysis to intuition' (Kohl 1965: 25). It may thus be the case that many times we need to obtain an intuitive grasp of some phenomenon before we can begin to analyze it in detail. The same point is made by Piaget when, in his later experiments, he speaks of the process of *cognizance* in problem-solving, as a stage prior to a conceptualization of the various elements constituting the problem (1976, 1978).

A third issue that is relevant in the comparison of apprehension and comprehension, in some ways opposite to the second consideration above, relates to the acquisition of complex skills, where one begins with conscious, deliberate action, and ends up with automatized, effortless action. A dramatic example is recounted by Treffert (1989), about a research student called Benji Langdon who studied the amazing mathematical abilities of idiot-savant twins (two autistic boys). As Treffert tells the story, Langdon decided to learn to replicate the twins' abilities. To this end he practiced day and night for a long time, without any appreciable effect. Most of us would presumably have given up and been content with a vicarious description, but Langdon persisted. Suddenly, overnight, a 'quantum leap in ability' occurred, and Langdon became as proficient as the twins, effortlessly performing the most complex calculations. Interestingly, it was found that Langdon's capacity 'migrated' from the left brain to the right brain at the time of his breakthrough. Relating this back to language development, we might speculate that 'hard work' at practicing language might eventually pay off in a similar way, and that many linguistic routines, ready-made expressions, formulas, and conversational scripts may be right-brain resident, thus contradicting the common assumption that language is a left-brain affair.

The above points are consonant with A.A. Leont'ev's discussion of *habit* as a dual notion (in the context of learning Russian as a foreign language):

> A habit may be generated 'from below' as the result of 'continuous realignment' and imitation, or 'from above' as the result of automatization and reduction . . . we shall call these two types of habits 'unconscious' and 'conscious' respectively. Let us emphasize, however, that this terminology is purely a matter of convention. (Leont'ev 1977: 468–90)

It is a truism that different things are learned in different ways. For example, learning to play a C chord, a G7 chord, and an F chord on the guitar, while at the same time trying to sing 'The leaving of Liverpool' is different from learning how to maintain your front lawn, which is different again from learning about the history of the Inquisition and its relations with the Vatican (and it is not really possible to say which one of these is 'more difficult'). I propose that language learning, both first and subsequent, is complex enough to be like all of the above, and much else besides.

The complexity of learning language can also be explored by looking at the problem in terms of Peirce's categories (or 'modes of being') of *firstness, secondness*, and *thirdness* (Büchler 1955). Firstness is awareness, perception, intuition, or feeling; secondness is interruption, change, the intrusion of the outside world; thirdness is synthesis, learning, thought. In Peirce's view, all of life and human knowledge is based on these three categories of firstness, secondness, and thirdness. In this scheme, apprehension would be firstness; noticing salient things in the linguistic environment, and the role of 'the other' in social interaction, would be secondness; and comprehension (including, interestingly, the ability to make *predictions* about future facts of secondness) would be thirdness.

Peirce's triadic model may be an excellent means of organizing the complexities of language learning (see chapter 6 for a more detailed discussion; see also Oller 1990). There are many other useful models, including the Vygotskyan and Piagetian ones, and the model of autotelic learning by Csikszentmihalyi (1990; see also p. 13 above). It is not necessary for us to 'adopt' one of these models and reject all others. Becoming a 'follower' of one model or another (including, of course, the one set forth in this chapter!) would mean abandoning the theory of practice. Rather, all of the models mentioned, and potentially many others, offer useful metaphors to assist us in our understanding of the language students in our classes, and all of them share the common themes that I have formulated as the AAA principles.

From intake to proficiency

I mentioned above that, for engagement with language to lead to intake, mental structures or networks must be *activated*. This activation can spread more or less broadly or deeply (Anderson 1983 speaks of *divergent* and *convergent* activation spreading; see Levelt 1989 for an accessible account), depending, e.g., on emotional involvement (see Schumann's discussion of the role of the *amygdala*, 1990; see also Damasio 1994; Humphrey 1992), on intensity of engagement, on degree of familiarity, and so on. In this way new connections are made and existing ones strengthened (others weakened, or severed perhaps), and this is part of what we mean by cognitive processing. However, according to Figure 4, more work needs to be done.

In plain terms, we need to remember the material we have learned. This means that it must be *retained* in memory, in such a way that it is *accessible* with facility at appropriate times and places. In addition, certain operations (stress assignment, inflections and agreements, gender and case assignment, and so on) and routines and sequences (e.g. ritual expressions, collocations) must be *automatized*, so that their use becomes progressively more energy-efficient. Some kind of *rehearsal* is therefore likely to be necessary for these kinds of language abilities to develop. In a connectionist model, learning takes place 'through repeated experiences with the same or similar entities . . . and with contrasting types of entities' (Potter 1990: 13). How much (or what aspects) of language learning depend upon various kinds of rehearsal (including repetition for a variety of purposes; see Schmidt & Frota 1986 for interesting suggestions), and how much of it simply and sufficiently occurs through apprehension (or cognizing), is not a question I can usefully address here. Nor can I do justice to the far more interesting and probably crucial interplay between apprehension, comprehension, and rehearsal (see chapter 7, on *contingency*, for ideas related to this). Rather, I take the reasonable position that, given the above, as a teacher I need to provide opportunities for rehearsal when it appears that students need them. It is part of the principle of autonomy that students basically learn to decide for themselves when, what, and how to rehearse.

The work (including rehearsing) that needs to be done in order to move from intake into mastery (uptake), and from there to proficiency, can take a wide variety of different forms. It is convenient to refer to much of it by the well-known general term *practice*, though we must remember at all times the heterogeneity of activities that this catch-all term includes.

Practice

As folk wisdom has it, *practice makes perfect*. Does this apply to language learning, or only to such activities as knitting, brewing beer, and driving in New York City? Most people who have studied a foreign language, or have learned to read, write, or speak in public in their native language will say yes, practice is definitely essential in learning those things. What is meant by practice in these cases, and are these people right?

Rod Ellis, who is one of the few people to have studied the notion of practice in the second language classroom setting in detail (1988), provides a description of the commonly accepted meaning of practice:

> The purpose of practice is to activate the new knowledge [obtained in the *presentation stage* that precedes the practice] to the point where it can be used automatically and correctly in normal communication. For this reason the learner is required to engage in *extensive production* of utterances containing the new structure. (Ellis 1988: 21)

In many cases (e.g. Harmer 1983, Hubbard *et al.* 1983) a progression from *controlled practice* to *communication* (or *free practice*) is assumed. Harmer, for example, speaks of pre-communicative and communicative activities. A few years earlier, in a very influential textbook, Bratt Paulston distinguished between *mechanical, meaningful,* and *communicative* practice (Paulston & Bruder 1976), again advocating a sequential progression, and taking perhaps a somewhat mechanistic view of the learning process. Wilga Rivers' classic distinction between *skill-getting* and *skill-using* illustrates a related view (Rivers and Temperley 1978).

We might thus say, without undue exaggeration, that there is a received or canonical view of practice which assigns it a prominent and well-defined place in the sequence of classroom learning. However, the agreement is by no means unanimous. In Krashen's input hypothesis, where, as we have seen, all that is required is comprehensible input in an affectively supportive environment, practice is largely regarded as unnecessary, or even counterproductive, given that it leads students to focus on form rather than on meaning. The same point is made by Prabhu (1987), who also discusses another important drawback of the types of practice advocated by Harmer and the others mentioned above. Incorporating a 'stage' of practice in language lessons implies, according to Prabhu, a pre-selection of forms, and this assumes that it is possible to decide beforehand what students are ready to learn (or ready to practice), or need to learn (or practice) at a particular point. To the extent that practice is conducted as a whole-group activity, it furthermore assumes that all students need / are ready for exactly the same kind of treatment at the same time.

Both Krashen and Prabhu are essentially correct in their rejection of regimented, timetabled practice sessions.[7] The 'pre-communicative to communicative' or 'controlled to free' progression assumes a uniformity and controllability of internal processes which, however convenient this would be, simply does not exist. It is as if doctors were to give to all their patients a cough syrup on Monday, a laxative on Tuesday, an appendectomy on Wednesday, and so on, regardless of what, if anything, was wrong with them. Doctors do not have a syllabus that tells them that on Friday their patients all need to have their left leg put in a cast. Yet language teachers often have a syllabus that tells them that on Friday their students all need to practice the sentence 'How often does your brother brush his teeth?'

Having condemned traditional views of language practice in this way, it is tempting to reject the notion of *practice* altogether, but this would mean the confusion of one argument with another. Saying that you cannot predict that on Monday everyone will need a cough syrup does not imply that nobody ever needs a cough syrup. Many people do, and some may even need one on Monday. Furthermore, a ritual practising-together may well hold a great deal of value in ways that remain invisible if we merely focus on purposeful skill building. Thirdly, we cannot summarily assume that the presentation of certain linguistic items can never make a group of students ready to practise those items in some concerted fashion: clearly, lessons have been designed for many years with that purpose in mind. Rather than throwing out the concept of practice, therefore, we have to carefully examine our policies regarding the provision of opportunities for practice. We have to learn to distinguish *practice* from *malpractice*.

Similarly, the argument that practice focuses students on form rather than meaning does not hold for the notion of practice *per se*. Learners (spontaneously or deliberately) focus on different aspects of the exposure-language they are encountering, and very often they focus on aspects of 'form' (though in most cases form and meaning are not neatly separable, as we shall see later on). When it appears that some kind of practicing or rehearsing is in order, then opportunities to do so must be available. The crucial difference is that the focusing is not imposed or forced (in the way that a camera is focused by the photographer), but motivated by the language learning work that is going on. When we focus more of our effort on understanding our students and what they are doing, rather than on translating preconceived lesson plans into the actions that seem to be warranted by those plans (notice how the *plans* here take precedence over *local understanding*), we should be able to give practice its rightful place.

In reviewing studies of language practice, Ellis (1992) makes a distinction between *focused practice*, which is designed to provide the learner with opportunities for performing a target structure repeatedly, and *free practice*, which is analogous with communicative language use. As Figure 5 suggests, focusing is the result of a *selectivity* (directionality) and *intensification* of attention. This focusing is a gradable activity, that is, it can be done to a lesser or greater degree. Further, in the methodological literature on language practice, the term focusing almost exclusively refers to focusing on *form* (as opposed to *meaning*, or *function*). Thus, a focus on meaning is usually excluded from the concept of language practice (except in the wider sense of free practice or communication, as mentioned above), and issues of selectivity or intensification are not normally addressed in this context. Focusing therefore seems to be routinely associated with form, although a language learner may of course focus with equal intensity and selectivity on meaning, or on a form–meaning compound, and indeed, on different aspects of form and meaning (the expression *focusing on language* is therefore preferable).

In addition to focus, practice can vary in terms of the degree of *control* over the linguistic actions that is exercised by some agency external to the learners themselves. If there is no such control at all, the term language practice would not normally be considered appropriate. Language practice typically refers to a situation in which someone has designed some sequence of specific linguistic actions for a learner or a group of learners. Two things must be noted here. First, control by others (external control) must be distinguished from self-control (or self-regulation, to use a term familiar from Piagetian and Vygotskyan studies). The former does not necessarily preclude the latter, but it is important to realize that external control does not necessarily *facilitate* self-control either (to say the least).[8] Secondly, the design of practice may involve a selection of formal items (e.g. grammatical structures) in some sort of predetermined sequence. In general, designed collections of language practice may be very useful for language learners, since the quality and the breadth of tasks may far exceed that which the learners themselves would be capable of. To the extent that the learners need practice, therefore, ready-made practice collections can be very useful. However, if the provision (selection) of language practice is determined (predetermined) by a language curriculum which itself is based on a piecemeal progression of linguistic items (whether formal or functional), one may question the utility of practice along the lines of Prabhu's and Krashen's arguments mentioned above.

The upshot of all this is that pedagogical practices (or malpractices) may well have given language practice a bad name, but that we should not conclude that 'practice is useless,' or some such sweeping statement. Rather, it is more reasonable to assume that practice is essential, but that the institutionalized practices in which it is embedded need to be examined.

Let us look at practice from a more 'liberating' perspective, taking the two continua of *control* and *focus* as defining parameters, as shown in Figure 6.

Below is a tentative description of the resulting four types of practice, with some likely components :

I. *Controlled and narrowly focused practice*   This category will include many varieties of mechanical and audiolingual drills, fill-in exercises, transforming or translating sentences, and so on. What, how, and when to practice is here controlled by the syllabus, the teacher, or the textbook.

II. N*ot controlled but focussed practice*   This includes practice which is self-regulated, such as inner speech, private rehearsal, planning and language play. Here the choice of what to practice, when, and how, is the learner's. On the surface, this type of practice may actually *look like* the types mentioned under I, but it may also occur covertly, and hence escape a teacher or researcher's notice.

III. *Controlled but not (narrowly) focused*   This type of practice might include such activities as guided dialogs, role taking, simulations, certain information-gap tasks, and so on. The choice of activity is made by the teacher (etc.), but the range of verbal actions that are appropriate may be broad and varied. The less controlled such activities are, the closer they move to type IV. The focus may well fluctuate unpredictably between form and meaning or some combination.

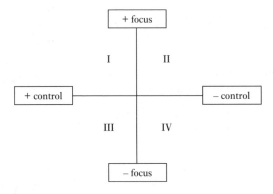

Figure 6   Four types of practice

IV. *Not controlled and not focused*   This category means communicating *per se* (i.e. conversation), and might not normally be regarded as practice at all, although of course it is a way of practicing.

As far as controlled practice (our type I, though possibly not type III) is concerned, we may note Ellis's conclusion:

> We are led to conclude that in the case of controlled practice the old axiom 'practice makes perfect' may not apply to language learning or, at least, not in the way that many teachers and methodologists think it does. Practice may only facilitate acquisition directly if it is communicative, i.e., meaning focussed in nature. (Ellis 1988: 38)

If, for the sake of argument, we agree with Ellis's verdict, we may return to the discussion about focusing and controlling of a couple of pages ago. I suggested there that we should examine *institutionalized practices* rather than assuming that *language practice* itself is useless. I suggested that externally determined control of practice, and a transitive form of focusing (i.e. an external agency focusing the student on something) might not be efficient ways of guiding the students' learning activities. To be more precise, guidance for practice should be grounded in local judgments based on the learners' developing interlanguage, and not on long-distance, remote-controlled preparations of sequenced and graded lesson materials. The teacher thus makes choices and provides practice opportunities, rather than following a method. How this is to be done suggests a considerable research program for classroom and action research. The next two chapters will give some suggestions, but at this point a few classroom episodes illustrating different kinds of practice may be instructive.

1. The first example comes from Ellis (1992). I will just quote a few lines to capture the flavor of the activity.

T   Now can you say, 'I didn't know that that was the father whose daughter was there.'

.
.

L19   Erm, ich habe das nicht erm gewusst
T   Ja, richtig, Ich habe nicht gewusst . . . . komme.
L19   der
T   Dass! Ich habe nicht gewusst dass . . .
L19   erm dass erm oh God! der war
(etc.)

According to Ellis, the teacher wants the student to translate a complex sentence in order to practice verb-final placement in subordinate clauses. We can see here that the teacher both controls and focuses. The student is not ready to produce the required structure (eleven turns later the teacher supplies the right final form), and therefore does not 'get' the intended practice. We might say that the student is actually 'being practiced upon,' rather than doing practice. We may further note that the targeted unit is a sentence rather than an utterance. Sentences are units of written language, and utterances are units of spoken language. This distinction may be crucial for practice: sentences are creative, but to some extent carefully designed, constructions, and generally not suitable for automatization. Utterances (particularly expressions), however, are. One might imagine practicing (with the right intonation and rhythm) utterences such as: 'I had no idea it was him!' (The other person: 'Who?'). 'The father of the girl who was there! Wow!' (The other person: 'Yeah, isn't it amazing?'). Such utterances, rather than sentences, are *practiceable*. One can learn them and then use them a number of times in contexts (fake or real) to 'get them down pat.'

2. The next example comes from a Spanish lesson. Two students are doing a practice conversation about current events (the spelling ('ley', 'muchow' etc.) is intended to indicate a strong American accent).

```
1  S1   si . ahm . . . entonces er cuandow ley parecey si: hablamos er ahora
         sobre er eventos er .. er que: ocurio oc-oCUrrio ocurri ocurEY=
2  S2                                                        ocurriO
         = ocurre . ocurre . ahora . en el mundo . . . . . . sabe- sabe usted er sobrey
         .. los elecciones er en er estey f- s- en estey: pasado semana en er en Chile?
3  S2   er no e::r el verdad er la verdad er es . que . er no e::r se er sobre e::r er
         esas lex- estas elecciones . . . perdone . . . lo siento . lo siento muchow
4  S1                            bueno        e:r        eh he he he he
```

Broad translation   1: yes, er . . . so when seems it to you if we talk now about event which occurred – occurry – occurro. occurr . now in the world . . . . . . know- know you about .. the elections in this- in this past week in in Chile? 3: no, the truth is that I don't know about these lex- elections . . . I'm sorry, I'm very sorry.

There are some similarities as well as some differences between this extract and the previous one. On the one hand, the students themselves are apparently controlling the progress of the acitivity, and they themselves also decide when to focus, and on what. However, we also note that, just as in the previous example, they appear to be engaged in the laborious construction of sentences, rather than the practicing of utterances. An exception is S2's 'lo siento . lo siento mucho'. My suggestion is that the students conduct their practice conversation this way because they have been fed a diet of sentence patterns, and they have internalized the sentential expectations of their various teachers. Under different circumstances one might expect a conversation somewhat as follows:

1 S1 Hablamos sobre las elecciones?
2 S2 Lex- elecciones?
3 S1 Este: pasado semana en Chile.
4 S2 No se sobre esas – estas elecciones. lo siento . lo siento mucho.
5 S1 Bueno. sobre qué hablamos entonces?

Broad translation   1: Shall we talk about the elections? 2: Lex- elections?
3: This: past week in Chile. 4: I don't know about these- these elections. I'm
sorry. I'm very sorry. 5: OK, about what shall we talk then?

This hypothetical conversation does not contain the verb 'occurre' with
which S1 had so much trouble. But can we say that S1 in actual fact
practiced that verb? Or did he just try to construct it as a component of a
structure? Imagine that we see Diana cutting a thin branch from a tree,
stripping it, and trying to bend it to stretch a string from end to end. We
ask: 'What are you doing?' She says: 'I'm practicing archery.' We would
be surprised at that answer, because she is constructing a bow, not practicing shooting arrows at targets (the normal meaning of 'to practice
archery'). In a similar sense, constructing sentences in the way indicated
by extracts (1) and (2) above is not practicing language.[9]

3. This extract is from Butzkamm 1980: 247. L stands for teacher
(Lehrer), S for student unidentified by name (Schüler). The model
exchange in the textbook read: 'What about your class? Is it a lively class?
Yes, it's the liveliest class of all.' Butzkamm uses what he calls a 'verbal
play' episode to elaborate on this type of exchange. The following is a
brief excerpt.

L	Wie steht's eigentlich mit Jack? ((laughter))
S	What about Jack?
L	Ist er schrecklich, ein schrecklicher Typ, schreckliche Person? ((laughter))
S	Is he dreadful?
L	Yes. Isn't he a dreadful person?
Cath	Isn't he a dreadful person?
L	Nein, er ist der netteste, den ich kenne. ((laugher, protest)) Alice! Bernie!
Bernie	No, he is the nicest boy of all. (etc.)

Despite the techniques of translation and imitation, which might strike
some readers as old-fashioned or mechanical (though we must examine
the reasons for making such a judgment!), this example comes much
closer to the view of practice which I am advocating. The teacher creates
a conversational structure, a *scaffold*, we might say, with slots for which
students may propose appropriate contributions. Several characteristics
can be noted which set this apart from the previous examples:

(a) Linguistic material from the texbook is used as raw material or 'Leitmotif.'

(b) There is a natural sequence or 'flow' of utterances, so that the practice session has a syntagmatic dynamism (a sense of one thing following another naturally, of utterances 'fitting in,' as opposed to example (1) above).

(c) The students have considerable freedom in framing the contributions offered, and may themselves decide whether to be 'safe' or 'daring.'

(d) The difficulty level is to a large extent self-regulating, that is, it is determined by the dexterity of the students.

(e) The teacher's contributions are designed to make access to the activity easier for the students.

It may be concluded from this brief examination of examples of language practice, that certain forms of practice, particularly those that force a manipulation of complex syntactic patterns, using the sentence (a 'disembodied utterance.' Farr 1990: 28) as a unit, might more aptly be named grammar *malpractice*, or the *dissection of linguistic cadavers*. To quote Wordsworth:

> Sweet is the lore which Nature brings;
>   Our meddling intellect
> Misshapes the beauteous forms of things:-
>   We murder to dissect.
>   (Dennett 1991: 21).

Conclusion

In this chapter we have explored language learning from a predominantly *intrapersonal* perspective. I have argued that the growth of proficiency is a lengthy, complex, and finely articulated affair. In Figure 4 it is represented as a series of phases or cycles, each one with its own conditions and outcomes. I have warned against taking a two-dimensional and linear view: on the one hand, the sociocultural nature of learning is obscured; on the other, the cyclical and cumulative dynamism of the process is not shown adequately. As far as the former is concerned, it will be discussed in detail later on under the heading of *contingency*. As regards the latter, perhaps we can draw an analogy to a picture of a four-stroke engine: we can draw the four steps separately, but to know 'how it works' we have to imagine a process where everything is in continuous and interdependent movement. Even better, we can think more organically (cf. Rutherford 1987), perhaps in terms of continuous metamorphosis and transformation, rather like the change from egg to butterfly (both Vygotsky and Piaget frequently emphasize transformational processes in development, see, e.g., Kozulin 1990).

Using Figure 4 as guidance (with the reminder that authenticity remains to be discussed), the following points have been made in this chapter:

1. Quality of exposure is more important than quantity of exposure.
2. Quality is determined by access. Comprehensibility, contextuality, familiarity, assistance, affective factors, and participatability (for want of a better term) are all part of the quality of exposure.
3. In engagement with language, perceptual processes (including attending and focusing) are of central importance. The application of these processes presupposes receptivity.
4. In order to turn language affordances into intake, both social and cognitive processing are required. Two kinds of understanding are involved: apprehension and comprehension. These processes require cognitive, emotional, and physical investment on the part of the learner.
5. For intake to become uptake, i.e. language that is retained in memory and can be effectively and appropriately accessed, various kinds of practice, including rehearsal, may be necessary. Although language practice in classrooms is often shown to be ineffective, this does not mean that the notion of practice *per se* is useless.

To close on a general note, It appears likely that in language learning many different processes are involved in interrelated (as yet scarcely explored) ways. Different subsystems of language may require different learning procedures, so that for some strands of learning extensive practice is required, for others not. For some, gradual increments can be discerned; for others, instantaneous acquisition may seem to take place. To take such a heterogeneous, multidimensional view is not to abandon scientific parsimony or to surrender to chaos. Rather, it is the entirely practical consequence of viewing language as a highly complex, multisystemic functional organism, and language use as a process which takes place in an equally complex social world.

Notes

1 Some current critical and social discussions of *literacy* take a similar stance, see, e.g., Gee 1991, Graddol, Maybin & Stierer 1994.
2 To be precise, comprehension is not *monolithic*, i.e. it is not one unchangeable property; it is not *monotonic*, i.e. more is not always better; and, finally, it is not *monochromatic*, i.e. it does not consist of one single type of process.
3 Think, for example, of a mother and infant playing 'peekaboo' or 'pattycake.'

Comprehensibility is in such a case clearly an irrelevant notion. The essence of the game is *playing it*. Language development is primarily a question of active *engagement*, not the *transfer* of linguistic items from one person to another.

4 Notice that in English we *pay* attention. In Spanish we *lend* it, in French we *make* it, and in Dutch we *give* it. Let us not make too much of these idioms in cultural terms, but note that in all cases it involves a deliberate action. See also Chafe 1994.

5 The role of consciousness is a very complex one (see Schmidt 1990, 1994 for detailed discussion and definitions). The question: 'conscious or unconscious?' may be superfluous at the level of *awareness*, though it is a crucial one when we discuss *autonomy*.This topic will be developed in more detail in chapter 4.

6 Exceptions may be the work of Krashen who speaks of a 'feel' for the language in the case of acquired language, and McLaughlin, who makes a distinction between controlled and automatic processing (1990); both researchers appear to have a somewhat similar underlying distinction in mind. However, both writers appear to oppose 'rule' to 'feel,' and this is a serious mistake which rests on a confusion about the meaning of 'rule.' Furthermore, both writers ignore the crucial interdependence of the two kinds of knowledge.

7 For other non-traditional views on practice, see Breen & Candlin 1980, Legutke & Thomas 1991, Carter & McCarthy 1994).

8 There is a significant amount of psychological literature in the area of *locus of control*, which interested readers may like to follow up on. For an overview, see Deci & Ryan 1985 (see further, chapter 5).

9 We may also want to call the construction of written sentences (in writing) a form of language practice, but it is one in which planning and editing play crucial roles. Perhaps the essence of malpractice is forcing students to treat written sentences as if they were spoken utterances.

4 Language awareness and learning to learn

Introduction

The scene is an 'Open House' in an elementary school. Open House night is an important event: parents have a chance to see what the classroom looks like, examine folders containing their child's work, and chat with the teacher about the curriculum, the progress of their child, and so on. In this particular classroom, most of the children were Hispanic, and many of the parents spoke little or no English. As people were milling about among desks and examining projects displayed on tables and on walls, the following conversational fragment was overheard:[1]

Teacher:	Does your mother have any questions?
Child:	Dice la profesora si tienes alguna pregunta. *(the teacher asks if you have any questions)*
Mother:	Aah . . . pues, ¿cómo se porta mi hijo? *(aah . . . well, how does my son behave?)*
Child:	How do I behave?
Teacher :	Oh, he behaves fine.
Child :	Dice que me porto bien. *(She says that I behave fine)*

Examples such as this of real-life language use in educational settings can tell us many things, if we are prepared to listen carefully. An immediate observation is that communication can be severely reduced between teacher and parent when they do not speak each other's language. That in itself is hardly an earth-shattering observation, although the potential consequences of such a *gap*[2] between school and home in terms of the academic prospects of the student must not be taken lightly. On a different note, the obvious ability of the student to act as interpreter might be used to enrich the linguistic interaction between parent, child, and teacher (as well as to give the child a sense of achievement and pride in his bilingualism). It should not be difficult to work out guidelines for turning the rudimentary communication illustrated here into a substantive exchange of ideas between the parties involved. All it takes is an awareness of the potential of language and the resources available, and we can turn a *constraint* into a *resource*.

Let's look at another scene, this time in a high school world history class. This is a so-called 'sheltered' class, which means that the students are non-native speakers who have reached a threshold proficiency in

English which enables them to take a subject-matter class in English for the first time. The teacher has worked out specific strategies to help students cope with the mainstream curriculum through the medium of their second language. The topic of *voter apathy* has come up, and the teacher explains that an apathetic person is one who is not involved, is not emotionally engaged, and so on. One student raises his hand and says: 'Teacher, so you are pathetic?' The teacher must now explain the humorous nature of this remark, and show how *pathetic* is not the opposite of *apathetic*, even though the student's derivational reasoning is perfectly sound and would have worked in most other cases (*typical – atypical, moral – amoral*, etc.). As this anecdote shows, language awareness can be fostered and exploited in classrooms on countless occasions, unplanned as in this instance, or systematically planned in lessons.

In this chapter we will examine language awareness and learning awareness as essential ingredients in successful language learning in educational settings. I will argue that language teachers and language learners benefit from an overt stimulation of their linguistic consciousness, including awareness of language use in relevant settings, of learning processes, of the power of language to enslave or liberate, and so on. To begin with, we will explore some central concepts such as *consciousness* and *awareness*.

The role of consciousness in language learning

In chapter 3 I suggested that many of the cognitive (including perceptual) actions associated with learning can be carried out with or without deliberate oversight by the individual concerned. For example, we can focus intensely on a story without being conscious of doing this focusing. At the meta-consciousness level we were therefore not conscious, yet it makes no sense to say 'I listened to the story unconsciously.' We would rather say something like 'I was oblivious of my surroundings,' or 'I was totally absorbed in the story.' This suggests that there are several different kinds and/or levels of consciousness that can mean quite different things.

Schmidt (1994) distinguishes four common senses of consciousness:

1. Consciousness as *intention*. This means something like 'on purpose.' In learning it highlights a contrast between intentional and incidental learning, i.e. learning one thing while doing another.
2. Consciousness as *attention*. This includes such notions as noticing and focusing.
3. Consciousness as *awareness*. In this sense, consciousness means 'having knowledge of,' either perceptually or cognitively. In language

learning it often refers to knowing rules, but it could also refer to noticing, in which case it will be hard to distinguish from consciousness as attention.

4. Consciousness as *control*. We often perform routine tasks (including language-using tasks) with a great deal of automaticity, and without conscious effort. In such cases we might say that control has been 'delegated' to automatized routines, and consciousness has been freed up for higher tasks (or perhaps for daydreaming).

Schmidt's types of consciousness can be of great help to gain some understanding of the complex notion of consciousness,[3] though it by no means solves all the problems with the term. For example, it is clear that the categories overlap and intersect in a number of ways (2 with 3, as I pointed out, but also 1 with 4, and surely in many other ways as well). Rather than try to elaborate or complexify the classification, or present one more of a myriad of alternative classifications, let me take an example to illustrate the different ways in which consciousness may come into play in language learning.

I refer back to the example of the student who came to class with the expression 'BIG DEAL!' written on his 3 × 5 card (see chapter 3). Recall that the students were asked to bring cards to class on which they had noted things they heard around them. It is possible that, had it not been for this task, the student might have heard 'BIG DEAL!' without 'registering' it, that is, he would not have actively *noticed* it (Schmidt 2). Was this an act of deliberate (rather than incidental) learning? Certainly, the student wrote the words down *intentionally* (Schmidt 1). He was clearly *aware* (Schmidt 3) of the expression (otherwise he would not have noticed it) , and may have realized a difference between the contextual meaning (as an idiom) and the literal meaning of the words 'big' and 'deal,' which he knew, i.e. he 'noticed a gap' (Schmidt & Frota 1986) between actual target language use and his own interlanguage (Gass 1991 refers to such noticing as apperception). When he repeated the words in class and we practiced a few exchanges in which 'BIG DEAL!' might be an appropriate response, his language use was *controlled* (Schmidt 4), i.e. he thought about the outlined situations, and took care in pronouncing BIG DEAL! in the way that he remembered hearing it. Afterwards he might go around and, on occasions he judges appropriate, use the expression 'BIG DEAL!' in conversation (Schmidt 1, 2, 3, and 4 all rolled into one, it would seem).

This small example shows how consciousness, in its multiple roles and guises, enters into language learning in a myriad of different ways at numerous points in the learning process. Anyone who says that all or most language learning occurs unconsciously must therefore have a very special definition of consciousness in mind, one which does not reflect the richness of the different senses described by Schmidt. One may also note, incidentally, that the activities associated with the 'BIG DEAL!' example (apart from the 3 × 5 card and potential in-class practicing) can occur equally whether or not the person is enrolled in classes, i.e. is engaged in 'formal instruction.' Taking into account the various roles of conscious involvement, therefore, the categorical distinction between formal instruction and informal language learning may need to be reexamined. Further, the role of consciousness is by no means limited to attention to form, explicit knowledge of and reliance on rules, and so on.

Up to this point I have discussed consciousness primarily as a property of an individual mind, something that resides in the brain of each and every person, as an intrapersonal concept, in other words. I would now like to discuss consciousness and also the related concept of awareness in a broader sense in which it allows for increasing self-regulation, for deeper processing, for more efficient learning actions, and for feelings of knowing, unknowing, and appropriate levels of confidence in one's own abilities. This is a more organic sense of consciousness which regards it as an *interpersonal* construct, which originates in interaction with the world and is closely tied to sociocultural development. Consciousness is thus a sociocultural construct as well as a cognitive one (see also Lee 1988).

This social and cultural perspective on consciousness can be found in the work of several psychologists, e.g. Vygotsky (1978), Csikszentmihalyi (1990), Bruner (1986), but also in the work of the anthropologist Clifford Geertz (1973) and that of the philosopher Ludwig Wittgenstein (1958b). Below, I will review some of the more prominent and interesting – from the latter perspective – conceptualizations of consciousness.

Vygotsky defined consciousness as 'the objectively observable *organization* of behavior that is imposed on humans through participation in sociocultural practices' (Wertsch 1985: 187). The emphasis here is on the *organizational role*, and the *social origin*, of consciousness. In Vygotsky's view, consciousness constitutes the highest level of mental activity. It has two subcomponents: *intellect* and *affect*. These two subcomponents of consciousness are dynamically interconnected, transforming one another constantly. Consciousness, then, organizes human activity – socio-cognitive activity, in Vygotsky's scheme – through intellectual and affective processes. Note that we may or may not 'be conscious' of these activities of consciousness, in the sense of meta-cognition. Another definition by Vygotsky, of consciousness as 'an awareness of the activity of the mind', is thus a special type of consciousness, a meta-consciousness in effect.[4] Being conscious of being aware, or of attending, is thus also a special kind of consciousness. It appears that this 'meta' sense cuts across all of Schmidt's categories, as in fact the prefix *meta* itself suggests.

Consciousness in the more dynamic and organic sense[5] of Vygotsky's first definition clearly has a crucial place in language learning. In it, intellectual (e.g. memory) and affective (e.g. the emotional value assigned to an action) processes are responsible for the organization of learning. What sets these processes in motion? In Vygotsky's view, sociocultural activity in the zone of proximal development (ZPD), the innate attention-focusing preferences of the child, and (increasingly) the autonomous, self-regulated actor him or herself.

Consciousness, thus defined, has several practical implications for the teacher in the classroom:

1. It is important to find the appropriate social interaction to allow learning to take place (as a case in point, see Tharp & Gallimore's (1988) *instructional conversation*; see also chapter 7).
2. We should seek, be prepared to stimulate, and guide natural attention-focusing tendencies in the students, since they are likely to be in the ZPD. As an example I would like to refer back to the 'entry ticket' activity mentioned in chapter 3. This type of activity assumes that the students, in collecting field data, focus on the kinds of language they are ready to learn.
3. We must educate the students to make their own decisions increasingly, and in order to do that we must make sure that they know what they are doing. Eventually they are best served by being able to regulate their own language learning.

Initially the teacher acts as the student's 'vicarious consciousness' (Bruner 1986: 72) but gradually, by a process of scaffolding, he or she hands over increasing responsibility and autonomy to the student, remaining 'forever on the growing edge of [the student's] competence' (*ibid.*:77).

The second view of consciousness we will consider is that of Csikszentmihalyi, in his work on the notion of *flow* (see also p. 49 above, Csikszentmihalyi 1990). In his view, consciousness, although the result of biological processes, is *self-directed*, i.e. has developed the ability to override its genetic instructions and to set its own independent course of action (1990: 24). Csikszentmihalyi's functional description of consciousness is worth quoting in full:

> The function of consciousness is to represent information about what is happening outside and inside the organism in such a way that it can be evaluated and acted upon by the body. In this sense, it functions as a

clearinghouse for sensations, perceptions, feelings, and ideas, establishing priorities among all the diverse information. Without consciousness we would still 'know' what is going on, but we would have to react to it in a reflexive, instinctive way. With consciousness, we can deliberately weigh what the senses tell us, and respond accordingly. And we can also invent information that did not exist before: it is because we have consciousness that we can daydream, make up lies, and write beautiful poems and scientific theories. (Csikzentmihalyi 1990: 24)

Consciousness, then, means the *organizing*, *controlling*, and *evaluating* of experience. Without it, we might still be able to respond appropriately to the environment, but it would be more like the leaf of a plant which moves in the direction of sunlight. It is clear that the bulk of human learning, being the complex and protracted activity that it is, can only be accomplished by a conscious person. This point seems so obvious that one might ask why it needs to be made at all. More specifically, from our perspective in this chapter, we need to ask why consciousness is an issue in language learning. There are several reasons why consciousness and language learning have enjoyed an uneasy relationship over the last few decades. Let me list a few of these reasons:

1. B*ehaviorism and audiolingualism*: the rejection (as phenomena worthy of scientific attention) of higher mental activities for which no direct, overt evidence could be found, exemplified in the work of behaviorist psychologists such as Thorndike, Watson, Skinner, and the rote learning and drilling associated with it, e.g. the 'mim-mem' (mim-icry-memorization) method of so-called audiolingual foreign language learning.

2. *Explicit and metalinguistic knowledge*: the equation, particularly by those working in classical and grammar translation methodologies, as well as their detractors, of conscious learning with explicit formal knowledge of linguistic features, such as grammar rules and structures.

3. *Universal grammar and innatism*: idealists, from Bühler to Chomsky, see language development (and, to a variable extent, the development of other higher cognitive functions) as the gradual unfolding of inborn qualities, in which the person's relationships with the environment play only incidental triggering roles. The role of the individual's growing consciousness, mediated by social activity, is minimized in such innatist views.

For reasons such as these the debate about consciousness in language learning has focused on two positions, both of them erroneous. These positions are, on the one hand, the assumption that consciousness does not matter, either because it is not an object of scientific interest, or because language learning is innate, and on the other hand, the assumption that conscious language learning means explicit knowledge about language structures and rules. Both assumptions ignore the real functions of consciousness and its perceptual component, awareness: the functions of *organizing*, *controlling* and *evaluating* experience.

Referring back to the discussion on the *Growth of Proficiency* in chapter 3, it should be clear that, without consciousness as defined in this way, it is simply not possible to realize the conditions (receptivity, access/participation, investment/practice, and commitment) that make progress towards proficiency possible. By the same token, outcomes or processes such as focusing attention, comprehending, memorizing, and creative language use require the involvement of a conscious mind (in interaction with its environment) which is aware of what it is doing and what is going on.

We must therefore study language awareness and learning awareness from the perspective that conscious involvement in language learning is essential, but that such conscious involvement does not equate with explicit grammatical study, although we cannot rule out that such study might have a role to play for certain learners in certain circumstances. A full discussion of this issue is not possible here, but the next section will give the reader some ideas to think about, and some avenues for further exploration. My main aim is to prevent simplistic conclusions one way or another.

Metalinguistic awareness

> He who knows something knows at the same time that he knows it and he knows as well that he knows what he knows. (Spinoza, quoted in A. Brown 1987: 70)

Metalinguistic awareness can be seen as the result of an increasing 'objectification' (Birdsong 1989) of language, that is, the ability or tendency of the child to see language as something that can be controlled, manipulated, and played around with. Cazden (1976) distinguishes between *transparent* language use, when the focus is on meaning, and *opaque* language use, when aspects of language become objects for observation and analysis in themselves.

It is fairly well established that even quite young children attend to language and engage in verbal play of various kinds, either on their own or assisted by caretakers. Children also invent words and expressions when they need them, showing that they can exert control over the building blocks of language. These abilities gradually increase and fully develop between the ages of four and si§x, and are crucial for the acquisition of literacy (Gombert 1992 distinguishes between *epilinguistic* control – manifested in word play and manipulation – and *metalinguistic* control – in which verbal description of linguistic features is possible).

Related to the transparent/opaque distinction is the distinction between subsidiary and focal awareness made by Polanyi, and illustrated in the following example:

> My correspondence arrives at my breakfast table in various languages, but my son understands only English. Having just finished reading a letter I may wish to pass it on to him, but I must check myself and look again to see in what language it was written. I am vividly aware of the meaning conveyed by the letter, yet know nothing whatever of its words. I have attended to them closely but only for what they mean and not for what they are as objects. If my understanding of the text were halting, or its expressions or its spelling were faulty, its words would arrest my attention. They would become slightly opaque and prevent my thought from passing through them unhindered to the things they signify. (Polanyi 1958: 57)

We might say that focal attention is a limited resource which cannot be directed towards several targets at once (cf. Chafe 1994). Our linguistic skills are such that peripheral attention to words, utterances and sentences is sufficient to allow us to focus on the meanings. However, when something goes wrong, either with the language, or with our ability to make sense of it, then our focal attention would be required to address the language directly in order to sort out the problems. In reaching higher standards of language knowledge and use, it seems reasonable to assume that it will be inevitable, as well as necessary, from time to time, for language to become opaque so as to allow 'construction work' to be conducted to bring the language data and our interpretive skills closer together, or to coordinate expressive requirements and linguistic resources. The function of metalinguistic abilities, whether of an intuitive or explicit kind, is to assist in such construction work.

The metalinguistic abilities of children are expressed in many different ways, and most parents and caretakers can undoubtedly relate numerous examples, such as the following, of the metalinguistic activities of their children My son, at five years old, showed an example of invention when he was playing 'bald eagle' with a towel across his shoulders and a white washcloth on his head. When the white cloth fell off, he said:

> 'Oopsie! My bald falled off.'

This utterance shows the creative ability to use a word in a new functional context (from adjective to noun), to create a 'grammatical metaphor,' in Halliday's terms (1989). On another occasion, at age six, when seeing a sign in the St Louis Botanical Gardens that read 'Violators will be prosecuted,' he showed that he knew that language can be turned around to playful effect by saying:

'Prosecutors will be violated.'

Our question is, what role, if any, such metalinguistic activities play in the linguistic (and social, and cognitive) development of the child. In answer to this, most researchers appear to judge the influence of metalinguistic processes to be a positive one, though it may fall anywhere between being merely facilitative to crucial (Birdsong 1989).

Further, the role of metalinguistic phenomena (whether expressed as *awareness, intuition, knowledge,* or *performance*) in other language learning scenarios requires examination. There seems to be no controversy about the importance of talking about language when it comes to literary appreciation. Next, in the teaching of writing, ESP (English for Specific Purposes), public speaking, acting, and other specialized registers and discourse worlds, at least *some* explicit focus on language is normally considered sensible. It is in the realm of L2 learning that we encounter a significant controversy about the alleged benefits or otherwise of metalinguistic awareness.

> For some years, particularly in the seventies and eighties, a significant number of L2 professionals, for example those influenced by Krashen's claims about the subconscious nature of acquisition, regarded all talk and knowledge *about* language superfluous and, indeed, counterproductive (1985). Explicit (*learned*) knowledge interfered, on this view, with acquisition, in the same way that thinking about every move interferes with your ability to ride a bicycle. More recently, the consensus has begun to shift again towards a greater role for explicit knowledge. The same can be noted in discussions about language awareness following the introduction of the National Curriculum in Great Britain (discussed in more detail later in this chapter). Whenever a conscious focus on language is promoted, whether for correct grammar, spelling, formal writing or speaking, the issue of metalinguistic terminology becomes controversial: to what extent do students need to know and understand the technical language for talking about language (terms such as plusquamperfect, clauses of unreal condition, ditransitive verb, and so on)? As I shall argue, the crux of the matter is not the need for explicit knowledge of metalinguistic terms in itself, rather, whether or not such knowledge should be specified and itemized beforehand in a syllabus. In the latter scenario, I suggest, we would remain stuck in a transmission-based view of instruction, rather than in the process view which I am recommending in this book. As a general recommendation, therefore, the need for explicit knowledge and for technical terms should naturally arise from the work that is being done, and in that case its introduction would be motivated. If the need does not arise, the use of technical (metalinguistic) terminology is simply not necessary.
> Predetermination of such issues, therefore, is not appropriate in the AAA curriculum.

I will not go into a detailed discussion of this issue here (for particularly instructive discussions, see Gass 1991, Sorace 1985, Swain 1991), but refer back to my discussion of awareness and attention in chapter 3. I spoke there of various kinds and intensities of awareness and attention, from relaxed to focused, and from noticing to vigilance. Different kinds of learning tasks benefit from different kinds and intensities of awareness and attention. The conscious learner intuitively regulates his or her processes of attending, assisted when necessary by a skilful teacher. The young L1 learner, when given adequate support (e.g. through scaffolding) to secure access and participation, can rely on innate attention-focusing mechanisms, focusing naturally (though perhaps not always in the same way, or equally effectively) on strategic 'hot spots' along the developmental road (Birdsong 1989: 175). The L2 learner does not have these innate devices available, and will need other kinds of help and support structures. One of the support structures that may help guide the L2 learner to focus attention effectively is a metalinguistic awareness and a store of metalinguistic knowledge. Of course, for this to work properly the learner's metalinguistic knowledge and proficiency (respectively, *declarative* and *procedural knowledge*, in Anderson's terminology [Anderson 1982]) must operate in a synchronized fashion; if not, the former may well interfere with the latter (Birdsong 1989). We must not be misled into thinking, however, that it is the *amount* or *extent* of metalinguistic knowledge or skills that somehow interferes with L2 learning. It is the way in which we bring it to bear on our linguistic tasks that makes the difference. Eating too much food at one time, or gobbling it down, interferes with our health. However, no one would claim that it is the amount of food in the refrigerator, or even on the table, that is to blame for one's indigestion or weight problems. We are in control (one supposes) of the amount of food we take in.[6] If we are overweight, it's little use blaming the refrigerator. On the other hand, it is clearly better for one's health to have a well-stocked refrigerator than a bare cupboard.

In the last two sections I have attempted to provide some conceptual clearing for a productive discussion of language awareness and learning to learn. I hope to have shown that 'conscious or unconscious?' is the wrong question to ask, and that '*either* focus on language *or* focus on meaning' is a false choice. The language learner has to be conscious, aware, and attentive. The unconscious person is asleep, or in a coma perhaps, the unaware person goes through life in a daze, and the inattentive person will sooner or later get run over by a car.

Next we will look at current efforts to improve language teaching through language awareness.

The Language Awareness movement

The Language Awareness (LA) movement, a grassroots organization of teachers and teacher educators, started in Great Britain in the early 1980s. Its origins can be traced back to the Bullock Report, 'A language for life,' the result of a government investigation into the state of British education (DES 1975), and to the influence of Michael Halliday (e.g. through the Schools Council Programme in Linguistics and Language Teaching, see Hawkins 1992), Eric Hawkins, and other linguists involved in educational projects and programmes. It was a response to increasing demands for a more systematic and efficient approach to language education and language use in schools and academic institutions (Donmall 1985). Following the Bullock Report there were several other British government publications focusing on language education, e.g. the Swan Report, the Cox Report, and the Kingman Report. Although this emphasis on the importance of language in education was – to my knowledge – nowhere as marked as in Great Britain, similar recommendations have recently also been made elsewhere, e.g. in Australia (Literacy and Language Task Force 1990), Canada (Ontario Ministry of Education 1984), and the USA (Tucker 1986, van Lier 1991b).[7]

In the United States, a movement close in spirit is the *Whole Language* movement (Goodman 1986, Cazden 1992), which promotes rich, multi-faceted language experience in the schools. A difference is that the Whole Language movement tends to be concentrated in the early years of the elementary schools, with an emphasis on teaching literacy skills, whereas the British Language Awareness movement has focused primarily on the secondary level. Furthermore, the ever-present forces of simplification threaten to push the discussion over the merits of whole language into a trivial argument for or against the use of phonics, and this is perhaps not all that different from the current argument in Britain over LA as either a renewed focus on correct grammar and proper usage, or a critical focus on power, manipulation, and prejudice in language (Carter 1992). Such simplification by stereotyping is perhaps the greatest danger to the future of both language awareness and whole language, and it is of vital importance to combat it energetically.

To return to the Language Awareness movement, this expresses, in general, a concern about the quality and scope of language education in the schools, a concern which is voiced by different parties in different ways. These differences in themselves can lead, and I have already hinted at this, to quite divergent conceptions as to what LA actually is, or ought to be, and what its agenda should be. Whenever we hear the term LA being used, we must be acutely aware of this multiplicity of agendas. In the following section I will discuss several views of what LA is, and in the process some of the more prominent agendas will come to light. After that I will focus on one particular agenda which I find in accord with my three pedagogical principles of awareness, autonomy, and authenticity, and explore its educational possibilities and implications.

What is language awareness?

Awareness of language has played a role in human consciousness for a very long time, and I assume it can be found in essentially very similar ways among hunters telling stories in caves in ancient times, and among modern businessmen drafting marketing documents in tall buildings. I don't want to go too far back, but in 1937 a Dutch educator called A.J. Schneiders wrote an interesting little article about the concept of 'language understanding' (*taalbegrip*).[8] He presented language understanding as something new, and compared it to another concept, much more accepted in every day usage, 'language feeling' (*taalgevoel*). The brief article has a very modern feel to it. It contains a discussion of both the intuitive and the reflective aspects of language knowledge, and Schneiders considers the traditional grammar-analytical approach a violation of language and language education: the language is learned in order to be unlearned ('aangeleerd om ze af te leren'). We might even say that Schneiders was quite some way ahead of his time, since he accepted the primacy of *language feeling* (or intuition), but also argued for a second metalinguistic entity, *language understanding* (or cognition).[9]

In 1982, in Birmingham, England, a Language Awareness Working Party (first chaired by John Trim, then by John Sinclair), which was set up by the National Congress on Language in Education (NCLE), agreed on the following definition of LA:

> LA is a person's sensitivity to and conscious awareness of the nature of language and its role in human life. (Donmall 1985: 7)

This definition, simple though it sounds, leaves itself open to an enormous variety of interpretations (Candlin, in his preface to James & Garrett 1991a, said of this definition that it 'clearly needs unpacking'), but this is not necessarily a bad thing in the early stages of a new endeavor. After all, when a field is not yet well staked-out, one must leave room for emerging meanings and metaphors. However, eventually more precision will be called for, if not in terms of a single definition, at least in the form of a concerted program for action. Unless this is achieved the field may fizzle out or become fragmented.

Eric Hawkins (1987a: 4), offers a more concrete and practical definition, based on some central objectives of LA. His proposals, aimed at the 11–14 age range (a transition period between primary and secondary education), include:

- facilitating the start of foreign language studies
- assisting with 'the explosion of concepts and language' introduced by new subjects
- connecting different aspects of language education (English, modern languages, minority languages)
- challenging linguistic prejudice and parochialism through open discussion and greater awareness

In addition to these general objectives, Hawkins makes a number of more specific suggestions in his book, including contrastive study in foreign language classes, increased 'adult time' (in American English, this might be translatable as 'quality time with the teacher'), and 'learning to listen' (1987a: 5). Hawkins' general rationale, even more so than the definition from Donmall quoted above, gives a clear indication of the educational ideals of many proponents of LA:

> We are seeking to light fires of curiosity about the central human characteristic of language which will blaze throughout our pupils' lives. While combating linguistic complacency, we are seeking to arm our pupils against fear of the unknown which breeds prejudice and antagonism. Above all we want to make our pupils' contacts with language, both their own and that of their neighbours, richer, more interesting, simply more fun. (Hawkins 1987a: 6)

A third conception of LA, perhaps a spin-off or a subset of the more broadly based recommendations from Donmall and Hawkins, is referred to as *knowledge about language* (KAL; see Carter 1990, Hawkins 1992). In principle this term should be compatible with any conception of LA, all the way along the continuum from the most utopian to the most utilitarian position. It all depends on how narrowly or broadly, how formally or functionally, how objectively or subjectively, we define *language*. However, in the media and elsewhere KAL is often interpreted as a renewed call for formal grammar teaching. KAL, when it focuses narrowly on formal aspects of language, or on language as *linguistic product* (rather than as *dynamic process*), is constantly in danger of reverting to the old days of sentence parsing, rote memorization of rules and exceptions, or even prescriptive ways of using a particular preferred ('standard') variety of language 'properly.' Such approaches, popular in the 1950s (and before and after, of course) in many countries, are referred to by various contributors to Donmall (1985) with picturesque names such as 'grammar grind' and 'the ghost of grammar past.' There are no doubt many traditionalists who wistfully look back to those good old days when people used language 'properly' and when language teaching was conducted 'solidly' and 'decently.' We will return to this question of prescriptivism in the section on teacher education below. Meanwhile, it is refreshing to see that pioneering efforts in KAL in the schools in Britain are able to bring language to life and avoid slipping into meaningless formalism (see, e.g., Carter 1990, Bain, Fitzgerald & Taylor 1992).

A narrow, form-focused approach to KAL is also a trend in the USA among those who advocate LA (e.g. those who attack *whole language*, see above), using arguments from work on metalinguistic awareness which is usually measured through formal features such as detection of ungrammaticality, understanding of structural ambiguity, and so on. In second language acquisition, discussions on LA center around the need for various types of *negative evidence* (corrections, statements of rules, and so on). In a variety of ways, many applied linguists argue for or against explicit language teaching using separate sets of terms, such as implicit, subconscious, acquisition, and the whole language, on the one hand, and explicit, conscious, learning, and phonics, on the other.

In these two groups of views, LA is by some associated with the latter list of terms rather than the former. This division (which, of course, we do not have to buy into) might push some of the work done under the banner of *consciousness-raising* into a traditional grammar direction, although Rutherford (1987: 154–5), one of the originators of the term consciousness-raising, contrasts his 'grammar-driven pedagogical programme,' which he calls *organic*,[10] with traditional grammar teaching, which he calls *mechanic*, and which regards grammar as an end in itself rather than as a means or a facilitator. A further important distinction Rutherford makes is between 'teaching grammar' and 'teaching learning.' Thus, consciousness-raising must be sharply distinguished from prescriptive grammar teaching which sees language knowledge as an end in itself, and which has conformity to specific language standards as an overriding goal. KAL, with the exception of the work of Carter and his associates (e.g. 1990), has not so far clearly adopted a definition which takes a stand on the issue of *prescriptivistic control* versus *autonomous development*, two positions which would appear to be incompatible, indeed, mutually exclusive. This means that, under the single umbrella of LA, one might end up finding approaches that are diametrically opposed to one another, in terms of ideology as well as methodology! Readers should note, therefore, that it is very important to carefully check the principles on which any particular LA proposal is based since, like the word *sanction*, the term can come to mean its own opposite.

The fourth and final view of LA that I want to present is known as *critical language awareness* (CLA). As the name suggests, this approach squarely confronts issues of power, control, and manipulation in language use in society. However, to see it simply as a politicized version of sociolinguistics would be a mistake. In its careful scrutiny of language as a form of social practice, or *discourse* (Fairclough 1989: 20, 1992a, 1992b; Gee 1991; Bruce 1991), CLA brings to light important language processes which people in education need to think about. The Open House scene in the introduction to this chapter is an illustration of one such process: the reduced dialogue between teacher and parents that can result from language differences. CLA, in examining the 'institutionalized discourse' (Corson 1990: 59) of the school (as well as, of course, many other discourses in society), can contribute to forming new school policies in which administrators, teachers, and students collaborate to identify problems, try out solutions, eliminate errors, and establish policies in democratic ways (Corson 1990: 70, following a formula first proposed by Karl Popper).

When such CLA is applied to curricula for students or student teachers, the meaning of LA may not coincide with plans for KAL that educational authorities have in mind, particularly if these authorities see LA as a means to legislate ways of language use which promote a specific agenda, such as the creation of Foucault's 'homo docilis' (Foucault 1977). As an example, the LINC (Language in the National Curriculum) materials developed by a team led by Ron Carter under a government grant were rejected by the British Government for not following a traditional model of grammar study (Carter 1992, Hawkins 1992; see further the section on teacher development below). This argument cuts both ways, of course: CLA promotes critical thought and democratic decision-making, and therefore should not push a political or ideological agenda that goes beyond clearly articulated basic human values (in my case they are expressed in AAA: awareness, autonomy, and authenticity).

Summary: the scope of language awareness

A useful summary of the different things LA can mean is Carl James and Peter Garrett's discussion of the five domains of LA (James & Garrett 1991a). In Figure 7 I give an overview of these domains, adding some information of my own to the descriptions provided by James & Garrett. It must be understood that there is broad overlap between the different domains.

Domain	Description	Reference
Affective	• relation between knowledge and feeling (including feeling of knowing) • consciousness includes intellect and affect • language awareness involves 'forming attitudes, awakening and developing attention, sensitivity, curiosity, interest and aesthetic response' • affective filter, humanistic approach, learner-centered second/foreign language teaching	Sorace 1985 Vygotsky 1978 Wertsch 1985 Donmall 1985: 7 Stevick 1976, 1980 Moskowitz 1978
Social	• linguistic tolerance • relations between ethnic groups • bilingualism, biculturalism	Trueba 1989 Romaine 1989 Rampton 1987
Power	• 'conscientizacão' • exploitation • social practices • literacy	Freire 1972 Bolinger 1980 Fairclough 1989, 1992a, b Gee 1991
Cognitive	• relations between language and thought • metalinguistic awareness • cognitive academic language proficiency (CALP) • learner training	Vygotsky 1986 Birdsong 1989 Cummins 1989 Willing 1989
Performance	• relations between declarative and procedural knowledge • automatization and control • communication strategies • language practice	Anderson 1982 Bialystok 1990 Tarone 1988 Ellis 1988

Figure 7   Domains of language awareness

Lest my listing be regarded as an act of unsolicited inclusion, I must emphasize that not all the writers mentioned in the table would necessarily refer to their work as LA. However, the various aspects of awareness-raising work discussed in this section, and summarized in the table, have broad ramifications in a range of activities in educational linguistics. I will now turn to more specific aspects of LA work in schools, first of all by discussing its relevance for teacher education.

Language awareness in teacher education (LATE)

There is incessant talk these days of a crisis in education, the need for reform and restructuring, the erosion of basic values in society, and the decline of standards of every sort. Multitudes of experts and non-experts voice their opinions about the reasons for the current mess and what needs to be done to get us out of it. Proposed solutions of all stripes abound and, although many of them clearly make eminent sense, we keep hearing that they will not work because they have all been tried before to no avail. Educators feel that, barring a profound upheaval of such enormity that it cannot be humanly engineered, they have to make the best of a bad situation, effecting whatever small changes and improvements they can inside the severe constraints of the system in which they are forced to operate. In a context such as this, claims for improvements in teacher education must be subject to the same limitations put upon all other forms of educational action.

I mentioned above that one project for LA, the LINC project headed by Ron Carter, didn't meet the expectations of the British Ministry of Education for employing a vision of LA that appeared incompatible with the official version, even though the materials were originally commissioned by the Ministry. It turns out that the government's reasons for doing LA were very different from those of the Carter team. As Carter explains (1992), for the government – and a segment of society in general – LA should lead to 'proper' language use, and 'proper' language use is packaged with a particular conception of the ideal (or, at least, 'decent') citizen. This view of LA is expressed frequently in editorial comments in the media, as well as in political speeches and diatribes on the bus and in the cocktail bar. From a number of press extracts collected by Ron Carter (1992) I select one particularly striking example:

> we've allowed so many standards to slip . . . teachers weren't bothering to teach kids to spell and to punctuate properly . . . if you allow standards to slip to the stage where good English is no better than bad English, where people turn up filthy . . . at school . . . all those things cause people to have no standards at all, and once you lose standards then there's no imperative to stay out of crime. (Norman Tebbit, Radio 4, 1985)

In such views, good English is associated with discipline, good manners, basic values, hygiene, patriotism, law-abiding behavior, and so on, and it is obtained by teaching grammar, spelling, and correct style in the ways this used to be done, before things took a turn for the worse (before 'the overthrow of grammar,' as an article in the *Observer* put it). Without such good teaching, the result is bad language, which is associated with such things as indiscipline, improper clothing and hair styles, academic nonsense (as Prince Charles put it), crime, and perhaps even socialism or worse. Unless language is taught properly, therefore, 'environmental wackos' will proliferate and all kinds of 'freaks' and 'weirdos' will demonstrate on the streets, aided and abetted, no doubt, by language teachers. Such a prescriptive approach to language education has been condemned by many educators and linguists for a long time. People as diverse as Charles Fries and Michael Halliday have argued against 'the traditional grammar of usage' (Fries 1952: 275) and 'teaching the do's and don'ts of grammar' (Halliday 1973: 59). In spite of this long history of condemnation, however, the teaching of language as linguistic etiquette persists and currently appears to be enjoying something of a revival.

I have painted the opposing forces of LA, the 'controlling forces' and the 'liberating forces", as we might call them, in strong terms, though the reader is encouraged to check newspapers and other media to decide for him or herself if I am exaggerating – which I do not believe I am. So far as *appropriate action* is concerned, the teacher educator has any number of options which it is not my place to legislate or lecture on. Suffice it to say that my approach, as I indicate on numerous occasions in this book and elsewhere, is to focus with care and caution on the encounter between teacher and student.

In making proposals for Language Awareness in Teacher Education (creating the not altogether inappropriate acronym LATE for this occasion), I therefore want to begin by focusing, not on sweeping changes or reforms of great magnitude, but on one small moment in the educational process: teachers and students talking to each other. Since large-scale reforms have had such a dismal track record by and large, there may be some merit in starting at the other end for a change: with the act of communication between participants in the educational process, particularly the teacher and the learner. While we thus potter away at the chalkface or the talkface of the classroom, the optimist in us may keep the 'butterfly effect,' familiar from chaos theory (Gleick 1987), in mind. According to this notion, a butterfly stirring the air today in Peking can transform storm systems next month in New York. We know that small actions can make big changes, as the old folk poem in Figure 8 tells us.

We will explore the details of classroom interaction in chapter 7, through the topic of *contingency*, as well as on various other occasions throughout the book. Right now I will review the prospects of LATE and make some recommendations for a greater role for educational

For want of a nail
The shoe was lost;
For want of a shoe
The horse was lost;
For want of a horse
The rider was lost;
For want of a rider
The battle was lost;
For want of a battle
The kingdom was lost;
And all for the want
of a horse-shoe nail.

Figure 8   For want of a nail

linguistics in teacher education programs. I want the reader to understand, via the last couple of paragraphs, that my focus on the minutiae of
educational language use is not due to a disregard for the wider social,
cultural, and political issues surrounding education. Indeed, the AAA
principles should make my commitments and ideological position clear.
My micro-educational focus reflects the belief that lasting educational
changes, at least those to which an educational linguist can contribute,
start in the classroom, in the interaction between teacher and learner. It
is from this perspective that I shall approach LATE here (see also
chapter 2).

In chapter 2 I argued for a more balanced interaction between
research, theory, and practice, particularly from the perspective of the
reflective teacher whose theories are shaped by everyday reality, and
whose research is directed towards improving aspects of that reality. I
suggested there that we, as teachers and teacher educators, have to work
towards a *theory of practice* which is aimed at understanding the shaping
and reproduction of educational systems (Bourdieu 1990). For the relationship between linguistic theory and LATE a similar recommendation
can be made. Language teachers (and teachers in general) need a more
systematic language component as part of their professional preparation,
but this does not necessarily mean that they need courses in linguistics,
grammar, and so on, modeled on academic linguistics programs.

It is instructive to investigate what teachers report about their language training in the past, and how they currently view language as a
subject. In a study of this type, Mitchell and Hooper report a series of
revealing, though perhaps not altogether unexpected findings (Mitchell
& Hooper 1991). Although they qualify their findings as preliminary, I
will summarize some of them in my own words (see Figure 9), since I
believe they have a fairly wide validity across different settings:

Past training	Current practices
• component of language in teacher training is very slight, if not non-existent	• little cooperation between language departments
• general background literature-based	• knowledge about language (KAL) is a marginal issue
• main emphasis on methodology	• for L2 teachers, 'talk about language' generally limited to grammar, parts of speech, etc.
• suspicion about linguistics: it's not helpful	• L1 teachers feel need to teach variation, standard/non-standard distinction, punctuation, spelling 'rules'
• possible perceived (not expressed) feeling of inadequate preparation in language	• highly varied perceptions about usefulness and applications of KAL

Figure 9   Language training and language practices

Out of such tentative and relatively informal comments, a picture emerges of a language teaching profession without a clear language preparation or a well-defined language program. Unless this problem is attacked at the teacher education level, there is little hope for an adequate language education policy, whether in individual subject classes or across the curriculum. Ideally, linguists and language teachers would have to cooperate to design innovative language courses. As Halliday has said:

> I would like to reject categorically the assertion that a course of general linguistics is of no particular use to teachers. I think it's fundamental. But I don't think it should be a sort of watered down academic linguistics course. It should be something new, designed and worked out by linguists and teacher trainers together. (Halliday 1982: 13)

It is unfortunate, however, that very few linguists – and even a decreasing number of *applied* linguists, who now often call themselves second language researchers – concern themselves with educational matters. This in spite of the fact that, at least in the USA, there are 'serious dangers ahead for the linguistics profession,' and the Linguistic Society of America 'has started a Fund for the Future of Linguistics' (Pullum 1991: 20–1). It would in my view be more beneficial, for the future of both linguistics and education, if more linguists occupied themselves with language-educational issues, in the classroom and in the larger social arena.

For LATE courses to be effective, a transmission-oriented methodology, which views language as a body of facts to be paraded before the students and offered for assimilation and periodic regurgitation, is going to be worse than doing nothing at all. If we wish to educate for *awareness, autonomy*, and *authenticity*, or any other set of clearly articulated principles, language education must be approached in an entirely different manner. To take a case in point, an *introduction to linguistics* course usually imparts a series of facts about phonology, morphology, syntax, semantics, and so on, probably enlivened with humorous cartoons and the usual quotes from Alice in Wonderland, but not often embedded in teaching practice and educational reality. A LATE course would examine the reality of language use in relevant educational settings, preferably incorporating classroom observation and gathering of data by students, and activities reflecting the kinds of language teaching we wish to promote (see Sorace 1985 for an example of work going in this direction; see also van Lier 1992).

Apart from making the subject matter (language) come alive and be more relevant to the student teacher, this way of working has another important advantage. When teachers are called upon to teach language in schools, they will hark back to the way in which they themselves were taught language (often the strongest influences on teaching practices are past classroom learning experiences; see Krahnke 1987). Teachers who were taught in the old grammar grind ways or not at all will either teach parsing and diagramming, and explain obscure points of structure, or they will turn away from LA in frustration and exclusively focus on literature instead (Brumfit 1991).

In workshops and staff development seminars, teacher educators tend to shy away from overtly addressing linguistic issues (except when relevant in skills-based units such as the teaching of reading, teaching listening or writing, etc.). Comments such as the ones summarized in Figure 9 above suggest that the main reasons are that the teacher educator does not want to frighten, bore, or otherwise turn off the audience, that he himself or she herself feels insecure in this area, or perhaps that overt language issues are not felt to be relevant. In spite of this, there is definitely a growing interest in linguistic issues, or let us be precise and say in educational linguistics. There are even occasional LA presentations at linguistics conferences, though the few that I have witnessed can do little but give LA a bad name (see further below).[11]

If we are serious about teaching LATE, there are three things we need to do:

1. *Take an experiential approach to LA*, one which acknowledges that teachers have a great deal of knowledge and know-how of language,

and which systematically draws upon that experiential base. As Brumfit puts it:

> linguistics must start where teachers are themselves if it is to have any impact on the [LA] movement: and not to have any impact on the movement is effectively to claim that it is not really the study of language at all, but some more esoteric glass-bead game that should be left to high priests of the cult while we get on with the real work of understanding language under some other name. (Brumfit,1991: 35)

2. *Reject language-as-product*, i.e. focus not on language as a body of content matter which can be transmitted piecemeal to an audience, but rather as a living thing which shapes our existence and which we use to make sense of our world and our work.

3. *Study language critically*, i.e. emphasize that language study is not only relevant to teacher education and classroom practice, but that it is essential to human growth and self-fulfillment. A critical view of language shows the interrelationships between text (any piece of language produced in a specific context), sociocognitive processes (the relationships and thoughts expressed in language), and the socio-historical context (the conventions, presupposed roles, and dominant views inherent in the setting).

Themes in educational linguistics

There are a number of excellent introductory textbooks to linguistics, although they are generally not written with the above recommendations in mind. All of them take the 'transmission-of-knowledge' perspective and are therefore insufficient as syllabuses for groups of teachers. I hasten to add that such books do have a definite place in LATE courses, my point being that they cannot form the core of the syllabus if we want to do appropriate LA development based on the guidelines above.

Instead of the usual linguistic subtopics of phonetics, syntax, discourse analysis, and so on, I propose that we identify language-related themes from the teachers' sphere of activity, that we take an *emic* approach to educational linguistics, in other words. I have experimented with some of these, but I would be loath to recommend a definitive list. The best way to proceed might be to encourage the teachers themselves to generate such a list of themes on the basis of awareness-raising exercises of different kinds, and field-gathered data to whichever extent is possible in the context in which we work.

Themes that are almost certain to come up include the following:

1. *Correctness*, with possible subthemes such as standard versus non-standard language, error treatment in spoken and written work,

systematic differences between spoken and written language.

2. *Bilingualism*, language choice, language policy, code-switching and related issues.

3. The language of specific *professions* (computer technology, the catering – or 'hospitality' – industry, education, and so on).

4. *Classroom talk* between teacher and student, and between student and student. Issues of control and management, initiative, contingency (see chapter 7), use of L1 versus L2, etc.

5. *Language use* in the relations between school and home, conversations between teachers and parents (including across language and ethnic boundaries), children's language use at home and in the neighborhood.

Within each theme, it is inevitable that straightforward linguistic phenomena of phonology, syntax, discourse, etc. will need to be explored at some point. This exploration will necessitate a certain amount of linguistic study in the traditional sense, but it is very important that such study is now motivated by a real-life question that requires an answer. Interestingly, in this scheme of LA development, we treat 'the teaching of linguistics' in a way that is very similar to the way in which we treat 'the teaching of grammar' in a task-based communicative approach. We do not teach linguistics 'because it is there,' but because it helps us to solve language problems in real-life tasks.

Since in a LATE course, teachers ideally collect their own data and conduct field observations, individuals or groups are likely to wish to explore certain issues that are of interest to them or that are problematic in their own setting. They can subsequently report their findings to the whole group, tying them back in to the global topic.

Learning to learn

According to Foucault, the school is one of many institutions characterized by a *disciplinary technology*, the aim of which is to create 'a docile body that may be subjected, used, transformed and improved' (Foucault 1977: 198). In Western nations the aims of schooling are usually expressed in terms of creating 'productive citizens,' who can make a decent living and not be a burden on the state. In times of economic crisis we are often told that the nation must 'invest in its children' to stave off economic disaster in the long run. Such advice focuses on the utilitarian goals of education, and speaks of students as marketable assets rather than as individuals who might find fulfillment in numerous different ways.

Education from the perspective of the AAA is incompatible with such views of education, and seeks to transform the process from the classroom up. So far as learning to learn (or learner training, as it is often called) is concerned, the aim is to encourage students to develop lifelong learning skills. Such skills crucially include the ability to deal with the unexpected, to make informed choices, to develop sharp observational skills, and to construct useful knowledge in one's interactions with the world, while guided by internal values, convictions, and reasons.

Learning to learn therefore goes well beyond training in study skills or other academic activities (such as test-taking), strategies for reading, making inferences, communicating, the management of grades and assignments, and so on. Although it might seem that a thorough grounding in a representative list of such skills and knowledge would prepare a person adequately for academic (and professional) success, as perhaps it does for certain populations, we are aiming for deeper conceptions of learning.

The concept of learning presupposes that one continues to improve.[12] This is only possible when one is not yet perfect and when there are problems in one's engagements with the world. It is also useful, of course, that the learner *wishes* to improve, though natural curiosity ('epistemic hunger,' Dennett 1991; unfortunately curiosity may be just as hard to find in some classrooms as a desire to learn!) is also a powerful initiator of learning, as is the ordinary activity of getting through one's days as best one can. In a sense, then, students do not really need to learn how to learn, rather, the desire to learn must be awakened or re-awakened, and sustained. Once that condition obtains, there should not be a need to go through a predetermined regime of learner training; instead, learners can be guided in the exploration of their own and each other's ways of learning.

We now return to the nitty-gritty of the classroom, where such lofty recommendations could well ring hollow unless backed up by practical actions.

Learner training, even when conceived of in general idealistic terms, requires certain practical action programs at the classroom level. A few examples follow (see further chapters 8 and 9).

1. If we want students to cooperate with each other, using each other's areas of strength and compensating for each other's weaknesses, we must ensure that they receive adequate training in cooperative learning and group work. This goal cannot be achieved instantly,[13] since it involves a range of organizational and communicative skills, as well as possibly a

profound change in learning habits. Many beginning teachers embark on group work with great enthusiasm, only to find that the class degenerates into an unmanageable chaos. They have probably selected an interesting and challenging activity which will take a group of students (perhaps four or five in one group) ten minutes or longer to do, implying a division of labour, a great deal of synchronization of talk and action, and a joint final product. They do not realize that, unless students have been carefully prepared, they are not likely to be able to carry out such concerted work independently.

2. Autonomous work (which does not primarily mean individual work, but rather work which implies choices and responsibilities) requires a range of academic and social 'housekeeping skills' which take time to build. Students must learn to organize their notes and their binders, and also their portfolios, in those settings where these form part of assessment. They must learn how and where to look for information, and how to build auxiliary structures for their memory, not only in their own head, but also in their environment: they have to know how to 'be reminded' of the right things at the right time, in other words, they have to become *resourceful*, literally and figuratively.

3. Since different people learn in different ways, i.e. have different *learning styles*, students should be aware of their own ways of learning, building on their strengths, and perhaps also build up weak areas if they are essential for progress. So, for example, a student who is very visually oriented may use pictures and diagrams for note taking, but at the same time practice auditory skills so as to cope better with lectures and taped programs.

4. Above all, students must learn to articulate their *needs* and *goals*, both long-term and short-term. 'Going to a good university' may be one such goal for a high school student, but it may conflict with a short-term goal of 'buying a cool car or designer clothes' to impress a boyfriend or girlfriend. Sometimes students' short-term purchases might require them to work after school to make the payments, thus conflicting with the long-term goal of obtaining good grades. Students need to learn to set their priorities, and this may be an extremely difficult thing to do in a society which applauds short-term consumer spending more than long-term prudence. If, as seems common in high schools in the US, the parking lot takes up almost as much space as all the classrooms combined, it may be difficult for students to develop the determination that educating themselves is more important than amassing consumer goods (parking a car in the parking lot may be a more significant event than parking one-

self in the classroom), and to realize that these two pursuits may run counter to one another at certain times in their life.

I have given just a few examples of what learning to learn might mean in an AAA curriculum. It should be clear that a teacher cannot simply transmit the sorts of skills and attitudes to learning that are required, nor can he or she *train* learners in the way that recruits are trained to march in step. This does not mean that transmission and training are never appropriate, only that they are subservient to the larger ideals of shaping one's own life.

Language awareness in schools

Finally, I want to say a few words about what LA in schools might look like. To begin with, there is no doubt that an enormous amount of LA work, both planned and unplanned, is going on in schools all over the world. It is important to find the best examples of such work and to allow teachers and students elsewhere to benefit from it.

The best place to start is Hawkins' Language Awareness project (Hawkins 1987a). The book contains the theoretical background and the rationale for doing LA, as well as a practical description of a series of seven small topic books published separately, for pupils aged between 11 and 14. These books are thematic, in the sense that each one deals with a different topic or area of language, and they are partially task-based in that a variety of activities and tasks (group and individual) are integrated with the textual information in the booklets. It is therefore very useful to study this series before embarking on any school-based LA program.

Other recommendations, and practical examples as well, are to be found in a collection of papers edited by Carl James and Peter Garrett (1991b), and in a collection of classroom reports on LA work in British primary schools, edited by Richard Bain, Bernadette Fitzgerald and Mike Taylor (1992). Although LA in schools is therefore not virgin territory (see also Tinkel 1988, Burrell 1991), a number of serious problems remain to be addressed (some of them have already been alluded to):

1. The extent to which metalinguistic knowledge (knowledge about language, or KAL) is beneficial in a range of academic activities needs to be empirically addressed. As I have pointed out, LA does not *have* to be limited to knowledge *about* language, nor does it *have* to refer exclusively to formal (e.g. grammatical) kinds of knowledge. Nicholas (1991) illustrates a range of different aspects of language awareness, such as *lexico-grammatical*, *interactional*, and *pragma-linguistic* awareness, and

proposes that LA address different aspects of language and language use in different age groups. It would therefore be a mistake to assume that LA is a unitary construct, the same for everyone all the time. Another very important consideration, particularly when it comes to evaluation or testing, is that one may be aware of language issues without being able to put that awareness into words (following Gombert, we may distinguish between *intuitive* and *reflective* awareness 1992: 36). Indeed, some of the most basic and deep-seated language phenomena may not be expressible through language in very clear-cut and precise ways (though metaphor and poetry might do the job, but such modes of expression are not very test-friendly!). I might refer back to the problematic differences between *knowing* and *saying* noted by Wittgenstein (see p.54). Is it, for example, easy to articulate why one finds it pleasant to listen to one dialect but not another? Or why one finds a certain pun hysterically funny (while perhaps no one else present does)?

All these caveats indicate that it is imprudent to take a narrow view of LA, or to presume that it is easy (or important) to write down a *list of contents* for it, and that it will probably be impossible to test LA along the traditional standardized models.

2. Point 1 can be said to refer to the *vertical* dimension of the curriculum (Hawkins 1987a; see also chapter 1). The *horizontal* dimension creates a series of problems of a different nature, since it involves synchronization across the school and collaboration among colleagues. Teaching is often described as a lonely profession, in which everyone looks after him or herself, where difficulties are often not shared since the public culture always expects everyone to always be 'just fine,' and time for collaborative efforts is not easy to locate among the daily duties. Teachers need to be trained not to expect their professionalism to reside uniquely within themselves, but rather to realize that it is to a large extent distributed among colleagues, and a crucial part of being an effective teacher is to find access to that distributed professionalism, through grassroots organizing, and 'networking,' to use a popular phrase. But that is only one side of the coin. Educational decision-makers cannot expect teachers to effectively synchronize their classroom activities, and to establish integrated curricula, without making scheduled time available for that purpose. As a simple example of the difficulties involved, numerous teachers have told me that it is virtually impossible for them to observe other teachers' classes in the same school, let alone to engage in systematic peer coaching (as part of INSET work, perhaps), since they have so many other duties and commitments, even during their lunch hour and their preparation period, if they have one. In an educational environment in which teachers are perceived to be 'at work' only when

they are in their classroom or engaged in various supervisory activities (such as policing corridors and playgrounds), not much innovative work can be expected or, indeed, demanded.

3. A programme of LA must take into account the essential interconnectedness of awareness with autonomy and authenticity. This interconnectedness has several direct consequences. One is that the student must be offered meaningful choices, and be held responsible for those choices (the requirement of autonomy). Another is that the raw material for awareness-raising is to be found all around the student, in the real world, rather than between the covers of a textbook (the requirement of authenticity). It is therefore not possible to legislate for LA, in the form of a sequenced, graded, and packaged set of texts and exercises. At the same time, however, it is necessary to ensure quality and accountability. Not having a tangible and finite (i.e. *predictable* and *controllable*) syllabus, and on top of that, not having convenient and objective ways of testing for achievement (as I explained above), makes such quality control and accountability very different from the standard ways our educational systems are familiar with. But that does not mean that it cannot be done. If it is worth doing, then surely a way to do it can be found. A promising way, for example, may be the concept of *portfolio assessment*, of which more in chapter 9. This allows students to justify their choices and to express their achievements in creative, yet effective ways.

Conclusion

In this chapter I have painted a picture of LA full of uncertainties and fraught with potential conflict and divisiveness. Controversy seems to be a natural companion of language debates, as Gramsci has pointed out:

> Every time the question of language surfaces, in one way or another, it means that a series of other problems are coming to the fore: the formation and enlargement of the governing class, the need to establish more intimate and secure relationships between the governing groups and the national–popular mass, in other words to reorganize the cultural hegemony. (Gramsci, quoted in Carter 1992)

The fact that language issues cause so much debate is itself an indication of the importance of language awareness work in education. It may not be immediately obvious to a student, or any language user for that matter, how crucial language is for humanity. As has often been said, a fish may not know how important water is, or even that there is such a thing as water. It is too familiar to even be noticed.

We use language all the time to conduct our daily lives, to improve our circumstances, and even to dream. Schools are full of language, from the teacher's lecturing, the counselor's good advice, the textbook's factual information, and the vice principal's voice blaring through the intercom, to the whispered wisecracks of a friend and the scribbled comments in the notebook. There can surely be no doubt that something so central to all human activity should be the centerpiece of all educational endeavors. Yet, attention to language has always for the most part been haphazard and selective (except, perhaps, for the rhetorical education of elites in the Middle Ages), not at all reflecting the informational and communicative centrality of talking and writing.

The crucial question seems to be how to get hold of this essential faculty of language and how to subjugate it for educational purposes without trivializing it. Subjugation seems to imply simplification and abstraction, so that we 'murder to dissect,' to borrow the words of William Wordsworth (see p. 65). In this way language teaching has focused on grammatical rules and other formal aspects of the language. Displaying knowledge of these in exams is not the same as being an aware language user. In recognition of this, language teaching methods and theories have at times rejected all overt reference to language forms, claiming that language learning occurs naturally and subconsciously as a byproduct of meaningful language activity, both social and cognitive.

I have shown in this chapter that consciousness should not be confused with a deliberate focus on language form, and that awareness of language implies a lot more than metalinguistic awareness. Consciousness, as the organizing, controlling, and evaluating of experience, as the agency that allows us to override physical and biological tendencies, and as the integration of intellect and affect, is a *sine qua non* for all learning, regardless of the amount of genetic priming that exists. All healthy children learn to walk, but they are intensely focused on the task for long periods of time, expending vast amounts of energy, giving up the safer and seemingly much more efficient method of crawling in the process. Learning language is a vastly more complex and protracted affair, tightly interwoven with social and cognitive development as well, and therefore requiring enormous investments of energy and conscious effort.

Learning a second language is a different process from learning a first, for many reasons I need not go into here (see, e.g., Pfaff 1987, Birdsong 1989, Ringbom 1987). The urgency for learning is not there to the same extent as it is in the first language, and the desire to learn can therefore not be taken for granted in the same way. The techniques and the tools for learning may be similar, though some tools for learning may work better, others worse, but the crucial difference lies in the will to learn, as I pointed out in the section on *learning to learn* above. In the next chapter we will look at this issue under the heading of *motivation*.

Notes

1 This exchange was written down from memory that same evening, and there-fore perhaps not necessarily verbatim. See also van Lier 1995a.

2 For earlier comments on the detrimental effect of gaps of various kinds, see p. 43 above.

3 Wittgenstein said of the word think: 'It is not to be expected of this word that it should have a unified employment; we should rather expect the opposite' (quoted in Armstrong & Malcolm 1984: 69). The advice is equally valid for the word *consciousness*. It is not possible here to conduct an exhaustive survey of all theories and aspects of consciousness. For the interested reader, there are now several excellent books on consciousness, e.g. Dennett 1991, Flanagan 1992, Humphrey 1992.

4 According to Wertsch, Russian has two words for consciousness, reflecting the two different meanings shown here. For a discussion of other problems relating to translations of Vygotsky's work, see van der Veer & Valsiner1991.

5 It may have been this sort of consciousness that Wittgenstein had in mind when he said that one can pretend to be unconscious, but not to be conscious (Wittgenstein 1980a: 165). Note, on the other hand, that one can pretend to pay attention as well as pretend not to pay attention. Attention therefore *presupposes* consciousness in this global sense.

6 If there is too much food, or ill-balanced food, on your plate, cultural con-straints may force you to eat unhealthily. In a similar way, too much or the wrong kind of metalinguistic information in class may lead to unhealthy learning conditions. Throwing all food away is not the solution for bad eating practices, and throwing all metalinguistic work out is not the solution for bad classroom practices.

7 Corson 1990 provides a comprehensive overview of various national as well as private initiatives relating to language education.

8 I am grateful to Arthur van Essen of Groningen University for generously providing this and other sources.

9 Dutch applied linguists have long been interested in LA. Another term that is used in the literature is *taalinzicht*, or 'language insight' (Royen 1947). See further van Essen 1992.

10 The term *organic* stands not only for grammar, but for language as a whole, and for consciousness as well. An organic view should guard against a tech-nical approach to teaching and a piecemeal progression of items as the basis for a syllabus.

11 Such efforts, at least those that I have witnessed, too often aim to convey lin-guistic information to the audience. They do not take as a starting point the language knowledge, skills, and attitudes of the participants, nor do they illustrate the task-based, critical approach to language which is essential for LA success.

12 As Minsky says, learning is 'making useful changes to the workings of our minds' (1985: 120). To reflect that learning is not only a mental, but also a social process, we might add: 'and improving our dealings with the world in which we live.'

13 For example, Nolasco & Arthur (1988) propose a ten-week plan for group-work training.

5 Motivation, autonomy, and achievement

Introduction

The nature of life is always to overtake itself.'
Jean Piaget 1971, quoted in Deci & Ryan 1991: 239

The last chapter dealt with the complex and slippery concept of consciousness. In this chapter we will tackle a notion that is probably even more slippery: *motivation*. Yet, unlike consciousness, which some regard as helpful and others as hurtful, experts and amateurs alike agree unanimously that motivation is a very important, if not *the* most important, factor in language learning. The applied linguist Pit Corder once remarked, in a bold and blunt statement in this respect:

> *given motivation*, it is inevitable that a human being will learn a second language if he is exposed to the language data. (Corder 1981: 8)

Experts in other fields, from the pioneer Italian educator Maria Montessori (1965) to the prominent American psychologist Abraham Maslow (1971), have also forcefully argued the crucial role of motivation in learning.

Parents, teachers, and children are, for once, in full agreement with the experts here. Note the following conversation between Sylvie and Bruno, in which the complex relationships between ability and motivation are neatly exploited:

> 'Well, how much have you learned, then?'
> 'I've learned a little tiny bit,' said Bruno, modestly, being evidently afraid of overstating his achievement. 'Can't learn no more!'
> 'Oh Bruno! You know you *can* if you like.'
> 'Course I can, if I *like*,' the pale student replied; 'but I can't if I don't like!'
> (Carroll 1991: 193)

My position here is in essential agreement with all these views on the importance of motivation. However, such a position does not absolve us from the need to find out what motivation really is, where it comes from, and how it does its job. Once these questions are posed, the admirable unanimity of opinion that we noted above evaporates instantly.

It is clear that in language learning (as in most other pursuits), people are motivated in different ways and to different degrees (or intensities). Some learners love doing drills, others hate them; some enjoy role playing and acting out, others would rather solve or discuss problems. Some put effort into whatever they do, others apply themselves sparingly or selectively. Somehow, out of all of these varied circumstances a coherent and efficient classroom needs to be built. For this task to succeed, teacher and students must study and understand their own and each other's motivational resources and limitations.

In this chapter, motivation will be regarded as an interplay between *intrinsic* (innate) and *extrinsic* (environmental) factors. I will assume that all learners possess intrinsic motivation to learn, in common with all active organisms (i.e. intrinsically motivated activity is inherent in the nature of life, as the opening quote from Piaget indicates; see also Deci & Ryan 1991). Learners (of all ages) are naturally curious, seek optimal challenges, and enjoy activities that capture their attention. In addition, human beings learn that there are demands and norms set by the society in which they live, and they may to varying degrees, and with more or less coercion, engage in activities which further social and societal demands, even when they do not coincide with intrinsic interests.

In the best of worlds, intrinsic and extrinsic motivations act in concert, or at least in peaceful coexistence. In less than perfect worlds (including terrible ones), extrinsic demands interfere with, or kill off, intrinsic motivations, reducing the individual to carrying out externally imposed actions, to forced labor, essentially. In practice, most of us live in circumstances where there is much externally controlled action, but also at least a little bit of room for self-initiated activity. The importance of the study of motivation for language learning lies in the realization of this interplay between intrinsic and extrinsic factors. We begin by realizing that without intrinsic motivation all language learning, first or subsequent, is impossible. We next hypothesize that in most educational environments extrinsic factors (often in the form of mandated assessment[1]) tend to dominate, often to the detriment of intrinsic motivation. Our task therefore is to stimulate intrinsic activity, while at the same time acknowledging that society puts on all of us certain extrinsic demands that we need to deal with, whether we like it or not (so, we may as well like them, the optimist in us will say). Promoting intrinsic motivation in our classrooms is therefore not equivalent to recommending to our students to do whatever they feel like, and only when they feel like it, nor does it equate learning with 'fun.' What we need to seek is a responsible course of action which balances intrinsic and extrinsic resources and constraints, and the needs and goals of the individual with the needs and goals of society.

What is motivation?

What motivation means depends very much on the particular theory of human nature that is used. Deci and Ryan (1985) distinguish between two broad theoretical orientations: *mechanistic* and *organismic*:

> Mechanistic theories tend to view the human organism as passive, that is, as being pushed around by the interaction of physiological drives and environmental stimuli, whereas organismic theories tend to view the organism as active, that is, as being volitional and initiating behaviors. (Deci & Ryan 1985: 3–4)

For behaviorists such as Thorndike and Watson, motivation was not a very useful construct since it was not immediately observable, measurable, or manipulatable. For the first half of the twentieth century, while behaviorism held sway, non-motivational accounts of behavior predominated. However, some empirical work was done during this period on the notion of *drives*, four of which were identified: hunger, thirst, sex, and avoidance of pain (Hull 1943). In this view, motivation was based on drive reduction principles, e.g. the hunger drive would motivate a search for food, for the purpose of consuming it and thereby reducing the hunger.

However, as early as 1950, Berlyne published results of studies that showed that monkeys (and rats) engaged in exploratory behavior even if it meant enduring hunger and pain. Monkeys exhibited curiosity-related behaviors such as exploration and manipulation purely for the enjoyment of these behaviors themselves, and the term *intrinsic motivation* was soon used for this by researchers such as Harlow (1950; see also p. 48 above) and Hunt (1971). Such findings could not be accommodated in the drive theories, and eventually the need for new motivation theories of a more organismic kind was recognized (see Hebb 1955). This has led to much work on constructs such as *locus of control* and *causality orientations*, which are important in studies of intrinsic motivation. In addition, the Freudian concept of 'ego energy,' and the influence in educational circles of Montessori, Piaget, Maslow, and others who put motivation central in their pedagogical writings (e.g. Dewey's [1938] notion of 'growth motivation,' White's [1959] notion of 'competence motivation,' and Hunt's [1971] 'intrinsic motivation'), contributed to a renewal of interest in a more organismic account of motivation.

As we saw in the chapter introduction, a complete account of motivation considers both intrinsic and extrinsic factors. However, not all extrinsic factors can be included under motivation. For instance, if I cut my finger while chopping onions, I can hardly be said to have been motivated to cut my finger. Although some things in the environment, a constellation of extrinsic factors (a sharp knife, a slippery peel, clumsiness), caused the cut, we do not speak of motivation in such a case. If a robber with a gun orders me to hand over my wallet, I will probably do so, but it seems a bit strange (though not unthinkable) to say that I was motivated to hand over my wallet. Other extrinsic factors, however, are not so easily dismissed as non-motivational. If a teacher tells me to do my homework or else I will flunk the class, can this motivate me? What if people tell me that I should work hard so that I get good grades? And what if everybody tells me to study in order to get a good job? Or to make my parents happy? Or to be proud of myself?

These examples, and a myriad of others that can readily be imagined, make it clear that the question: '*Where does motivation come from?*' is not easily answered, particularly also because I may work hard for several of the reasons mentioned above, and many more besides, all at the same time. The next question: '*What sources of motivation are most conducive to learning?*' is of crucial importance to education. We might argue that there is just one kind of motivation, one 'force' that impels learning behavior, which might be generated in a number of ways, from threats to rewards to enjoyment. This would mean that one can be *more* or *less* motivated, but not motivated in different ways. This appears to be Robert Gardner's position when he says that 'the source of the motivating impetus is relatively unimportant provided that motivation is aroused' (1985: 169). This does not solve the problem that, if you do not understand the sources, you may not be able to 'arouse' motivation in the ways and at the times that you want to, in yourself or in others.

Alternatively, we might argue that it *does* make a difference where motivation comes from, and that the different *sources* of motivation lead to different *kinds* of motivation, most notably *extrinsic* and *intrinsic* kinds of motivation, depending on whether the stimulus for the behavior originated outside or inside the individual. People taking this view are likely to value intrinsic over extrinsic motivation, perhaps saying things such as: 'He went through the motions because I told him to, but his heart wasn't in it.'

In this discussion it is unlikely that we shall get to the bottom of this issue of *degree* versus *type* of motivation. My approach is, roughly, to regard motivation a bit like money which in itself is neither good nor bad, it just depends what is done with it. Further, extrinsic motivation is like borrowed money, an investment which may eventually pay off, whereas intrinsic motivation is like money you own. Being very highly motivated is like having a lot of money, and, like money, motivation can be wasted or well-spent (this qualifies Corder's statement, quoted in the introduction, that motivation is sufficient; it may in actual fact be *necessary*, but not *sufficient*). In education, motivation is organismic energy-capital to be spent in the learning market. Some of it we bring with us as a genetic endowment, but we may need to learn how to invest it. Some of it we borrow from adults and peers in the form of extrinsic stimuli and coercion.

Actions are judged as motivated on the basis of a combination of factors, most commonly *intensity of engagement, attention, effort,* and *persistence* (see, e.g., the useful overview by Crookes & Schmidt 1991). These are the kinds of things that can be directly visible (and perhaps measurable) in observations and research. They are also the kinds of things learners themselves might be more or less *aware* of. In the film *Stand and deliver*, the teacher Jaime Escalante (played by Edward James Olmos) told his students that the key to academic success was to have '*ganas*,' a concept not easily translated into English, but including ingredients such as enthusiasm, energy, in short, all the factors just mentioned. Many teachers in the US are familiar with the agglutinated monsterword 'stick-to-it-iveness,' which highlights the persistence factor.

Apart from these visible manifestations of motivation, there are other, less tangible, and at the same time more basic, ingredients to motivation. The most central ingredient, in most current theories, is the notion of *intention* (Deci *et al.* 1991). Thus, essentially, *motivated behavior is intentional behavior.*[2] Intentionality is closely related to *choice* (which presupposes the availability of *options*), a concept that is prominent in Crookes & Schmidt (1991), and they quote the following simple definition by Keller as being representative of current thinking:

> Motivation refers to *the choices people make* as to what experiences or goals they will approach or avoid, and the degree of effort they will exert in that respect. (Keller 1983: 389, my italics)

A definition in much the same spirit, but emphasizing the crucial elements of emotion and agency, is provided by Martin Ford in his useful theoretical survey:

> Motivation is defined as the organized patterning of three psychological functions that serve to direct, energize, and regulate goal-directed activity: personal goals, emotional arousal processes, and personal agency beliefs. (Ford 1992: 3)

For further development of the essential nature of motivation, it is useful to return to Vygotsky's conception of consciousness as being composed of intellect and affect (see chapter 5 for a brief discussion; see also Humphrey 1992). Affect (or emotion), in Vygotsky's scheme, refers to the *volitional* side of human nature (Wertsch 1985) and, interestingly, we are now able to make a link between *intentionality/choice*, and *affect*. A further ingredient, following Keller's definition (and, indeed, in our everyday conception of motivation as well), is *effort*, and I suggest that with this tripartite cluster of concepts we can capture the essence of motivation. It may be worth defining these concepts, or at least clarifying them, so as to get a clearer picture of how they might, in concert, bring about the phenomenon that we call motivation.

1. *Intentionality (choice)*: defined by Dennett (1991: 333) as 'aboutness,' 'the processes that are actually involved in keeping a mind in enough contact with the things in the world so that they can be effectively thought about: the processes of attending to, keeping in touch with, tracking and trailing.'
2. *Affect*: 'experiences of emotion' (Dennett 1991: 45). Ryle (1949: 81ff.) distinguishes four kinds of emotion: inclinations (motives), moods (frames of mind), agitations, and feelings. Humphrey refers to 'sentiments,' a combination of sensations and affect (1992: 146–7).
3. *Effort*: Sullivan and Conway (1989) say that 'cognitive effort refers to the investment of deliberately initiated thought in some activity, such as problem-solving, decision-making, or mental arithmetic.' As Chafe (1994) argues, cognitive energy, or the focusing of attention, is limited to one central focus at a time. The ability to direct cognitive/affective energy in ways that are conducive to learning (in other words, the creation of learning opportunities) is therefore crucial in learning, and this may well be the essence of motivation.

These three facets of motivated conduct stand in dynamic relationships with one another. First is *intentionality*, the tendency of living things to 'point to' external things, from the simple pointing of a green leaf toward the light, and the chasing of an antelope by a lion, to the unraveling of the concept of 'free will' by a philosopher. As a result of intentionality, *affect* may be aroused in different ways and intensities. Finally, intentionality accompanied by affect influence the amount of *effort* expended in the actions of the organism.

Leaving the world of plants, and to a certain extent animals, behind, we can next relate motivation to consciousness. As we saw in the previous chapter, consciousness allows us to override our genetic 'equipment' and hence take control of our own activities, including learning. The addition of consciousness also relates to the emphasis which I have placed on *choice*, and the availability of *options*. Such an emphasis would be spurious if there were not a consciousness to do the choosing with, and the manufacture, through socialization and cultural membership, of *reasons* for choosing. We thus end up with a construct of intrinsic motivation which contains at least two layers:

(a) a basic, organismic motivation consisting of intentionality, affect, and effort
(b) a specifically human motivation, grafted onto this organismic one, consisting of consciousness and choice (hence, deliberation)

This compounded human motivation exists by the grace of a world which offers options and opportunities to develop and deploy it. The human activity made possible in this way is *learning*, and the result is *learnedness* (in the sense of 'having learned things').

We can now proceed to apply this view of motivation to language education, so we will be moving again from the more abstract to the more concrete, and from the more general to the more specific. In the next section we will look briefly at the way motivation has been discussed in the field of foreign and second language teaching.

Integrative and instrumental motivation

In the second and foreign language teaching field, virtually all discussion of motivation has been heavily dominated by the distinction between *integrative* and *instrumental* motivation, which originates in the research of two social psychologists, Robert C. Gardner and Wallace Lambert (Gardner & Lambert 1972, Gardner 1985). On this view, integrative motivation refers to a learner's identification with the speakers of the target language, and potentially a desire to integrate with their group, and instrumental motivation refers to goals such as getting a job, a promotion, or passing an exam. As Crookes and Schmidt point out in their survey (1991), this approach to motivation suffers from two limitations:

(a) It is social-psychological, and emphasizes language learners' goals, in terms of attitudes towards the speakers of the target language and the target cultural group(s), or professional aspirations. As an example, in a recent paper R.C. Gardner (1991) consistently uses the expression 'attitudes and motivation' as a unit, without either distinguishing between them, or showing how they interrelate.
(b) It has tended to lump affective factors and motivation together, and has thus been unable to provide a clear definition, or at least a fine-grained description, of motivation as a construct in learning.

It is possible to add a third limiting factor to the two proposed by Crookes and Schmidt:

(c) It identifies motivation with long-term goals and purposes, and does not consider here-and-now interest in the task, the joy of exploration or working together, natural curiosity, and other factors operating in the immediate learning context.

According to Csikszentmihalyi and Rathunde (1993), most motivational theories have focused on *past* and *future* sources of motivation, and have thereby ignored *present* or emergent sources.[3] Using this distinction we can show instrumental and integrative motivation in perspective by way of the diagram in Figure 10.

Past	Present	Future
drives, needs, learning, or other responses programmed in the individual	enjoyment of performance in the present; intrinsic motivation, emergent motivation (= FLOW)	goals in directing action; instrumental, integrative

Figure 10   Sources of motivation

The view of motivation in the work of Gardner and Lambert is thus at one and the same time too narrow and too broad in its scope of application. It is too narrow, in that it ignores a range of phenomena relating to intrinsic motivation (see below), and too broad, in that it insufficiently specifies potential components and contributing factors of motivation. [4]

Similar limitations can be seen elsewhere in the language teaching literature as well. In Krashen's influential model of second language learning, for example (the monitor model, e.g. Krashen 1985), the whole area of motivation receives the mechanistic title 'affective filter.' High motivation equates with a 'low affective filter,' and a high affective filter equates with high anxiety. It would seem that in such an account high motivation would be equivalent to low anxiety, and vice versa. This means that related issues such as boredom, challenge, attention, and effort are neglected.

A richer view of motivation emerges from Allwright and Bailey's study of classroom interaction (1991). Their key term for motivational factors is *receptivity*, following Earl Stevick's influential discussion on this issue (1976). Under this rubric they discuss such related factors as attention, anxiety, competitiveness (see also Bailey 1983), self-esteem and reinforcement. As I have suggested in chapter 3, *receptivity*, when viewed in conjunction with *engagement* and *investment*, can go a long way towards understanding successful intake.

The importance of investment is brought out very clearly in Csikszentmihalyi's dynamic construct of flow experience, as shown in Figure 11 (Csikszentmihalyi 1985: 102).

Csikszentmihalyi and his associates have over several decades conducted research on the so-called flow experience (comparable to Maslow's peak experience, 1971), an experience, in work or play, when time seems to be suspended, everything happens just the right way, and one is totally absorbed in the activity. Preconditions for this state of flow are a perfect balance between available skills and challenges. Anxiety results from insufficient skills or insufficient challenges, and learning means that skills and challenges are increased in order to promote opportunities for 'hitting the flow channel.'

It would seem reasonable to assume that, in an experiential and task-based language learning environment such as is universally promoted these days, a richer and more dynamic view of motivation would be inevitable. However, the literature leads us to conclude, in broad agreement with Crookes & Schmidt 1991, that motivational research in language education has hitherto been rather partial, even though a promising agenda can be constructed for future research in this area. It is particularly important to broaden the social-psychological outlook which has predominated with information from psychology and education, and also, again in line with recommendations by Crookes and Schmidt, to broaden the research agenda to include ethnographic research, case studies, action research, as well as experimentation.

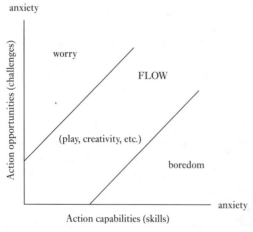

Figure 11   Flow

In the next section I contribute to this agenda by discussing the educational psychology of *intrinsic motivation*.

Intrinsic motivation

The earlier sections in this chapter have raised some questions and made some proposals that stand in need of further discussion. My general thesis, which echoes much of the language learning literature, is that motivation is central to language learning. Following on from that premise, I have argued for a reconceptualization of motivation, proposing a new construct which has at its core an *intrinsic motivation* which interacts dynamically with various forms of *extrinsic motivation*.

In this and subsequent sections I will discuss the following questions, along with some suggestions for research on possible answers:

1. What is intrinsic motivation, and why might it be crucial for learning?
2. If intrinsic motivation is innate, how does it relate to social needs and cultural influences?
3. What is the interplay between intrinsic and extrinsic motivation?
4. How do we stimulate motivation in the teaching/learning process?

Let us consider definitions first. The concept of intrinsic motivation is closely linked to a number of others in the psychological literature. In an exhaustive survey, Ford (1992: chapter 6) lists no fewer than 32 different theories of motivation (he does not include Gardner and Lambert's socio-educational model, however), several of which might fall under the general umbrella of intrinsic motivation, with names such as actualization, self-determination, personal investment, self-efficacy, effectance, and optimal experience. What unites all these theories, and justifies our grouping them together under the general heading of intrinsic motivation, is their focus on present, rather than past or future influences on motivation (see Figure 10 above). It is this focus which has been most conspicuously absent in studies on motivation in language education, and it is therefore important to make intrinsic motivation part of our research agenda.

Edward Deci and Richard Ryan, who are among the most prominent researchers in this area (e.g. Deci & Ryan 1985, 1991), regard intrinsic motivation as voluntary and spontaneous in nature, not dependent on reinforcement or biological drives, but inherent in the nature of life, and needing no other reward than the affects and cognitions accompanying the intrinsically motivated activity. The notion that there are behaviors that occur in the absence of any apparent external reward, challenges the main tenet of the branch of behavioral psychology known as operant theory (Skinner 1953), which is that all behavior is a function of external reinforcements. Thus, Deci and Ryan speak of intrinsic motivation as a *non-derivative motivational force* (Deci & Ryan 1991), i.e. one which cannot be traced back to environmental stimuli or feedback, but rather, which comes from within (or: is caused by) the person.

If motivation in general can be seen as an organism's response to a certain need (e.g., the *drives* mentioned earlier in the chapter), intrinsic motivation arises out of certain basic psychological needs which are innate in the human being. Deci *et al.* postulate three such innate needs: the needs for *competence*, *relatedness*, and *autonomy* (or self-determination):

> Competence involves understanding how to attain various external and internal outcomes and being efficacious in performing the requisite actions; relatedness involves developing secure and satisfying connections with others in one's social milieu; and autonomy refers to being self-initiating and self-regulating of one's own actions. (Deci *et al.* 1991, p. 327)

The innate needs of competence, relatedness, and self-regulation are translated or transformed, by the individual and through cultural membership, into goals. This transformation from innate needs into goals is, to my knowledge, not discussed in the intrinsic motivation literature, but is of crucial importance in education. It determines how motivational universals are channeled into widely differing directions, ranging from true self-actualization (Maslow 1971) to extreme helplessness (Seligman 1981, Peterson & Seligman 1987). Clearly, individual characteristics play a role in this, but more important, from the viewpoint of the educator (whether teacher or parent) is the realization that social interaction and cultural patterns to a large degree determine the particular (attainable, desired, valued, etc.) route taken, the means that are deemed appropriate in this pursuit, and the final destination of the child's needs for competence, relatedness, and autonomy.

The needs → goals transformation process is thus at the core of all pedagogical action. Its implications reach from the most fundamental questions of individual and society, to the smallest pedagogical actions in everyday classrooms. One simple example should suffice. Let us say that, in a cooperative learning context, students experience anxiety regarding their competence on a particular task. The teacher advises these students to repeat to themselves in such stressful moments the slogan: 'I am enough!' This stresses autonomy and self-determination. However, one might equally well, within the tenets of cooperative learning, recommend the chant: 'I am not enough!', thus emphasizing relatedness, and the need for intersubjective assistance. Which (if any) of these slogans is appropriate, effective, and socioculturally preferred in a given context depends on many factors which educators need to discuss and reflect on.

In Csikszentmihalyi's division of motivational theories into past/present/future orientations, as discussed above, intrinsic motivation connects organismic needs (past) to human goals (future). Intrinsic motivation is thus located in the present, in the processes of carrying out activities. Searching for the qualities that characterize flow activity, Csikszentmihalyi proposes that intrinsic motivation *emerges* when an appropriate balance between skills and challenges is achieved (hence his term *emergent motivation*). In such a situation, people may experience what German psychologists have called *Funktionslust*, i.e. pleasure in the activity itself (Csikszentmihalyi 1990: 250), something we usually see in children rather than in adults.

Teachers, with the best of intentions, often assume that 'feeling good' and 'boosting self-esteem' is sufficient to bring about motivation and academic success, and this may result in affective tinkering such as the ritual shouting of slogans (as exemplified above), or hanging placards around students' necks. As the following quote shows, such efforts have nothing to do with intrinsic motivation, since they ignore the characteristics of pedagogical action itself:

> In junior high, educational professionals made everyone in my science class hang placards around our necks that proclaimed, 'I am lovable and capable!' That didn't make me feel good; I still didn't know any science. (Cizek 1993: 24)

We have so far addressed questions 1 and 2 above. We have seen that intrinsic motivation refers to universal human needs, such as competence,[5] relatedness, and autonomy. These needs, translated into goals, energize human behavior. The individual's social circumstances, within the family, a specific social group, an ethnic entity, and so on, and the cultural norms and practices that are in force, govern the transformation of universal motivation into desired outcomes in terms of competence, social relatedness, and autonomy. The various forces that bear upon the individual's learning activities include a range of factors known as extrinsic motivation. The next section will look at these in more detail.

Intrinsic and extrinsic motivation

In our complex world there are many things which, if we were left to our own devices, we would rather skip. These things include such necessary evils as commuting in snarled traffic, wearing ties or high heels, jogging and, especially when we were young, eating spinach and being polite to visiting relatives. Other things we might not get involved in are backbreaking or mindless jobs and (seen from the perspective of young people) countless hours of tedious schooling. Yet, somehow we manage to put up with these and many other unpleasant situations and activities. It would seem that intrinsic motivation alone would be insufficient to account for all the – pleasant and unpleasant – things we get involved in.

If we regard intrinsic motivation as the human response to innate psychological needs for competence, relatedness, and autonomy, a partial explanation for engaging in unpleasant activities becomes available. Remembering Berlyne's finding (1950) that rats will endure pain and hunger just to satisfy their desire for exploration, we can assume that humans will likewise be prepared to engage in unpleasant tasks in order to explore and to satisfy their curiosity. Moreover, we can assume that adult humans are able to see a greater ultimate good beyond a present evil, and therefore actions that are not 'fun' do not necessarily conflict with intrinsic motivation. However, most teachers and parents will attest to the prevalent view that children and students will not move with sufficient enthusiasm and alacrity towards the goals of exemplary citizenship and outstanding academic achievement, if guided by nothing more than their intrinsic motivation. This means that there is a need for extrinsic motivation, in the form of such well-known educational tactics as tangible rewards, praise, coercion, punishment, and so on.

What we are basically saying here is that, for humans, participating fully in civilized society is impossible on the strength of intrinsic motivation alone. According to Deci *et al.*, 'intrinsically motivated behaviors are engaged in for their own sake – for the pleasure and satisfaction derived from their performance' (1991: 328). While this may well characterize the bulk of intrinsically motivated behaviors, especially for children, I want to propose another category of intrinsically motivated behaviors, those to which the child is 'driven' by genetic instructions. For example, the act of walking seems, at the beginning, a painful, dangerous, and inefficient means of locomotion as compared to the safe and efficient method of crawling. Yet, all physically capable children will make the transition from crawling to walking, with varying degrees of extrinsic assistance from others.

Deci and associates propose that their two types of motivation, intrinsic and extrinsic, are basically unrelated. Even though their conception of these two types has changed from the early research in which they were viewed as antagonistic, to a more recent view of broad compatibility (Deci *et al.* 1991: 328), their theory does not consider the possibility of a dynamic positive relationship between intrinsic and extrinsic factors. Yet, such a relationship is visible in all fields of human learning and activity, from earliest childhood onwards. This relationship is also the natural consequence of a Vygotskyan view of learning in which innate and sociocultural forces go hand in hand. What we therefore need to do is to take the very useful research of Deci and associates, and look at it from a Vygotskyan vantage point. In this view, intrinsic motivation and extrinsic motivation are like two forces which may well start out as being separate, but which converge and intertwine ever more closely, until it may well become impossible to tell one from the other most of the time.

Having established the need to see intrinsic and extrinsic motivation as two interdependent forces which increasingly fuse in an individual's actions, we next have to consider how extrinsic motivation can be used to marshal the productive forces of intrinsic motivation. Looking around us, we can see that external motivators work in a myriad of different ways. It is possible to get someone to do something at gun point, by threats to life or safety, by promising various things such as food, money, grades, diplomas, or eternal happiness, by a smile or a pat on the back, by appealing to the actor's sense of decency, duty, or intelligence, and so on. In some cases, the person in question may continue the behavior after the external incentive is removed, in other cases not. In the former case we may say that the incentive is *internalized*, in the latter case it clearly is not.

Deci and Ryan (1985) identify four types of extrinsic motivation according to the degree in which the motivation is internalized, or is other-regulated or self-regulated: *external, introjected, identified,* and *integrated* regulation. A brief description of these four types of extrinsic motivation, and a few typical examples provided by Deci and Ryan (1985) follow.

1. *External regulation* refers to behavior initiated by another person, e.g. by means of the offer of a reward or the threat of a punishment. Avoidance of parental confrontation, or the desire to be praised, are examples given by Deci and Ryan of external contingencies regulating actions. This is the least self-determined form of extrinsic motivation. Here a controlling person is present or at least potentially present (as in Jeremy Bentham's sinister *Panopticon*).[6]
2. *Introjected regulation* 'involves internalized rules or demands that pressure one to behave and are buttressed with threatened sanctions (e.g. guilt) or promised rewards (e.g. self-aggrandizement)' (Deci *et al.* 1991: 329). This form of extrinsic motivation , although within the person (i.e. a controlling person does not physically have to be present), is not part of the integrated self, and can therefore not be considered to be self-determined, or to entail true choice. Deci *et al.* quote an example of a student coming to class on time so as not to feel like a bad person.

3. *Identified regulation* occurs when the individual values the activity and has identified with it. In this form of extrinsic motivation, the behavior has become 'more fully a part of the self, so the person does the activity more willingly' (Deci *et al.* 1991: 329). The person now feels a sense of choice or volition about the activity. An example would be a student who does extra work in mathematics because it is important for him or her to continue to be good in math. The motivation is extrinsic because the behavior is not undertaken for its intrinsic interest or an urge to explore, but rather as an activity instrumental to a goal of 'success at math' (Deci *et al.* 1991: 330). At this point I part company with Deci *et al.*, since I believe that here intrinsic and extrinsic motivation may have converged so that external goals (being good at math, and obtaining high grades and scholarships) and internal needs (competence, and so forth) form one unity.

4. *Integrated regulation* is 'the most developmentally advanced form of extrinsic motivation' (Deci *et al.* 1991: 330). It refers to activities which are fully self-determined and primarily part of adult stages of development. In the view of Deci *et al.*, the distinction between integrated regulation and intrinsic motivation is that in the former case the activity is personally important for some valued outcome, whereas in the latter case it is interesting in itself. My criticism of this is that in such cases activities tend to be both valued in terms of outcome, and in terms of their intrinsic interest, so that these activities are at one and the same time extrinsically *and* intrinsically motivated.

The view of externally motivated behavior as falling along a continuum from external to internal regulation is a useful one. An excess of externally controlled behaviors, especially if they do not attempt to tap into intrinsic motivations, leads to helplessness and amotivation (Deci & Ryan 1985). In my conception of motivation, externally controlled actions can only be beneficial if they gradually fall in step with intrinsically motivated actions, so that other-regulation can become self-regulation. The most effective way to do this is to stimulate intrinsic motivation, so as to take advantage of natural interests, curiosity, and emergent rewards. Not doing so is like sailing into the wind. Placing an undue emphasis on threats, monetary rewards, or grades, may suppress the energizing forces of intrinsic motivation and all the crucial stimulants for learning it carries with it: focused attention, positive affect, depth of processing, intensity of engagement, and so on.[7]

To sum up, not only is there no opposition between intrinsic and extrinsic motivation, they are actually two essential forces that must work in concert to stimulate learning. In many activities in everyday life, including scholastic activities, both intrinsic and extrinsic motivation play a part. For example, language students may participate in classroom discussions because they are interested in obtaining good grades, they want to make their parents happy, they like the target language and want to spend a year abroad there, and they also enjoy the activity itself because it is challenging, it makes them feel competent, and it is entertaining. To ask such students whether they are intrinsically or extrinsically motivated to do the activity, appears a rather spurious question. On the other hand, there are also activities which are clearly only extrinsically motivated, as well as others which are engaged in purely for their 'fun' value. It is important to find out, in a particular educational context, what kinds of activities they are, and use the information to judge the pedagogical value of these activities. As part of an illustration of learner training in a graduate context, I have used adaptations of several motivation questionnaires (Ryan & Connell 1989, Vallerand *et al.* 1989) to raise the students' awareness about motivational issues, and to initiate a discussion about their value. It was, incidentally, in this context that it became apparent to me that no sharp distinction could be drawn between intrinsic and extrinsic factors, at least not for groups of professional adults (there are no doubt sharper distinctions in younger age groups). An example of such a questionnaire is shown in Figure 12, and I recommend readers to use a suitably adapted version of it in their classes, since it can lead to much useful discussion in a learner-centered program. Note that each question has a code written after it, meaning that the question addresses a particular type of motivation, as follows:

E   external regulation
IJ   introjected regulation
ID   identified regulation
IN   intrinsic motivation

The types of questions chosen follow quite closely the examples given in the questionnaires mentioned above. The reader may like to imagine a current or recent academic situation and attempt to answer the questions as a mind experiment.

Motivation in classrooms

Discussions of motivation in classroom work tend to gravitate towards issues relating to intrinsic versus extrinsic motivation, where the former focus on the benefits of exploration and interest, and the latter on external

Academic motivation

> 4 = very true
> 3 = sort of true
> 2 = not very true
> 1 = not at all true

Why do you want to do well in this program

Because I want to be a better teacher (ID)	1 2 3 4
Because I am having a good time (IN)	1 2 3 4
Because I want to learn as much as I can (ID)	1 2 3 4
Because I want to get high grades (E)	1 2 3 4
Because if I don't I'll feel bad about myself (IJ)	1 2 3 4
Because I love being a graduate student (IN)	1 2 3 4
Because people will nag at me if I don't (E)	1 2 3 4

Why do you read TESOL/SLA literature?

Because I want to be well-informed (ID)	1 2 3 4
Because I find the reading stimulating and worthwhile (IN)	1 2 3 4
Because I want to understand the subject (ID)	1 2 3 4
Because I feel guilty if I don't (IJ)	1 2 3 4
Because my professors tell me to read it (E)	1 2 3 4
Because I enjoy studying and researching (IN)	1 2 3 4

Why do you discuss and work in groups?

Because it's required by the professors (E)	1 2 3 4
Because I want my peers to see that I'm a good student (IJ)	1 2 3 4
Because it makes learning more enjoyable (IN)	1 2 3 4
Because it's important to learn to work in groups (ID)	1 2 3 4
Because it's great to debate and create projects with peers (IN)	1 2 3 4

Why do you participate actively in class?

Because I enjoy the classes (IN)	1 2 3 4
Because I want to get good grades (E)	1 2 3 4
Because I want to show that I know the material (IJ)	1 2 3 4
To find out if I'm right or wrong (ID)	1 2 3 4
Because it's expected of me (E)	1 2 3 4

Figure 12   Motivation survey

rewards of various kinds (stickers, certificates, grades, etc.; cf. Kohn 1993). It seems that the indestructible demon of experiential versus behavioristic learning rears its ugly head again here. Can learning be based on intrinsic motivation alone, or are some forms of (preferably positive, of course, following Skinnerian learning theory) external feedback necessary? Will students who are left to rely on interest alone ever progress from Nintendo to Shakespeare? A further question adds another very worrisome aspect to this already knotty problem: Do extrinsic rewards actually dampen motivation and lead to lower levels of performance? How this might work can be illustrated by the following two examples, one fictional, the other real.

Deci and Ryan (1985: 48) relate a story from Jewish folklore in which children in a Southern town would gather round a Jewish tailor's little shop, shouting 'Jew! Jew!' The tailor was at first distressed but finally came up with a plan in which he first paid the jeering kids a dime each, the next day a nickel each, and then a penny. Upon receiving the penny, the kids were so disgusted that they vowed they would *never* come again and call him 'Jew!', just for a lousy penny.

What one can see in this story is that external rewards can 'take over' from any intrinsic fun a particular activity might have. When the extrinsic rewards are subsequently removed (as they eventually always are), the activity is also discontinued. Another example comes from my own teaching. I once designed what I thought was an excellent grammar game, in which two teams (of graduate students) would compete for points to identify and exemplify grammatical rules. Unfortunately, the points-awarding mechanism of the game was less carefully designed than the grammatical problems were, and I happened to have some strongly competitive students in my class that semester. Pretty soon heated arguments started to erupt as to the fairness of awarding this or that point here or there, and any attention to the grammar work was lost in the fray. I am fairly sure that no grammar was learned that day, but I learned the lesson that external rewards (and social rewards, such as praise and group inclusion, are part of this) can be very seductive, and can detract from learning activities. They can *control* instead of *enhance* the activity to which they are applied (Deci & Ryan 1992).

In a recent issue of *Educational Leadership* (February 1991), we can see an interesting example of this controversy as it relates to cooperative learning. Alfie Kohn, a noted educational celebrity, accuses cooperative learning gurus (there are several competing models of cooperative learning in the current US educational landscape) of being nothing but crude behaviorists in disguise, who 'bribe students to work together' and, by doing this, actually decrease motivation and produce lower levels of performance. Kohn (1991a) quotes the noted psychologist Robert Sternberg giving a damning verdict from motivation research:

> Nothing tends to undermine creativity quite like extrinsic motivators do. They also undermine intrinsic motivation: when you give extrinsic rewards for certain kinds of behavior, you tend to reduce children's interest in performing those behaviors for their own sake. (Sternberg,1990: 144)

Indeed, I have often wondered, when observing highly trained cooperative groups in action, for example as they wave their fists in the air and chant 'We're the tadpoles, we're the greatest!', how great the distance is between such group behavior and marauding bands of soccer hooligans or skinheads committing racial atrocities. The analogy may be far-fetched, but I have an uneasy premonition of the kinds of havoc an unscrupulous instructor might wreak with children, using cooperative learning methods. And I have personally seen children in cooperative groups put intense pressure on others, in ways that would be wholly unacceptable in any other context. My unease about such pedagogies is similar to that expressed by Legutke and Thomas about humanistic (or 'therapeutic') approaches to language education, in which learners may be 'in danger of becoming pawns in the teacher's strategy to improve the learning climate without their having an opportunity to make this task their own' (Legutke & Thomas 1991: 67).

In the *Educational Leadership* issue I mentioned, Slavin (one of the most prominent proponents of cooperative learning) strikes back, saying that 'the idea that cooperative rewards can be dispensed with is wishful thinking, and the idea that such rewards will undermine intrinsic interest or continuing motivation is unproven or unlikely' (1991: 91). Slavin does, however, acknowledge that awards may undermine continuing motivation, but only

> in a narrow set of circumstances; it applies only to activities students would engage in without rewards, to short-term reward situations, and to concrete rather than social rewards. (Slavin 1991: 90)

What will be the final verdict on this rewards–versus–interest controversy? I suppose we must quote the usual cliché that the jury is still out. According to Deci and Ryan (1985), research to date indicates that external rewards, whether money, grades, or even praise, will all have the same motivation-killing effects, *if they are perceived as controlling* (Kohn 1991b: 94; see also Kohn 1993), that is, if the outcome is perceived to be controlled by the award-giver or praiser, rather than by the student.

There is much that we have yet to learn about the role of motivational factors in learning. The processes involved are vastly more complex than our research to date has been able to illuminate. Vygotsky's zone of proximal development, coupled with Bruner's notion of scaffolding, meanwhile, may provide a stable guide to the teacher. Teaching is the provision of temporary support for learners, and teachers have the power (and the duty) to guide learners across an ever-widening ZPD. There is little doubt that this power can be constructive as well as destructive. Theories of intrinsic motivation suggest that it is destructive when it leads to external rather than internal control, and other-regulation (including group regulation) rather than self-regulation. Bruner reports that a friend of his said, after hearing of Vygotsky's ZPD, 'It smacks so of twentieth-century liberalism.' Bruner continues:

> Is the Zone of Proximal Development always a blessing? May it not be the source of human vulnerability because the learner begins without a proper basis for criticizing what is being 'fed' to him by ones whose consciousness initially exceeds his own? Is higher ground better ground? *Whose* higher ground? And are those sociohistorical forces that shape the language that then shapes the minds of those who use it, are those forces always benign? The language, after all, is being reshaped by massive corporations, by police states, by those who would create an efficient European market or an invincible America living under a shield of lasers. Indeed, was not Vygotsky's famous example of conceptual development illustrated by how the mind improves when armed with the Marxist ideas of state? Yet, rather ironically in this case, it is Vygotsky's systematic analysis that, in the end, makes us most keenly aware of the dangers to which the critics of the future will address themselves. (Bruner 1986: 148)

I have quoted Bruner at length to point to the importance of another angle to the motivational question: the angle of critical language awareness (see chapter 4). Our decisions to praise, coerce, reward, and so on, are largely determined by our basic educational values, and the *meta-messages* we thereby send concerning control and competence, are largely shaped by our awareness and understanding of the role of language in the educational encounter. We can therefore not escape the essential unity of the pedagogical act, regardless of the amount of technical expertise we amass, and the efficiency with which educational actions march to a particular drum. This brings us squarely back to the basic curricular principles of awareness, autonomy, and authenticity, and to the need to articulate motivational issues with these principles.

Achievement, assessment, and motivation

> In a society such as ours, so strongly oriented toward achievement, individuals' personal value may be judged, even if inadvertently, in terms of their performance. To the degree that this is so, evaluations, even when they are positive and are not accompanied by rewards, surveillance, or deadlines, are likely to be experienced as highly controlling. (Deci & Ryan 1992: 18).

There are basically two ways to look at achievement, and they are visible in Figure 2 on p. 16. We can take an ideocentric or individual view, or we can take a sociocentric or external view (Heckhausen [1987] calls these *intraindividual* and *interindividual*, respectively). The most important task, within the AAA curriculum, for both the teacher and the learner, is to understand how personal and social constructions of achievement are *related*. It is only from this perspective that a focus on other factors such as self–esteem, assessment (or 'measurement'), feed-back, and rewards, is at all meaningful.

In the discussion of intrinsic motivation earlier in this chapter, we saw that Deci *et al.* (1991; see also Deci & Ryan, 1992) postulate three innate human needs: the needs for *competence*, *relatedness*, and *autonomy*. Achievement relates to all three of these needs: feeling competent in terms of knowledge and skills, being successful in one's relations with others, and being in control of one's actions and direction. But the specific ways in which these different aspects of achievement are constructed and manifested, can vary enormously from one person to the next.

Intrinsic motivation, which starts out as a fairly undifferentiated desire for action, and as a general interest and curiosity, becomes increasingly differentiated (i.e. oriented towards certain activities) as the child grows up, and intrinsic factors intermingle with extrinsic ones, in the way outlined above. According to Deci and Ryan (1992: 10ff.), the differentiation of intrinsic motivation depends on three sets of factors:

1. the relation of the child's abilities to the task demands (cf. Csikszentmihalyi's flow model, Figure 11 above)
2. the affordances[8] available in the environment
3. the degree to which the social context is supportive of autonomy versus controlling of behavior

There are thus a number of ways in which the environment influences intrinsic motivation and, by extension, achievement.

Before continuing, let us see if we can define what achievement is. What does the dictionary tell us? Webster's Collegiate Dictionary lists 'successful completion, accomplishment, a result brought about by resolve, persistence, or endeavor,' and then 'the quality and quantity of a student's work.' The latter meaning is immediately associated with the scholastic trappings of achievement: work that a student has to do, and which is assessed by others. Achievement in this sense is defined against program goals, objectives, standards, societal expectations, and so on. Indeed, a quick perusal of the latest issues of several educational journals shows the word achievement being used quite frequently, but in all cases in a context of evaluation and testing, and in most of those cases for the purposes of comparison between groups of students (particularly, in the educational sources consulted, the comparison of minority groups with the mainstream).

But that, as we have seen, is just one side of the coin. On the other side are self-perception (Bem 1972), personal knowledge (Polanyi 1958) and self-determination (Deci & Ryan 1985). Here the question of external standards and sequenced goals (as well as grades, exam results, and positive feedback) takes a back seat.

These two sides of achievement, the 'outer perspective' and the 'inner perspective,' as Ryan, Connell and Grolnick call them (1992: 167), should receive at least equal focus, though from the AAA perspective I would argue that fostering achievement in the personal sense is the true goal of education. Especially since the outer perspective appears to have dominated the discussion of achievement almost totally in recent history, an emphasis on personal achievement, focusing on self-knowledge, self-assessment, and self-regulation (the true meaning of autonomy) appears long overdue.

From the personal perspective, achievement is that which provides an answer to the question: 'How am I doing?' Information about this question can come from a variety of sources. In intrinsically motivated activity the answer lies in the activity itself and its successful conclusion, the pleasure of competent performance, the feeling of success, in sum, the sorts of things Csikszentmihalyi calls flow (1990). In other cases, to varying degrees, feedback from the environment helps provide the answer, in the form of approval, rewards, tokens of appreciation, material or social gain, and so on.

Research on intrinsic motivation and achievement suggests that there is a very delicate balance between a person's experience of competence and external feedback. As soon as such feedback is perceived as controlling, intrinsic motivation, creativity, and personal commitment tend to decrease (Deci & Ryan 1992). Not a great deal is known yet about the exact circumstances which lead instances of feedback to be perceived as either controlling or enhancing. As teachers we often tend to assume that positive feedback must be enhancing and negative feedback controlling (or demotivating), but this does not appear to be the case at all. Deci 1971, Smith 1974, Fisher 1978, among others, have found that positive feedback can be equally perceived as controlling, especially when it occurs in a context in which there is little self-determination.

To sum up, achievement, from the personal perspective, appears to be closely linked to self-determination. Feedback from others can enhance a person's knowledge of success but only if the person feels that the behavior was self-determined, and the context was one which facilitated autonomy. Does this mean that achievement from the social or institutional perspective, in the form of assessment and tests, is irrelevant to educational progress? Surely not, since a framework of expectations and goals can assist the individual enormously in charting a course towards success. Further, the question 'How am I doing?' has, for many people at least (excepting, perhaps, the truly authentic person), a comparative angle to it: 'How am I doing in comparison with other people in my situation?' (the *competitive* angle). Finally, people who are responsible for a particular job, such as educating children or adult learners, and who spend time and money in this pursuit, are understandably held accountable for the quality and efficiency of their activities. It is appropriate for this accountability to be expressed in terms of the achievement of the children or learners in their charge, and the testing industry (which, after all, is in essence a form of quality control) has arisen in response to this need.

In my view the problem with such expressions of accountability, i.e. with public measures called tests and examinations, is that they must *measure*. Unfortunately, one can only measure that which is *measurable*. It is quite possible that the deepest, most satisfying aspects of achievement, and the most profound effects of education, both in positive and negative terms, are entirely unmeasurable. For example, how does one measure a happy memory, or a dreadful one? What if we held educators accountable for the quality of the memories they gave their students, rather than for averages on national tests? A facetious question, it might appear to some, though no doubt such memories far outlast the memorized items addressed in test questions.

The institutional machinery of accounting and evaluating, the technical intricacies of designing tests which demonstrate achievement in terms recognized by sponsors or society at large, and the control of learning behavior by agencies charged with deciding what proper learning behavior is, these are all topics which I purposely set outside the AAA curriculum. This does not mean that I do not regard them as important, or worthy of constant study and debate. However, I see the task of the AAA curriculum as finding ways to ensure that proper attention is paid to the basic moral purpose of education: promoting the self-actualization of every learner, to the fullest extent that an imperfect institution can do this.

Conclusion

Language educators agree with admirable unanimity on the supreme importance of motivation in language learning. However, rather than doing justice to the construct by critically and analytically examining it in thorough and honest ways, educators attempt to capture the students' attention by various gimmicks such as putting on a show (the Rassias method of teaching a foreign language is an extreme example, see Oller & Richard-Amato 1983), providing stickers and grades, and a multitude of other superficial devices that I have touched on in various places in this chapter. I cannot escape the thought that all such 'motivating' actions at best relate to learning in the way that the supermarket version of 'have a nice day' relates to wishing someone well, or a TV cooking show relates to a family dinner. Somehow, many of the things done in the name of 'motivating the students' do nothing but sidestep the issue of true motivation. Education, in other words, is heavily polluted with surrogate motivation.

I have used Csikszentmihalyi's view of motivational theories as being oriented to the past, present, or future. As we have seen, in language teaching, discussions of motivation have almost exclusively focused on future goals, in terms of either instrumental or integrative motives. I have argued that this ignores innate curiosity as well as intrinsic enjoyment, both of them essential sources of motivation.

Achievement and motivation are closely related. External achievement, as measured via various forms of assessment such as tests, is only effective, from the personal perspective, if the learner buys into it, and does not perceive it as controlling. Personal achievement, in terms of knowledge, skills, and rewarding social relationships, is tied to intrinsic motivation through the person's self-determination and autonomy.

Looking towards the future person we want to become and we would like our students to become, we acknowledge the importance of growth in self-regulation and autonomy. Our ideal should be the *autotelic personality* of Mihalyi Csikszentmihalyi, the *self-actualized person* of Abraham Maslow, the *authentic person* of Jean-Paul Sartre. This turns pedagogy into a *project*, in the sense in which Sartre uses this word in *Being and nothingness*. The essence of project in this sense is *choice* of being, and *action* towards future ends (Sartre 1957: 633). This relates to the principle of *authenticity*, which will be discussed in the next chapter. After that, the practical examination of pedagogy in terms of choice and action will be the topic of chapters 7 and 8, on *contingency* and *curriculum design*, respectively.

Notes

1 We will return here to the second triad (see chapter 1) of achievement, assessment, and accountability, and particularly to the relationship between achievement and assessment.

2 This does not necessarily mean: 'done deliberately,' see Churchland 1988: 63. Intending means, rather, 'pointing to,' or 'orienting towards.'

3 Csikszentmihalyi's notions of emergent motivation and flow will be further discussed below.

4   In a reply to Crookes & Schmidt 1991 and other recent criticisms (Dörnyei 1994, Oxford & Shearin 1994), Gardner and Tremblay point out that research in the 'Gardnerian tradition' is far more varied and complex than a simple oppostion between instrumental and integrative motivation or orientation (1994). Indeed, it is likely that we tend to receive a rather simplified version of this work, as is so often the case when complex theories become popular. However, it remains true that Gardnerian research leaves the dynamic complexity of motivation relatively untouched, and focuses instead on orientations and attitudes towards learning and language. In the view expressed in this chapter, these latter issues are only parts of a much bigger puzzle.

5 It is instructive to recast the Chomskyan competence/performance distinction in terms of needs and goals, rather than assuming as usual that competence is a universal state, possessed as an innate good by every individual.

6 Bentham's proposed *Panopticon* is a set of buildings with individual cells which are all completely visible from a central control tower. The inhabitant of each and every cell may be constantly observed, but never knows if and when this is actually the case. Foucault discusses this concept frequently (see Rabinow 1984).

7 See several experimental studies described in Deci & Ryan 1985, in which monetary rewards were used as a variable, and which showed that such external rewards were ultimately detrimental to performance.

8 The use of this word suggests an interesting link to the ecological perspective of J.J. Gibson (1979), which I mentioned on p. 36. However, the reader may recall that an affordance, as conceptualized by Gibson, implies the complementarity of the individual and the environment. The notion of affordance therefore requires an active person, not a passive receiver of input.

6 Authencity

If you seek authenticity for authenticity's sake, you are no longer authentic.
Jean Paul Sartre 1992: 4

Introduction

S1   What's mean leave-taking?
T   Leave-taking. You say 'good-bye.' Okay?
     Sometimes when you leave somebody you say 'good-bye' or 'see you tomorrow.'
     Or what else can you say?
S2   See you later.
T   See you later, yes. What else? Huh?
S3   Take it easy.
T   Take it easy. What else? S4?
S4   Catch you later.

The above piece of language is quite easily *identifiable* as L2 classroom language. It does not take an expert to place the episode in its appropriate context. Why is that? And what does such an observation mean?

The fact that classroom language looks and sounds like classroom language is often taken as evidence of the artificiality of language lessons, and this in turn can then be used as an explanation for the lack of success of language instruction. 'Classroom language is unnatural' means in practice that language use in the classroom is different and distinguishable from language use elsewhere. In addition, it implies that language use is natural in all places, except in classrooms. To become more 'natural,' then, the classroom must try to be less like a classroom, and more like some other place. The people in the classroom must speak and write as if they were somewhere else.

In the interests of authenticity, the classroom must become inauthentic, as a classroom. We are therefore confronted with a paradox, and to unravel this paradox is central to any discussion of the issue of authenticity in language teaching. This is a crucial issue, one which goes well beyond the simple question of what materials to use, or what kinds of language to use in the classroom. It touches the core of what language lessons are supposed to do, what their purpose and realistic goals are. In this chapter we will examine authenticity as a basic principle of language education.

Let us begin by examining the following exchange which, I confess, I have just made up:

A   Open your mouth wide, please. Hold still for a moment, if you can.
B   ((mumbling through multiple gadgets)) Ish ick gowa 'ur'?

Most readers will have no problem identifying this as an interaction occurring in a dentist's office rather than, say, in a fast-food restaurant. It will further be clear at once that A is the dentist and B the patient, rather than the other way around.

As in the classroom example above, there is a clear relationship between the setting and the type of language use that occurs in that setting. The language is *tied* (indexed), in a number of ways, to the setting. But in the case of the dentist's office, no one complains about the artificiality of the language (though one might complain about many other things, of course), yet in the case of the classroom such complaints are common.

Now let us look at another exchange, once again at the dentist's surgery, and once again made up for the occasion:

A   ((drill poised)) Who are the Dodgers playing this Saturday?
B   ((unable to move or speak)) . . . Ungh . . .

Now we might say, with some justification, that there is something wrong with the language used in this setting. A requests a verbal contribution of B, while in the full knowledge that B is unable to make such a contribution in the circumstances. Indeed, A herself has *caused* B's inability to respond. But how would we characterize the problematicity of the discourse? Intuitively, it seems that *authenticity* is not the right concept here. Rather, we might want to say that the discourse is *defective* or *ill-formed* (regarding these terms, for the time being, as roughly synonymous).

Why is this exchange defective? We might say, informally, that there is no point in A's asking a question if she knows that B cannot possibly answer it. Then we can go back to A's question, and say that it is a *fake*, and not an *authentic* question. But we are not at the end of the argument here. A might say that she asked the question in order to divert B's attention from the approaching drill and thus avoid undue anxiety or even a panic reaction. Then the question, with its *overt* intention of requesting information, has the *covert* intention of putting the patient at ease.[1] We have thus been able to *rationalize* a speech action which appeared, on the surface, to be irrational. Our rationalization has 'fixed', so to speak, the defective exchange, and it has managed to *authenticate* the dentist's question. Authenticity, on this view, is not something that is a property of some piece of language, but rather, of a speaker's intention and a hearer's interpretation of the language used (ultimately, then, it becomes a question of *relevance*, in the sense of Sperber & Wilson 1986).

Bringing the argument back to the language classroom, these considerations are indicative of the complexity of the issues involved. Minimally, we should be very careful before we make judgments about the 'naturalness' or authenticity of classroom language. Merely being able to identify classroom language as such is irrelevant in a discussion of authenticity. In the following section we will attempt to develop a definition of authenticity that is relevant to language education.

What is authenticity?

The introductory problem-posing above has set the stage for a discussion of authenticity which goes beyond the usual domain of the term: that of authentic materials and authentic tasks. I will argue that the concept goes far deeper, and that we need to look at it as a *process* of engagement in the learning situation, and as a *characteristic* of the persons engaged in learning. As such, authenticity relates to who teachers and learners are and what they do as they interact with one another for the purposes of learning.

According to Giddens, 'the authentic person is one who knows herself and is able to reveal that knowledge to the other, discursively and in the behavioral sphere' (1991: 187–8). Authenticity thus relates to self-knowledge and to communication. But, warns Giddens, 'shorn of external moral criteria, the pure relationship is vulnerable as a source of security at fateful moments and at other major life transitions' (1991: 187). In other words, authenticity must go together with morality, or social responsibility.

In the classroom, authenticity relates to processes of self-actualization, intrinsic motivation, respect and moral integrity in interpersonal relations, and so on. In this way, both epistemology and axiology (see chapter 2) are essential in the description of authenticity. This is the view I will be sketching in this chapter, though I am well aware that the danger exists that I am making the construct of authenticity do much more work than is customary. However, I feel that this is valuable so long as important questions are raised that allow us to look at language education in a new light. To begin with, we will discuss some earlier views of authenticity in learning.

The notion of authenticity has been prominent in the L2 literature for some time. In 1979, Widdowson introduced the very useful distinction between *genuine* and *authentic* language use. In his description, genuineness is a property of some language sample not constructed for the purpose of language learning, perhaps a newspaper article, a recorded episode of a soap opera, or a poem. It therefore refers to the provenance of a piece of language, or its 'pedigree.' Authenticity, on the other hand, 'is a characteristic of the relationship between the passage and the reader and it has to do with appropriate response' (1979: 80).[2] In other words, if we clip an article from a newspaper, and bring it to class, then this is a *genuine* piece of language. Once introduced into the language lesson, we may proceed to ask students to do *authentic* or *inauthentic* things with it. Inauthentic things would presumably include such tasks as learning it by heart, conjugating all the verbs in it, or finding three synonyms for every concrete noun in it (I'm inventing these, they are not mentioned as examples by Widdowson). It is harder to say what might be authentic uses of the article, and Widdowson recognizes this problem. He says that our main problem is to induce the learner to treat such genuine instances of language 'as discourse, to adopt the same attitude to them as he would to written discourse in his own language' (*ibid.*). However, it is necessary to point out that one's attitude to written language in the native language is not necessarily authentic, as I expect most readers' experiences of school lessons will corroborate. We will therefore have to delve further to get to the meaning of authenticity in education.

Extrapolating to spoken discourse, authenticating genuine instances of spoken language might require the same stance as authenticating the written language does, but it might be even more difficult to achieve, particularly if it involved participating in a conversational interaction, since the classroom context is traditionally not set up to foster genuine conversational interaction. So, it is easy to bring genuine pieces of language into the classroom, but to create authentic opportunities of language use on their basis appears to be quite another matter. As Widdowson points out, *genuine* texts must be *authenticated* by the learners (*ibid.*), but the *conditions* for authentication are hard to pinpoint.

The next discussion of authenticity I wish to mention is Breen (1985). Breen relates authenticity to the actual text, the learners' involvements with the text, the language learning tasks based on the text, and the social situation of the classroom as a language learning environment. It is easy to see that these different senses of authenticity might lead to conflicts with one another. For instance, one might argue that a drill, or a recitation in chorus of an invented dialogue, can be authentic language-learning tasks within the social context of the classroom. Any language, used in any way whatsoever, can then be claimed to be authentic. However, as Widdowson (1990: 46) points out, in this way the meaning of the word authenticity is generalized to such a degree that it becomes virtually useless. Widdowson suggests that 'we retain the term to refer to the normal language behaviour of the user in pursuit of a communicative outcome rather than the language-like behaviour of the learner.' He concludes: 'Thus inauthentic language-using behaviour might well be *effective* language-learning behaviour, but to call the latter 'authentic' seems to me to confuse the issue' (1990: 46–7).

Both Widdowson and Breen make some valid points, and though they appear to be at loggerheads over the term authenticity, I believe that there is a broad measure of agreement between their arguments. This agreement can be brought out if we look at authenticity not primarily as a *product*, or a *property of language* or even *language use*, but rather as a *process of validation*, or *authentication*, to use Widdowson's own term, conducted by the participants in a language-learning setting. To give an example, let us return to the last dentist's exchange used above. I initially called this defective, and I suggest it would be so if it were validated (authenticated) by one interlocutor (e.g. the dentist) but not the other (the patient). This defectiveness would be *covert* if neither of the participants demonstrated their justification/rejection, and such a situation might cause friction, or irritation, or 'bad blood.' The defectiveness would become *overt* if the participants aired their discrepant views of the well-formedness of the exchange, and then they might engage in repair procedures to remedy the discrepancy. Such a repairing or remedying process might be called an *authentication process*. It establishes *relevance*, and it *endorses*, *rejects*, or *revises* prior utterances. Inauthentic discourse then happens when defectiveness (e.g. a discrepancy of interpretations) occurs which is not (successfully) repaired. In the classroom, this would occur, for example, when one participant's and another participant's language use are in conflict, and when this conflict is either ignored or not successfully repaired. It would also occur, in a much more covert and 'pathological' (in a pedagogical sense) way, if all participants were confused about means and purposes, a case of collective blindness, as it were. In many such cases it may be relevant to use Habermas's concept of *systematically distorted communication*, which can be described as the result of 'a confusion between actions oriented to reaching understanding and actions oriented to success' (in which case a situation of unconscious deception obtains; Habermas 1984: 332).

We are now gradually zeroing in on a conceptualization of authenticity which is quite different from the one that is commonly used in the literature. It has nothing to do with the origination of the linguistic material brought into the classroom (Widdowson's 'genuine' text), nor even with the kinds of uses to which the material is put, i.e. the tasks and exercises devised for and executed in language lessons. The notion we end up with, foreshadowed by the term *authentication* as used by Widdowson, is much closer to the meaning the term authenticity has in existential philosophy. Such authenticity results from self-determination (knowing-what-you-are-doing), a commitment to understanding and to purpose, and transparency in interaction.[3] As Sartre says in *Being and nothingness*, like individuality, such authenticity is not given, it has to be *earned* (1957: 246). This means that authenticity is not brought into the classroom with the materials or the lesson plan, rather, it is a goal that teacher and students have to work towards, consciously and constantly (cf. Candlin 1993).

In a curious way, it seems to me that the traditional language lessons of the grammar translation type which I remember from my school days might lay greater claim to that sort of authenticity than some of the so-called communicative classrooms that I have had occasion to observe in recent years. I must emphasize that the old lessons seem to have been authentic *for me*, although they may well have been inauthentic for some of my class mates.

Authentication is basically a personal process of engagement, and it is unclear if a social setting could ever be clearly shown to be authentic for every member involved in it. However, given the privileged status of the teacher, it is reasonable to suggest that a teacher's authenticity may stimulate authenticity in the students as well. In terms of language teaching methods, one cannot say that any particular teaching method is more likely to promote authenticity than any other, regardless of whether or not it promotes the use of 'genuine' materials. Rather, the people in the setting, each and every one individually for himself or herself, as well as in negotiation with one another, authenticate the setting and the actions in it. When such authentication occurs *en masse*, spontaneously or in an orchestrated fashion (socially constructed authentication, so to speak), we may well have the most authentic setting possible. A good teacher may be able to promote such authenticity. It may be easier to achieve it in some settings than in others.

To sum up, authenticity is the result of acts of *authentication*, by students and their teacher, of the learning process and the language used in it. The teacher may be instrumental in promoting authenticity, although this may be a lot easier to achieve in some settings, and students, than in others. In the following sections, various aspects of authenticity and its promotion in language classrooms will be discussed.

Simplification and teacher talk

When we speak we have certain ways of conveying what we mean. We know that anything we say can potentially 'mean' many different things, and we are aware that listeners may need some help in deciding which one of all the possible interpretations we want them to go for. So, our talk is designed in order to avoid unnecessary ambiguity, to avoid the listener floundering about not knowing what we are getting at, and not knowing what we expect him or her to say next.

A central notion in any form of communication thus is *audience design* (Bell 1984). The speaker has some communicative intention, and this intention includes the intention to be understood as intended (in addition to the information, or 'message', being understood). Levelt 1989 (see also Sperber & Wilson 1986) calls this the speaker's purpose of *intention recognition*. We want the audience to understand us the way we want to be understood. In addition to the purpose of intention recognition, the speaker may also have such purposes as *attitude recognition* and *face recognition* (as well as possibly others). The speaker may signal a certain attitude towards the thing being said, such as sincerity, jocularity, sarcasm, emotion, detachment, and so on. The speaker may also want to or need to indicate observance of and respect for the sociocultural demands of the setting,[4] including decorum, etiquette, and mutual respect, in short, observe the demands of face, politeness, group membership markers, and so on.

Further, to the extent that the utterance is designed to convey *information*, or a *message*, it must also bear a proper logical or propositional form, it must fit in with other things that are being said, and it must have sufficient cohesive markers.

Finally, every utterance also has design features relating to interactional requirements of the setting, such as appropriate turn taking, topic management, relevance signalling, and so on. The *design features* of utterances include thus at least the following (possibly overlapping) components shown in Figure 13.

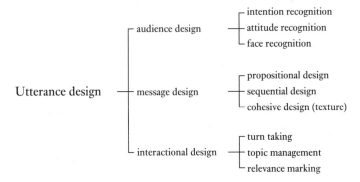

Figure 13   Utterance design

This exploration of the complexities of utterance design and interpretation is no more than a crude sketch, and its purpose is merely to give an impression of the accomplishments – routinely taken for granted by adult native speakers – evidenced by everyday language use. When these accomplishments are perceived to be lacking in our listeners, as is the case when we speak to small children or to foreigners, we *adapt* our language in various ways. The better we understand the problems our less-competent interlocutors face, the more efficient we are likely to be at adapting our language, and at deciphering what is said to us in return.

When we change our language for the benefit of a learner (or, in general, a foreigner), we are practicing some form of *accommodation* (more precisely, convergence; see Beebe 1988 for more detailed discussion of these terms). If we do not like the foreigner, harbor some form of resentment, or wish for whatever reason to create or maintain a distance, we may – deliberately or unconsciously – block this accommodation, with the result that the foreigner does not understand what we say, and vice versa (divergence). According to one well-known stereotype, Parisians do this to tourists who speak French less than perfectly. There may be other reasons why foreigner talk could be unsuccessful: perhaps we have insufficient experience with non–native speakers to know *how* to accommodate. In such cases, upon not being understood, we may merely repeat what we said before, only louder.

Foreign language teachers are expected to understand the kinds of problems their students have. They can therefore be regarded as being especially sensitive to and aware of what their students know and can cope with (in that sense they may be compared to parents and other caretakers of small children). Teachers are therefore eminently capable of adapting their language to accommodate their students' temporary imperfections. This leads to a paradoxical situation, however, since on the one hand teachers can accommodate effectively, but on the other hand, in doing so they deprive their students of the full array of language and expression that native speakers engage in. Efficient foreigner talk (or 'teacherese') would appear to be an authentic mode of communication for teachers in classrooms, but by the same token it does not reflect the richness of language as it is used by native speakers in the target-language world at large. The more the students depend on their teacher in terms of their exposure to genuine language, the more problematic this paradox is likely to be. It is not, strictly speaking, a question of authenticity of language. Teachers, in using teacherese to communicate effectively with their students, are using language authentically. Indeed, if they spoke to their students differently, now as if they were addressing a neighbour, now a car mechanic, and so on, they would be using language inauthentically. However, it may be desirable, or even necessary, to expose the students to the types of language used around front lawns, car service areas, and many other speech settings. Are we then doomed to be inauthentic in classrooms, whatever we do? Do we have to choose between classroom authenticity and 'real world' authenticity?

These questions, in various different formulations, underlie much of the perennial debate about language teaching methods. To resolve this debate, we need to go back to the notion of *authentication* discussed in the previous section. This notion is important, since it allows us to reject as unnecessary any choice between 'classroom world' and 'outside world' (or 'real world'). In the authentic language classroom, both a teacher's foreigner talk or teacher talk and demonstrations (or samples reproduced in one way or another) of language use from extra-mural settings can, in appropriate circumstances, be authenticated by the participants. This is commonplace in a myriad of classrooms, though the selective perception (not to say dogma) which characterizes most methodological positions often obscures this authentication. We will elaborate on ways in which such authentication may proceed at various points in this book, beginning here with a look at *simplification* or *teacherese*.[5]

The characteristic features of teacher talk have been described in many studies (see Chaudron 1988, Ellis 1994). Some of the issues that have been addressed in research, and some of the 'DOs and DON'Ts' offered to teachers in handbooks and workshops, are listed in Figure 14. It is not my aim here to prescribe or proscribe certain features of teacher talk, indeed, I suggest that the giving of such 'advice,' though it is quite common in teacher workshops, is either superfluous or counterproductive. It is superfluous where teachers clearly have an excellent rapport with their students. It is counterproductive where they do not, since merely changing some outward features of speech and interaction patterns is unlikely to change an unhappy teacher–student classroom relationship into a happy one. On the contrary, making superficial changes without addressing underlying problems is likely to exacerbate these underlying problems in the long run (it may also be insulting to many audiences). Instead, as part of teacher education, we might examine features of teacher talk such as the ones listed in Figure 14, rate them (on a scale from 1 to 5, say) according to their perceived usefulness in general or in specific classroom events, and discuss our ratings with colleagues. I think that such an exercise would be more beneficial than merely indicating that, for example, 'amplifying' is good, 'simplifying' is bad, however reasonable such a judgment may seem within a specific educational context and philosophy.

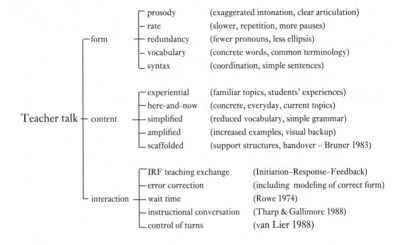

Figure 14   Teacher talk

Rather, it is beneficial for teachers – and teachers in training – to learn about teacher–student interaction patterns, to become aware of their own habits and practices in terms of teacherese and so on, and to reflect on the desirability of making changes. The study of teacherese thus becomes part of a teacher's self-monitoring and teacher research (in which peer coaching could be a highly effective component). When teachers become aware of their tendencies and practices of using teacherese in the classroom, they can ask themselves: 'How are we going to control it?' By *control* I do not mean *eliminate*, but rather bringing our patterns of speaking under the control of conscious pedagogical decisions, so that we can use teacherese to its best effect, without overdoing it or neglecting it. It can thus contribute to professional growth.

To sum up, as part of self-monitoring, teachers can ask themselves the following questions:

1. Do I use teacherese, and what is it like?
2. Should I use teacherese more or less? Why?
3. Should the quality of my teacher talk be improved? How?
4. When is using teacherese appropriate, and when is it not?

Although I do not wish to deny importance to questions 1 through 3, in my view question 4 is the most interesting one here. It suggests that teacherese can be brought under the conscious control of the teacher, and become a *strategy* to obtain certain outcomes. Most importantly, it suggests that teachers can use more than one register, or linguistic repertoire, in the classroom, thus increasing the range of expression available as exposure to the student.[6] Rather than being told that teacherese is necessary in order to provide comprehensible input, and then being given instructions as to how to do it, teachers can investigate their own teacherese and learn to use it as one tool among many. It thus becomes part of a teacher's theory of practice (van Lier 1995b).

Aspects of authentication

When we use teacherese we bring into the classroom a type of language specially designed to make the job of learning easier for the students. This is language which is in some respects (see Figure 14) different from the language as it is used in most other places. In addition to the teacher's speech, books, tapes, worksheets, and other materials may also be constructed to contain language specially designed for the benefit of the students. I argued above that in itself there is nothing wrong with this, given that audience design is a natural feature of language use. However, if we let the natural forces of audience design take their course unchecked, or promote various forms of teacherese for the sake of 'comprehensible input,' we may end up with a narrow range of language in the classroom, one which does not afford the students sufficiently rich and varied exposure, and challenging practice. The question is thus, how can we satisfy the natural demands for audience design, while at the same time providing a rich and varied linguistic environment?

On p. 127 I suggested that authenticity is the result of a process of *authentication*, a validation of classroom events and language, and an endorsement of the *relevance* of the things said and done, and of the *ways* in which they are said and done. This suggestion, as it stands, may be interesting in the abstract. However, in practical terms it might be dismissed as spurious, for the same reason that Widdowson found Breen's interpretation of authenticity inadequate (see above p. 127). Students may be docile, naive, misled even; teachers may be pushy, persuasive, misguided, and so on. Unless we are careful, authentication may merely come to mean acquiescence or the absence of open revolt. We therefore need to specify in some detail what kinds of authentication can occur, and how the traditional view of authenticity as the use of genuine materials is compatible with a more expanded and process-oriented view of authentication.

There are many ways in which the notion of authentication can be brought into a description of language classroom practices. Let me illustrate a few of these before elaborating in more practical terms. First of all, it might be argued that authenticity is the natural result of awareness and autonomy, and at the same time that authenticity leads to increased awareness and autonomy. In other words, if you 'know what you are doing,' and if you are 'responsible for your own actions,' then you are 'being authentic'. Viewing the AAA curriculum as an organic compound of central values and knowledge schemas, one might propose the simple formula 'A + A = A'. Any one of the three principles might be placed in any one of the three slots in the equation, and in every case a sensible statement would result. Putting it another way, awareness without autonomy is pointless, autonomy without awareness is disastrous, authenticity without autonomy is a contradiction in terms, and so on.

It is also possible to look at authentication as the Peircean category of 'thirdness' (see above, p. 56). If awareness is firstness,[7] autonomy (one's stance *vis-à-vis* others and the object world) is secondness, and authenticity is the interpretation of that which unites awareness and autonomy. If we regard the three principles as truly interrelated (as, I think, is inevitable), then they form a genuine triad, in the Peircean sense. Any one of the three cannot exist productively (or be explained satisfactorily) in isolation from the other two, and a relationship between any pair of principles presupposes the remaining principle. This may seem a rather abstract and esoteric way of discussing authentication within the AAA context, but I think that some reflection will show its theoretical soundness, as well as its practical value. Let me give a few examples.

1. Let's say that we are interested in promoting language awareness (LA), as recommended earlier, and as advocated by a number of applied linguists, sometimes under the name consciousness-raising (Rutherford 1987, Sharwood Smith 1981). In the course of promoting LA we discuss issues such as language change, varieties and dialects, differences between spoken and written language, and so on (Donmall 1985, van Lier 1991b). Now, unless this awareness is increasingly a *critical* awareness (see also Corson 1990, Fairclough 1992a), we will end up discussing language as dead subject matter, decontextualized and dissected in lessons. A focus on language will then end up being a focus on grammar rules, textual analysis, and exercises and drills, in short, all the things which have justly been criticized in traditional language education. A language awareness which goes beyond 'dead form' will examine the role of language in life, and discuss issues of attitude, control, prescriptivism, creativity, and so on. Such study inevitably requires learner autonomy in terms of creating choices and setting directions, and authentication of the subject matter of language in terms of data, evidence, and the roles and purposes of the language-using subject (including, first and foremost, the learner).

2. A program of fostering learner autonomy, perhaps as a component of learner training (Willing 1989), aims to make learners responsible for their own learning, capable of making reasoned choices, assessing their own progress and achievement, and able to respect themselves and others. Such a program would be impossible without an awareness of what is going on, including in terms of language use, and without an authentic commitment to and involvement in the educational tasks at hand.

3. Finally, if learners are to successfully authenticate their language learning environment and activities, they clearly need to develop a critical awareness of language and of educational processes, and also develop the ability and will to take charge of their own learning.

We see therefore that the AAA are not just three principles that a good language education program needs to take into account, they are interdependent and interrelated, and thus form a genuine triad in the sense of Peirce's firstness, secondness, and thirdness.

There are a number of ways in which one can show the inner coherence of a genuine triad. For Peirce, the triad is the cornerstone of his logic of relations, and represents the structure of the mind. The true triad is undecomposable into dyads, and everything that is composed of four, five, or more categories can be reduced to triadic relationships (Apel 1981: 121). The best-known example of a genuine Peircean triad, highly influential in the field of pragmatics and the philosophy of language, is Peirce's distinction between icon (firstness), index (secondness), and symbol (thirdness).

To many readers this may seem a piece of obscure logic, and the question may arise what relevance it might possibly have for the theory of practice or the curriculum. But after some further thought it should become clear that a move away from dichotomous thinking will have far-reaching effects on the work of the thoughtful teacher. Some years ago, walking towards a plenary session at a conference with some colleagues, someone remarked that it seemed inevitable that we always think in terms of dichotomies or opposites: objective versus subjective, qualitative versus quantitative, focus on form versus focus on meaning, prescriptive versus descriptive, and so on forever. I remarked that 'Actually, according to Peirce the basic structure of thought is triadic, not dichotomous,' without at that time being able to elaborate on the consequences of a triadic rather than a dyadic view of reason. The difference is so subtle and yet so basic that it simply takes years just to get used to the idea of triadic thinking.

A triadic arrangement of the AAA principles along the lines of Peircean firstness, secondness, and thirdness, might proceed as follows. Firstness is exposure and its quality, and the receptivity of the individual. Secondness is the relation of the individual and the exposure, involving perception, noticing and social (inter)action. Exposure and perception are the basis for awareness. Thirdness is the social and cognitive processing that results in conscious activities of interpreting and purposeful linguistic action. Action and perception are the foundation of autonomy. And awareness and autonomy can bring about the organic transformation the concept authenticity implies. Visually, we might then show a first glimpse of the structure of language learning in the AAA mold as in Figure 15 (see Apel 1981: 23 for a precedent for such triadic constructions).

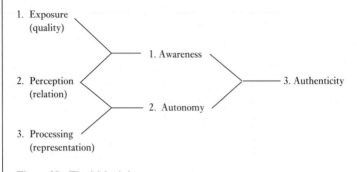

Figure 15   The AAA triad

Returning to the issue of authentication, we are now in a position to discuss its various ramifications within this expanded framework. In the following, I shall identify several types of authenticity as *conditions* under which authentication can take place.

The authentic classroom: conditions for authentication

It used to be that authenticity referred primarily to the provenance of the materials used as linguistic samples for the students (the kinds of things Widdowson referred to as *genuine*, as discussed above). The demand for authenticity in this sense can be seen as a reaction to rather unrealistic (or even surrealistic) textbook language and dialogs. Authenticity, in this sense, is a characteristic of a piece of text, and refers to where the text came from, and attests that it has not been adulterated or 'fixed.' The authentic text was originally created for people other than those who eventually end up struggling with it in the classroom. This kind of authenticity can be called *authenticity of materials* (mainly in terms of their provenance, intended audience, and so on), though I prefer the broader term *curricular authenticity*, for reasons that will become apparent (see Figure 16). In my view it is a very questionable practice to automatically prefer such authentic materials to materials specifically audience-designed for classroom learners. One might just as well condemn children's literature and children's songs as not authentic, since they do not reflect the full range of expression the adult language is capable of. Criticism of learners' materials should primarily be based on the intrinsic qualities of the texts, not on the mere fact that their audience is the learner rather than the native speaker. After all, one does not condemn a children's book because it was written for children.[8] Having given this important caveat, there remain several reasons why authenticity of materials might be an important criterion nevertheless:

(a) Texts for non-native speakers, especially at the more elementary levels, are often linguistically distorted and unrepresentative of the target language, much more so than texts for L1 children. Note that this may not *have* to be so, perhaps it just happens that they are often badly written and uninteresting. But then again, the same can be said for educational texts in other subject matters (history, economics, etc.).

(b) Learners can handle (and benefit from) texts aimed at native speakers, especially if the activities based on them are carefully designed (e.g. they are *scaffolded*, in ways to be elaborated later on in this book; see also Candlin *et al.* 1980).

(c) Learners may themselves prefer and choose to deal with texts of varying provenance, and to the extent that they have learned (and are allowed) to be autonomous, they may elect to work with genuine texts.

(d) The daily demands of survival or communication may press for the inclusion of genuine texts into a syllabus, particularly for immigrants, foreign students, and others who need to cope with the target language on a daily basis (Cathcart 1989).

This discussion of linguistic samples to be used as learning materials indicates that the question of creatorship or intended audience is not the only one that determines the conditions for authentication of particular texts. It may also be important where, by whom, and in response to which demands the text was *found*. For example, if in a class the topic of ethnic stereotyping were to come up, a student might come across or remember some ethnic jokes, and these texts (they might have to be *re-created*, or *recontextualized*, since they came from somewhere outside the classroom) would provide useful learning opportunities, regardless of exactly who invented the jokes, or where they were heard or read by the student. So, in addition to *creator authenticity*, we might speak of *finder authenticity*. Textbooks very often attempt to provide everything students might need (Krashen has aptly termed such efforts 'macho syllabuses' [Krashen 1990]) and, although this might seem advantageous, it actually prevents students (and teachers!) from being *finders* (or *discoverers*).

A further consideration is the actual *use* to which the material is put in the classroom. Texts can be used in many different ways, and some are undoubtedly more conducive to authentication than others. A third consideration relevant to authenticity of materials is thus *user authenticity*.

The second set of conditions for authentication can be loosely grouped together under the heading *pragmatic authenticity*. This includes as subsets at least the following:

(a)   authenticity of *context*
(b)   authenticity of *purpose*
(c)   authenticity of *interaction*

For a discussion of the importance of *context* I refer back to the beginning of this chapter, where I argued that all language used in settings bears significant features relating it to those settings. Aspects of context have been analyzed in numerous different ways,[9] but for our present purposes a simple componential view suffices. In this view (see van Lier 1988 for a detailed account), contexts of language use consist of *setting, participants, topic, and activity*.

To translate this into classroom terms, the *setting* is the physical description of the place where the language use occurs, in this case the classroom, with desks, tables, a blackboard, an overhead projector, computers, walls with pictures on them and windows through which things can be seen, and whatever else may impinge upon the acts of speaking. The *participants* are the people involved, the students, the teacher, perhaps arranged in groups, with different personalities, roles, assigned tasks, and so on. The *topic* is whatever it is that is talked about, perhaps the subject matter of the lesson, a theme running across a series of tasks, something brought up in a conversation, etc. Finally, the *activity* is the complex of rules and norms that govern people's involvement and participation. Around or behind (in a metaphorical sense, of course) these immediate contextual features are numerous other contextual (or macro-contextual) forces which impinge upon the speech event in the classroom. These include the students' family background, parents, siblings, friends, and neighbors; the teacher's pedagogical and methodological persuasions and practices; the institutional forces of school, educational bureaucracy, society at large; and the sociocultural influences of the place and the age.

Authenticity of context refers to language use which is tied to this context and all the factors which make it into what it is. This can include, of course, critical discussion of contextual features (and subsequent *transformation* of some of those features), and the realization that the speech event itself also in part creates the context. It does *not* include a classroom which is essentially a 'baby-sitting' operation or, in more general terms, a classroom in which the professed goals for the classroom are at variance with the practical actions purported to realize those goals (cf. the *systematically distorted communication* Habermas discusses, and which we mentioned briefly in the introduction to this chapter). The contextual authenticity of the classroom should of course allow for discussion of language and content from outside the classroom, whatever is deemed relevant to the purposes at hand. As Breen and Candlin (1980) suggest, the classroom can be a laboratory, a window on the language world, an arena for action, a planning center, and many things besides. But in being any or all of those things, the classroom should never have to deny being a classroom.

Next under the heading of pragmatic authenticity I list authenticity of *purpose*. This does not refer to the participants' educational aspirations or even to the types of objectives that are set. In a pragmatic sense, purpose simply relates to the intended outcome of a speech event, whether it be an instructional conversation, a role-playing activity, or a grammar drill. This criterion demands that a speech event is what it says it is, and does what it says it does. If it is supposed to be a conversation, then let it be a conversation, and if it is supposed to be a role play, then let's not behave as if it were a grammar drill (and vice versa). Basically, authenticity of purpose calls for *transparency* in classroom activities, something that has been advocated in different words by numerous methodologists (Keith Morrow, in one of his five communicative principles, referred to it as 'know what you are doing' [Morrow 1981]).

The third subcategory of pragmatic authenticity that I will describe is the highly problematic one of authenticity of *interaction*. I say it is problematic from an analyst's point of view, because in it are visible elements of all the other types of authenticity, which, in their capacity as conditions for authentication, constrain interaction in a variety of ways. At the same time, interaction directly serves the purpose (or obscures the prospects) of authenticating the educational enterprise. In spite of these analytical difficulties, classroom interaction can usefully be examined in terms of the opportunities it can provide for authenticating learning processes. For example, teacher–student interaction is often perceived to be of a highly controlling, circumscribed (or 'lockstep') nature, tending to stifle creativity and the development of autonomous and critical thought and action. It is important to investigate why this might be so, and to ask ourselves if it could be otherwise (see van Lier 1988 for the notion of *initiative* in classroom interaction; see Kinginger 1994 for research based on it).

Paulo Freire has said that you can only have dialog when you have equality. This statement, regardless of its possible value for literacy and empowerment of oppressed people, cannot be applied to the language classroom without careful analysis. After all, the essence of teaching is an inequality (of knowledge and experience, at least) between teacher and learner, yet we would not like there to be no possibility of dialog, nor would we wish the teacher to cease being a teacher so as to make dialog possible. Looking ahead to the next chapter, we might wish to distinguish *dialog* from *conversation* (and possibly other forms of verbal interaction, or *speech exchange systems*[10]). There are many ways to do so. For example, conversation might be used as a vehicle for the establishment of (temporary) equality for the express purpose of making subsequent dialog possible. A president and a pauper might thus converse (e.g. 'exchange pleasantries') prior to engaging in a dialogue concerning the plight of the latter and the commitment of the former to alleviate it. Two business persons may converse over aperitifs before discussing a joint venture involving billions of dollars and influencing the lives of thousands of workers. Further, conversation is, I fear, often used to avoid tackling substantive issues between unequal as well as equal partners. We will need to distinguish between *equality* and *symmetry*.[11] I think that there can be symmetry (that is, equal participation rights and duties) without equality (in terms of status and power), and there can be equality without symmetry (and symmetry, rather than equality, is a defining feature of authenticity). These distinctions are very important for everyday classroom work. We will discuss them in detail in chapter 7, but the issue is sufficiently central to authenticity to warrant some concrete examples here.

1. In a small student survey conducted as part of a recent graduate seminar, one student expressed an intense dislike of group work because, he explained, one of the group members usually monopolized the interaction and would not let the others get a word in edgewise. He preferred teacher-led discussion which he felt was more balanced and because 'one can ask a question and get a decent answer'. I take this to mean that *equality* does not always translate into *symmetry*. Other problems that may occur in student–student groups, and that may interfere with interactional authenticity, are a tendency to seek early 'closure' to a problem, and to summarize rather than analyze or synthesize (see Rudduck, 1991 for details).

2. Consider the following extract from a class in Russian as a foreign language:

  1 T   Try the next sentence, please.
  2 L1   Kakie produkty SShA vyvozila v Evropu, a chto ona vvozit v etom godu?

3 T   OK. You need to watch out for the noun 'produkty,' since it's a false cognate. It really means 'foodstuffs.' Do you know another word for 'products?'

4 L1   Tabary?

5 T   That's close. Try again.

6 L1   Oh, yeah. Tovary.

7 T   Right. Now read the sentence again.

Though the exercise being done here would be considered quite traditional by most current standards (the translation of isolated sentences), the interaction appears authentic in interactional terms, however difficult we may find it to define interactional authenticity (looking ahead to the chapter on contingency, I suggest that the Gricean maxims, coupled with Sperber and Wilson's notion of relevance (1986), may provide a fair shot at definition). We may of course criticize the episode as being methodologically unsatisfactory, objecting to the translation of isolated sentences, and to the excessive use of L1 in an L2 lesson, but the interaction, *qua interaction*, is authentic in my terms. Note that a teacher (higher status, clearly in charge, knowledgeable) is talking with a student (who is trying things out, defers to the teacher's authority), a situation of inequality, though, I would argue, at the same time of interactional symmetry. Now consider another extract, from the same lesson, between the same teacher and the same student, a short time later:

16 L1   Oh, yeah: the Shtaty part is nominative, right?

17 T   Uhuh. So that's the actual grammatical subject, right?

18 L1   Yeah, so the verb has to be vyvozili, right?

19 T   That's right. Why?

20 L1   Because it's past tense and so it needs to agree with Shtaty in the plural form.

21 T   Good. Try the sentence again.

It seems clear that this, even more so than the previous extract, shows symmetrical interaction between two participants. Note all the 'so' and 'right' tokens produced by both parties. Even so, the status and authority of the teacher have not changed, as turn 21 clearly shows. It is a mistake to suppose that inauthentic interaction is due to inequality in terms of status or even power. We may often find inauthenticity in such circumstances, but I suspect that it rarely – if ever – arises out of the inequality in and of itself (see further chapter 7).

3. Graman (1990) makes a distinction between *pseudodialog* and *authentic dialog*, defining the latter as entailing 'a straightforward discussion of ideas in which people are seeking mutual understanding' (p. 9). He quotes the following extract as an example of pseudodialog:

Carolina: Because people separate .. (pronounced [sɛpéret])
Teacher: Separate (pronounced [sɛ́prɪt]) – the adjective, and then
  [sɛ́pəreyt] – the verb) . . .

Although the teacher understood Carolina, she corrected the student's
pronunciation, rather than reacting to the content. According to
Graman, most teacher–student interaction is pseudodialog (characterized by predetermined answers and the production of correct forms);
indeed, all the examples of authentic dialog he quotes are of student–
student interaction. Can authentic teacher–student dialog occur at all?
One is tempted to suggest that it can occur only if the teacher does not
focus on accuracy, does not use authoritarian control, does not seek a display of linguistic skill, and so on.

Reasonable though such pronouncements may sound, I think they can
land us in waters that are troubled indeed. To start with, the above
extract from the Russian class appears interactionally authentic (at an
intuitive level, at least), even though it focuses squarely on form, and
does not use the target language communicatively. As regards the latter,
we may have an 'out' if we say simply that it is authentic interaction in
English, but not in *Russian*, and that authentic interaction in Russian
would be quite another story. As regards the former, we should remember that many students (and syllabuses) want, even demand, a focus on
form, and express a preference for being corrected and getting grammar
explanations. Withholding form-focused work in such settings would not
seem very authentic, pedagogically speaking. Perhaps two subcomponents of pragmatic authenticity – (*pedagogic*) *purpose*, and (*social*)*interaction* – have a tendency to conflict in a classroom, a conflict whose
resolution may cause methodological problems. Authenticity of (pedagogical) purpose and interactional authenticity may not always coincide,
and when they do not, a resolution of some sort must be found. Tharp
and Gallimore, in their discussion of *instructional conversation*, put it as
follows:

> The concept itself [i.e. instructional conversation] contains a paradox:
> 'Instruction' and 'conversation' appear contrary, the one implying authority
> and planning, the other equality and responsiveness. The task of teaching is to
> resolve this paradox. To most truly teach, one must converse; to truly
> converse is to teach. (Tharp & Gallimore 1988: 111)

A further problem with a roles-based view is the observation that interactional authenticity (indeed, pragmatic authenticity as a whole) may
have widely differing interpretations in different cultures and systems of
schooling. The authenticity of a specific instance of classroom interaction
cannot be judged or evaluated in isolation from the context of

educational history and ritual constraints on the teacher–student relationship. Authenticity of context therefore partly, and in some cases perhaps largely, determines authenticity of interaction.

The discussion has more or less turned full circle. Interactional authenticity is a crucial ingredient in the language classroom, but we cannot define it in isolation from pedagogical purpose and educational and cultural context. If the reader agrees with this verdict, studies of classroom interaction will clearly be extremely complex and tentative, and one must take care not to draw hasty conclusions from superficially identifiable interactional tokens. On the other hand, the intricacies of classroom interaction should lend themselves well to ethnomethodological analysis (Mehan 1979, van Lier 1988) or microsociology as exemplified in the work of, for example, Goffman (1981). Further, we must guard against making the mistake of equating *learning value* with *quality of interaction* (or with *quantity* of interaction). Unfortunately, we have insufficient knowledge to guarantee that there will be a complete and automatic match. As an analogy, someone who is learning to play the trombone may produce trombone sounds which are of high practice value but at the same time of low musical quality.

The final tier of authenticity is referred to as *personal authenticity*. Its three subheadings are:

(a) *existential*
(b) *intrinsic*
(c) *autotelic*

We are now getting to the core of the issue of authenticity. If interaction is the 'cut-and-paste' desktop, then personal authenticity concerns the purposeful actions of cutting and pasting. *Existential authenticity* refers to the personal commitment to and genuine interest in the activity in hand. It assumes identification on the part of the acting person with the goals and procedures that characterize the learning process. *Intrinsic authenticity* refers to the sources for the motivation to engage in learning activities. Intrinsic motivation was the topic of chapter 5, so we can be brief about it here. In general, the intrinsically motivated person does not depend on extrinsic rewards or coercion. Intrinsic motivation goes together with a sense of self-determination, a feeling of knowing (through monitoring one's own performance), and a view of the learning process as an end in itself. The person who exhibits all these characteristics is an *autotelic* person (Csikszentmihalyi 1990).

In personal authenticity all the elements of awareness, autonomy, and authenticity come together. Authentic persons know what they are doing, and attend in relaxed or focused ways, in accordance with the demands of the situation. Authentic persons are also autonomous, in the sense of feeling responsible for their own actions, and able to deal with choices. Finally, authentic persons validate (authenticate) learning opportunities as they occur, create their own learning opportunities when the circumstances allow, and need no coaxing to take learning action (see Deci & Ryan 1985). Clearly, 'the authentic person' is an ideal which we rarely see embodied in a particular person to its full extent. However, that does not mean that we should not strive to educate students towards that ideal, or that it would not be possible to make significantly greater strides towards personal authenticity than most educational practices currently do. In the classroom we can foster personal authenticity by incorporating and building on students' personal experiences, by working towards cooperation rather than competition, and by training the students to become autonomous. In our efforts to do so we will find that bureaucratic demands and practices, external controls in the form of tests and grades, perceived gaps between what is valued at school versus what is valued at home or in the peer group, and many other factors may constrain authentication in the classroom. Authenticity, like empowerment, innovation, restructuring, and various other key terms in our perennial educational debates, is therefore closely tied to political, ideological, and critical issues. That is why a view of authenticity as merely the choice of texts to bring into the classroom avoids the complex factors that govern authentication.

Conclusion

By way of summary, Figure 16 lists the various types of authenticity that we have discussed in this chapter. Under each main heading I have listed a few of the more obvious *constraints* and *resources* influencing authentication in the language classroom. The constraints may operate to impede authentication, and the resources can be seen as ways of overcoming or alleviating the constraints.

It should be clear, even after the brief and sketchy discussion in this chapter, that the issue of authenticity is by no means as simple as some communicative methodologists may lead us to believe. Authenticating language lessons is hard and sustained work, both on the part of the teacher and of the students. It includes looking at language and language use in all relevant contexts, in critical and creative ways, and reflecting on what it means to learn language.

Authenticity is part of the triad that forms the principled core of this book: the AAA. It can therefore not be defined in isolation from the

Type	Constraints	Resources
Curricular		
	• difficulty level	• student choice/gathering
creator	• availability/variety	• media/immediacy
finder	• comprehensibility	• scaffolding/amplification
user	• relevance	• visual/other expansion
	• interest	• familiarity/(background knowledge)
Pragmatic		
	• classroom/institutional	• study skills
context	• asymmetries/roles/status	• cooperative tasks
purpose	• communicative intent	• instructional conversation
interaction	versus educational	• contingency
	objectives	
	• time	
Personal		
	• bureaucracy	• experiential learning
existential	• standardized tests	• learner training
intrinsic	• low expectations	• cooperative learning
autotelic	• low perceived relevance	• fostering autonomy

Figure 16   Authenticity in the classroom

other two members of the triad: awareness and autonomy. The essential connections between these three principles have to be constantly borne in mind; in fact, the theory of practice consists of building and strengthening these connections. Given that many constraints operate in the pedagogical environment, authentication, and movement towards the AAA curriculum in its totality, constitutes a struggle which is at the heart of the profession of language teaching. It is in that sense that, following Sartre, we can say that authenticity is not given, but has to be earned (see p. 128 above).

In the next chapter we will focus on social interaction, particularly an examination of the property of *contingency* in interaction. In doing so, we will pull together many of the threads of chapters 3–6, and also deepen our understanding of one of the key ingredients of authentication.

Notes

1 For real-life examples, see Candlin *et al.* 1980.
2 The next big question of course is: 'What makes a response appropriate?' For an insightful discussion on this, see Fairclough 1992a.
3 This, interestingly, is closely related to the control/autonomy distinction

investigated by Deci, Ryan and associates (see the last chapter). The link between autonomy and authenticity may therefore be very close indeed.

4 With reference to setting-related 'decorum,' or the power of context, it may be instructive to reflect on the following sentence from Ellen Langer's book *Mindfulness* (1989: 35): 'We whisper in hospitals and become anxious in police stations, sad in cemeteries, docile in schools, and jovial at parties.'

5 Although my examples come primarily from foreign or second language classrooms, the general points apply equally to all teacher talk, including in native language classrooms.

6 This is an issue which needs to be addressed in the education of non-native teachers. To what extent are non-native speakers able to use teacherese (Milk 1985), or, in more general terms, vary their register? What ways can be found to compensate for the inevitable shortcomings of many non-native teachers in terms of proficiency?

7 As Figure 15 shows, I am suggesting that the picture is actually more complex than this.

8 Ruth Larimer has pointed out to me that one cannot validly compare children in the process of developing their cogntive capabilities with adults who may have to cope with survival needs in their everyday world. This is a good point (see point (d) below), which brings up the issue of relevance. The essential quality may be that of *engagement* of learner with language, and this will be partly determined by practical and cognitive demands.

9 For an excellent overview of the concept of context in pragmatics, see the introductory chapter in Goodwin & Duranti 1992.

10 See Sacks, Schegloff & Jefferson 1974 for descriptions of conversation and tentative comments on other speech exchange systems. According to Sacks *et al.*, and also Heritage & Atkinson 1984, conversation is the rockbottom form of verbal interaction, other forms deriving from it. Dialog, in Freire's sense, would presumably be a form of interaction focused on establishing such goals as agreement, mutual understanding, negotiated settlements, and the like. Conversation, by contrast, focuses on the harmonious (contingent, symmetrical, see chapter 7) exchange of utterances, pure and simple.

11 This distinction can clarify much of Habermas's work on communicative action (1984, 1987), and educational interpretations, such as Young 1992. Much of the confusion about the possibility of 'unconstrained discourse' (Young 1992: 50; this is actually a contradiction in terms, and therefore not a viable generalization) in an ideal speech setting, which might foster equality, is based on a failure to distinguish between equality and symmetry. See further chapter 7.

7 Contingency

Introduction

In earlier chapters I have on a number of occasions emphasized the centrality of social interaction in the pedagogical process. Now that we have discussed language learning primarily from the individual learner's perspective (in chapters 3–6), the time has come to move on to the next layer of theory in the AAA curriculum: *pedagogical interaction* (see p. 37). This will be done in two steps: first, in this chapter, an analysis of interaction itself, with the emphasis on classroom talk (and comparing this to conversation), and then, in chapter 8, a discussion of pedagogical strategies designed to facilitate the necessary kinds of interaction to engage language learning processes.

When I said at the beginning of chapter 3 (that social interaction is the 'engine' that 'drives' the learning process, I meant that the powers (or conditions) of learning – awareness (and attention), investment, practice, and commitment – are engaged, sustained, and augmented by learners' work of interacting with others, and this includes interacting (using language) with the world in general through reading, thinking about worldly things, and so on. In other words, social interaction, although it is first and foremost the use of talk in face-to-face encounters, includes many other word–world encounters as well. Social interaction (inter+action[1]), in this broader sense, means being 'busy with' the language in one's dealings with the world, with other people and human artifacts, and with everything, real or imagined, that links self and world. This view is important, especially for my discussion of contingency below, since otherwise we may well give a rather shallow and trivial meaning to social interaction, one in which talk is glorified for the sake of talk, rather than for the minds and worlds it connects, and the expanded horizons it might open up. The quality of social interaction resides in the things it *points to.*

In this chapter I will begin with a closer look at classroom discourse, picking up some threads from the discussion on teacher talk in the last chapter. I will review some proposals for improving the quality of classroom talk, and evaluate their merits. Then I will look at the critical side of the issue, the ideological and institutional forces that operate in classrooms. Since talk tends to be different inside classrooms and out (as we already saw in the last chapter), I will compare classroom talk to other kinds of talk-in-interaction, including ordinary conversation (see Drew & Heritage 1992 for a discussion of different kinds of talk). This leads naturally to a discussion of symmetry and equality, key elements in the construct of contingency. I will end the chapter with a multilayered view of classroom discourse, one in which the notion of contingency occupies a central place.

I want to reiterate, before we begin this discussion, the importance of the study of interaction for educational innovation. On p. 85 I referred to the 'butterfly effect' of chaos theory (or *complexity theory*, which has now become the preferred term for this way of theorizing, see Lewin 1993), which symbolizes the principle that 'tiny differences in input [can] quickly become overwhelming differences in output' (Gleick 1987: 8). The educational context, with the classroom at its center, is viewed as a complex system in which events do not occur in linear causal fashion, but in which a multitude of forces interact in complex, self-organizing ways, and create changes and patterns that are part predictable, part unpredictable. Such systems must be analyzed from the bottom up (Stites 1994), and this justifies sustained scrutiny of the details of pedagogical interaction. Recall Stephen Jay Gould's comment about biological systems (see p. 38): 'Details are all that matters: God dwells there, and you never get to see Him if you don't get them right' (1993: 14).

Classroom discourse: the IRF exchange

We begin by looking at a brief extract from a lesson in English as a Second Language (ESL):

1 A How many people are talking. Elly? . . . How many people?
2 B Two people.
3 A Yes, that's right, two people. And what are these two people talking about. Marcia.
4 C ((unintelligible)) people ask the way.
5 A Uhuh.

It will be at once clear to the reader that A is the teacher, and B and C are students. Next, it should be possible to take a pencil and draw a vertical line between two words, so as to divide the extract into two exactly symmetrical halves. This line will come between the words *people* and *And* in turn 3. The extract is thus divided into the following two equal parts:

1 A How many people are talking. Elly? . . . How many people?
2 B Two people.
3 A Yes, that's right, two people.

1 A And what are these two people talking about. Marcia.
2 C ((unintelligible)) people ask the way.
3 A Uhuh.

Both parts, each one called an *exchange*, have the following structure:

1 Initiation (or question, elicitation)
2 Response (or answer)
3 Feedback (or follow-up, evaluation)

There is probably nothing that symbolizes classroom discourse quite as much as this structure, the much-noted IRF exchange. It was first noted by Bellack *et al.* in 1966 in their pioneering classroom study. They called it the *teaching cycle*. Next, Sinclair and Coulthard (1975) made it into the centerpiece of their discourse analysis, calling it the basic unit of interaction, or the *exchange*. In traditional classes (where the focus is on *transmission of information*, see below), the percentage of utterances that fall neatly into this three-part structure may be over half: on my own count, between 50 and 60 per cent of the secondary-school data transcribed in Sinclair and Coulthard consists of three-part exchanges, and Mehan (1979) estimated about the same for his primary-school data. Wells (1993: 2) estimates up to 70 per cent (though he does not quote sources for this figure).

The IRF sequence is thus a prominent part of classroom interaction, and its rationale and pedagogical value must be examined carefully. Does it occur at all outside of lessons? Let's imagine the following:

1 A Excuse me, where's the Exploratorium?
2 B All the way down Bay Street and then two blocks to your right.
?3 A Good!

The third turn sounds a bit funny here (we'd rather expect 'Thanks!'). Perhaps this occurs in a classroom as part of an activity called 'giving directions,' rather than on the streets of San Francisco.

But it can get stranger still:

1 A Excuse me, where's the Exploratorium?
2 B All the way down Bay Street and then two blocks at right.
*3 A OK. Two blocks TO THE right. TO THE right.

In this case we are absolutely sure that we are not on the corner of Van Ness and Bay, but in a classroom, where A is a teacher correcting a student, B. If such correction were to happen in the street, the murder rate would skyrocket.

These hypothetical examples show clearly the classroom-specific nature of the IRF sequence. It is obviously *designed for instruction*, and a special kind of instruction to boot, namely one in which instruction is 'delivered,' and the deliverer must check constantly that the recipients are actually receiving, or have received at some earlier point, the instructional material or point in question. But why should it be so designed, and what might be its advantages and disadvantages?

Let's note, first of all, some of its main features:

(a) It is three turns long.
(b) The first and the third turn are produced by the teacher, the second one by the student.
(c) The exchange is started and ended by the teacher.
(d) As a result of (b) and (c) the student's turn is sandwiched between two teacher's turns.
(e) The first teacher's turn is designed to elicit some kind of verbal response from a student. The teacher often already knows the answer (is 'primary knower'), or at least has a specific idea 'in mind' of what will counts as a proper answer.
(f) The second teacher's turn (the third turn in the exchange) is some kind of comment on the second turn, or on the 'fit' between the second and the first. Here the student finds out if the answer corresponds with whatever the teacher has 'in mind'.
(g) It is often clear from the third turn whether or not the teacher was interested in the information contained in the response, or merely in the form of the answer, or in seeing if the student knew the answer or not.
(h) If the exchange is part of a series, as is often the case, there is behind the series a plan and a direction determined by the teacher. The teacher 'leads', the students 'follow'.

These design features have a number of consequences. First, the teacher is able to lead the students in a certain planned direction, in carefully measured steps, following a logical progression, more or less the way Socrates proceeded in Plato's dialogues.[2] Second, the student knows immediately whether the answer was correct or incorrect. Third, the noise and chaos of many students shouting answers at once, or the dangers of confusing or irrelevant commentary, are minimized. The IRF exchange thus allows the teacher to maintain control and conduct an orderly lesson. Moreover, at its highly skilled best, IRF interaction pushes the students to think critically and articulate grounds for their answers.

These are all quite positive consequences, to many teachers. Yet, upon studying the literature, we find that many researchers take a highly critical position towards the IRF exchange (see, e.g., Wood 1988, Drew &

Heritage 1992).[3] Let us therefore examine some of the problems or disadvantages of the IRF exchange.

Going back to Bellack *et al.*, Barnes (a strong opponent of IRF himself) reports that they found that nearly one-third of all teachers' moves were categorized as 'Rating', that is, teachers usually responded to what their pupils said not by replying to it but by evaluating it (Barnes 1976: 128). Indeed, the examples I have given above certainly all include third turns that seem to say 'Yes, that is correct' rather than 'Oh, how interesting', or 'Thank you so much'. This is different in three-part exchanges of a non-instructional nature:

(*adapted from radio commercial*)
1 A Don't you have a laptop?
2 B Eh- no.
3 A They're so:: useful. I always take mine on trips.

(*author's data*)
1 A Why do they call it Yule?
2 B I don't know . . . maybe we can look it up in the encyclopedia.
3 A All right.

1 A Why did the boy cross the playground?
2 B E:r . . . . I give up.
3 A To get to the other slide.

One difference, then, between classroom exchanges and other exchanges is that the former have an eliciting and an evaluating function, both of which are absent in the latter. In the IRF exchange, the student's response is hemmed in, squeezed between a demand to display knowledge and a judgment on its competence. This can turn every student response into an examination, hence the frequently observed reluctance to 'be called upon' and to participate, and the paucity of linguistic elaboration when responding to that dreaded call. In addition to evaluating – or validating – the student's response, the third turn closes the exchange, preventing the exploration of interesting avenues of thought initiated by the students. The IRF structure therefore does not represent true joint construction of discourse.

At times, then, the IRF structure makes it unattractive and unmotivating for students to participate in classroom interaction, since their responses may be evaluated or examined publicly, rather than accepted and appreciated as part of a joint conversation.

> It is important to emphasize that this is neither a necessary nor an exclusive consequence of the IRF structure, merely that this structure may favor such a state of affairs. Sometimes the IRF may actually facilitate a student's contribution, if the teacher's question is designed in such a way that the response is easy and predictable. Sometimes participating in a less formally

structured conversation is equally or more daunting for a student, especially a non-native speaker, since, in addition to figuring out the right thing to say, the student has to judge the right moment to say it (i.e. without being seen to interrupt, or to be incoherent), and how to say it (i.e. displaying the right conversational skill, tone, and so on). The IRF essentially strips the work of turn taking and utterance design (see Figure 13 chapter 6) away from the student's contribution, and this obviously has advantages as well as disadvantages.

However, the IRF can only be seen as advantageous if it is designed as a way of scaffolding interaction, and if this is so, then it must contain visible efforts to promote *handover*, so that students can grow out of IRF and into true dialog whenever the opportunity arises. Since IRF is strictly other-regulated, it can only be pedagogically beneficial if it contains within itself the seeds of self-regulation. All the data that I have examined, however, suggests that IRF is a closed rather than an open discourse format, and that it does not encourage a flexible progression towards self-regulation. As such it cannot be a valid candidate for interaction in the Vygotskyan ZPD, as is erroneously suggested in a number of studies (Tharp & Gallimore 1988, Greenleaf & Freedman 1993, Adair-Hauck & Donato 1994).

Greenleaf and Freedman, for example, claim that the IRF structure (they call it I-R-E, following Mehan 1979) 'can support a collaborative problem-solving session in which students play an important role in the construction of the problem's solution' (1993: 492). Close inspection of the data they present as evidence, however, makes it clear that the students' collaboration is largely coerced and that their role in the construction is minimal. Most student responses are elicited, several are marked in the transcript as unintelligible, sometimes repeated on demand, the majority are heavily elliptical (one of the hallmarks of IRF), and they include a telling 'I don't see what you're asking for' (1993: 479). The teacher's third turn closes the exchanges rather than opening up the interaction, and use, discard, or transform the students' offerings as if they were the teacher's exclusive property. The experience is thus a highly controlling one and, in the light of the literature on intrinsic motivation discussed in chapter 5, its value in terms of motivation, attention, and self-determination must be questioned. Later on in this chapter I will illustrate more responsive and contingent forms of interaction, and discuss how they may be more in line with Vygotskyan principles of learning.

As I indicated above (see note 2), the IRF is not an invariant, monolithic questioning procedure that has only one form and one function. Rather, it can vary along several dimensions, and in order to judge its place in education it is important to elaborate on the potential diversity within IRF. This will allow us, as teachers, to judge its value for our classroom. Below, I will distinguish between *conduct of initiation*, *response function*, and *pedagogical orientation* (or *purpose*), and look for possible variation in each of these dimensions.

In terms of its conduct, the IRF exchange can be initiated in two different ways, and teachers will have different reasons for preferring one or the other:

(a) General, unspecific elicitation: here the teacher addresses the question to all the students, either expecting someone to volunteer the answer or for those who wish to respond to indicate so by, e.g., raising their hand, so that the teacher can then choose one person from among those who are 'bidding for a turn.'
(b) Specific, personal elicitation: here the teacher selects one person to provide the answer, e.g. by 'nominating' them (as in the case of Elly and Marcia above), looking at them, or pointing at them, and so on.

The technique under (a) has the advantage that everyone thinks about the answer (at least theoretically), and that no one is forced to answer, but it has the disadvantages that some vocal or eager students get a disproportionate number of turns, and that several students may answer at the same time, thus making all the answers unintelligible, and perhaps making more noise than the teacher in the next room can stand.

The technique under (b) has the advantage that turn taking can be spread equitably across the room, and that participation will be orderly and clear, but it has the disadvantages that only one person may be making the effort of thinking about the answer (this can be overcome by nominating the student *after* asking the question, perhaps after a pause), and that a student may be forced to answer who is clearly not ready or able to do so.

We can see that the advantages of one procedure are the disadvantages of the other. Teachers therefore need to deliberate carefully and orchestrate continually to get the type of participation they want. Students have to learn the rules and play by them, no doubt occasionally having to be reminded ('Hands up if you know the answer!') of the proper conduct.

In terms of response function, the teacher can use the IRF format in at least the following four ways (here illustrated with brief – constructed – examples):

1. *Repetition*

    T   Refrigerator. Can you say that? Altogether-
    SS   ((in chorus)) Refrigerator
    T   Well done.

2. *Recitation*

    T   Which prepositions take the dative case? Kevin?
    S   Aus, bei, mit, nach, seit, von, zu, binnen, gegenüber
    T   Great! Are there any others, or is that all?

3. *Cognition*

    T   And why would Abigail tell on Sinbad?
    S   I think she was mad at him.
    T   Possibly. And why do you think she was mad?

4. *Expression*[4]

T   What's the water doing now?
S   Water is heating, it it's the one who's heating
T   Ahah, can you explain that in a little more detail?

As the above examples show, the IRF can be used to make the students repeat something verbatim, to require them to produce previously learned material from memory, to ask the students to think and then verbalize those thoughts, and finally, to ask them to express themselves more clearly or precisely. I suggest that these four response functions form a continuum from less to greater demand on students' mental processing powers, and from less to greater depth of processing.

The third dimension along which the IRF can vary is pedagogical orientation. Two broad orientations can be distinguished: a *display* or *assessment* orientation, in which students are required to show what they have learned so that the teacher can evaluate this, and a *participation* orientation, in which the teacher is concerned primarily with engaging and maintaining the students' attention, and drawing them into the discussion actively. While these two orientations can often both be present at the same time, they can usefully be distinguished since they have important consequences for the students' motivation and for the possibility of opening up the IRF into more mutually contingent interactional formats (see later on in the chapter). The various types of IRF and the relationships among them are shown in Figure 17.

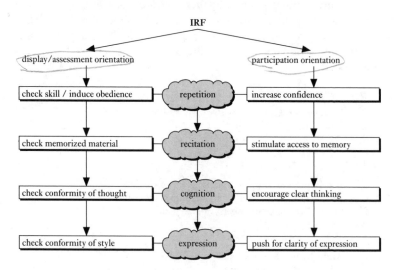

Figure 17 Types of IRF

From the AAA perspective, the sophistication and instructional value of the IRF increases as one moves from top to bottom, and is also greater in the participation orientation on the right, than in the display/assessment orientation on the left. This does not mean that the types nearer the top or on the left-hand side should be rejected: they may well have a place in our instructional practices, but they need to be judged in the context of our overall strategic plan.

One final point that needs to be made is the linguistic nature of the students' contribution in the IRF format, and this relates to the *paucity of linguistic elaboration* mentioned above. There is likely to be a continuum from linguistic restriction to linguistic elaboration as we move from top to bottom and left to right on the diagram. Linguistic restriction is quite clearly noticeable in many traditional teacher-fronted lessons containing a preponderance of IRF exchanges and exchange series. As an example, Figure 18 shows a tally of all the responses made by students in one of the lessons transcribed by Sinclair and Coulthard (1975: 90–111).

Type	Example	
Noun	'paper'	64
Non-verbal:	(pointing)	28
Noun Phrase	'paper clip'	14
Affirmation/negation	No, yes, yeah, etc.	12
Verb + Noun	'cuts metal'	5
Article + Noun	'a nail'	4
Article + Noun Phrase	'a nut and bolt'	3
One each:		
–Wow!		
–Cor!		
–It's like – cuts cuts metal things		
–They weren't sharp enough		
–The wood, the wood is hard		
–Because it's too hard		

Figure 18   Responses in IRF exchanges

In addition to these overwhelmingly truncated responses, there were four instances in which students produced talk falling outside the IRF structure, and three of these were requests to go to the toilet. The fourth one was a whispered: 'hacksaw isn't used for wood'. This last example is a highly revealing one, in that it is the only instance of student disagreement in the lesson, and it manifests the prevailing power structure by its very existence: it is *whispered*, and it is not made *inside* the IRF format.

Drawing up the balance sheet for a lesson like this, it is quite clear that the linguistic contributions of the students are of a reduced nature. Does it matter? That is a question we need to reflect on. If we believe that linguistic processing relates to cognitive processing, then we may want to encourage more elaborate forms of expression. Further, if we believe that practicing using language is important in language learning, then we must conclude that these IRF structures may not encourage sufficient practicing. Most importantly, however, if IRF discourse is perceived by the students as *controlling* (as seems inevitable, at least in the display/assessment orientation), then it will not foster motivation and autonomy (see chapter 5). In the IRF, both the *rationale* (the *raison d'être*) and the *value* of the student's utterance are determined by the teacher's agenda rather than by the unfolding talk itself, and the student cannot control this (except, perhaps, by figuring out what will trigger a positive reaction, and strategically manipulating this knowledge).

I have looked at the IRF exchange in some detail because it is so pervasive in classroom interaction, and because it has received so much attention in the literature on classroom research. It is particularly worrisome that it is sometimes regarded as a prototypical example of social interaction in the ZPD. An understanding of its 'inner workings' and its purposes are crucial for our discussion of contingent interaction below, and of pedagogical scaffolding in the next chapter.

To summarize, the IRF sequence, while it is effective in maintaining order, regulating participation, and leading the students in a certain predetermined direction, often reduces the student's initiative, independent thinking, clarity of expression, the development of conversational skills (including turn taking, planning ahead, negotiating and arguing), and self-determination. Its prominent status in the teacher-controlled class, and the notion of teacher control in general, must therefore be carefully examined and constantly reevaluated. On the other hand, by exploring the different types of IRF available, by deliberately pushing towards a participation orientation, clear thinking, and precise expression, and by moving away from a focus on display, repetition, and regurgitation, IRF use may be beneficial in securing students' engagement and building a bridge towards more contingent forms of instructional interaction.

Constraints on educational discourse

Talk in classrooms is often quite different from talk in other places. In the previous chapter we discussed this in terms of teacher talk, and we provided the caveat that talk in any setting tends to be to some extent different from talk in any other setting. In other words, talk tends to be situation-specific or context-determined to a certain extent.[5] We saw an example of classroom-specific talk in the previous section: the IRF exchange (actually, IRF exchanges may also occur in such contexts as parent–child interaction, for example when a parent reads a picture book with a toddler, see Bruner & Haste 1987).

It can be argued that classroom talk is the way it is because of the institutional constraints that operate in the setting, including the power relationships, the expectations of various parties involved, and the goals that have been set. In a sense, talk is symbolic of the power that the institution gives to or withholds from the individuals in it, and it serves to maintain and reproduce the power structures that define the institution and its purposes (Bourdieu 1991). The institution *endows* individuals with power, status, and resources of various kinds, and it endows the speaker with the authority to carry out the act which his or her utterance claims to perform.

Within a setting such as the school, the power does not in the first instance come from the language itself, but rather it is an institutional power which is embodied in the language and given to the persons who carry out the institutional tasks. Bourdieu uses as a metaphor the Homeric *skeptron*, which is handed to the orator who is about to speak, and which symbolizes that person's right to speak (1991: 109).

With the right to speak within and on behalf of an institution comes the requirement to speak in certain ways that are considered 'proper' ways of speaking within the institution, similar to language use in rituals. A good example of such institutionally mandated ritual language use is the performative utterance described by Austin (1962). As Bourdieu points out (1991: 8), these performative utterances are not ways of reporting or describing a state of affairs, but rather ways of acting or participating in a ritual. 'I pronounce you man and wife' can only be successfully uttered in the right place at the right time by a properly authorized person in a context of a series of actions that have to occur in the right way and in the right sequence, laid down in the ritual canons of a particular culture.

Similarly, the IRF exchange and other types of talk characteristically associated with the teaching profession can be seen as ways of acting, as ritual performances, rather than strictly as talk delivering messages (note how often teaching is called a 'performance'). Using Habermas's terminology (1984), we can say that the teacher's talk is *dramaturgical* action as well as *strategic* and *communicative* action. Or in Bakhtin's terms (1981), teacher talk, or social interaction in education in general, manifests several voices, often simultaneously.

Institutional ways of speaking in education are most strikingly visible when they are caricatured, for example when children 'play teacher,' or when TV commercials include teachers (who are generally depicted as humorless, cruel and controlling), and when the behavior (including speech) that society typically associates with their role is exaggerated. While in everyday classrooms extreme manifestations of teacher talk might be rare, there is little doubt that the institution places constraints on the kinds of talk that can occur within it. Bourdieu and Passeron (1977: 109) express these constraints in rather colorful terms:

The lecturer . . .

Elevated and enclosed in the space which crowns him orator, separated from his audience, if numbers permit, by a few empty rows which materially mark the distance the laity fearfully keep before the mana of the Word and which at all events are only ever occupied by the most seasoned zealots, pious ministers of the magisterial utterance, the professor, remote and intangible, shrouded in vague and terrifying rumour, is condemned to theatrical monologue and virtuoso exhibition by a necessity of position far more coercive than the most imperious regulations. The professorial chair commandeers, willy-nilly, the intonation, the diction, the delivery, the oratorical gestures of its occupant . . . Such a context governs teachers' and students' behaviour so rigorously that efforts to set up dialogue immediately turn into fiction or farce. (Bourdieu & Passeron 1977: 109).

We may find the physical setting described here quite different from the classroom in which we, as teachers, or even as professors, work, yet we must take seriously the question if the institutionalized educational enterprise, and in particular the culturally sanctioned workplace we call the classroom, force certain ways of speaking upon us which prevent true dialog or conversation from taking place, or at least, discourage it. In other words, do institutional constraints condemn the teacher to perpetual pedantry, and the student to zealousness or zombyism?

Curriculum innovation, such as that implied in an AAA orientation, can only come about through a fundamental change in the way educators and students interact with one another. As I have proposed in several places in this book, starting by a close examination of interaction itself, and transforming it according to sound pedagogical principles, would necessarily (though not instantaneously) bring about a transformation of the institution itself.[6] Reform thus occurs from the bottom up, one pedagogical action at a time. I have justified this approach by drawing on complexity theory, in which small changes in input can bring about fundamental changes in output (Gleick 1987, Lewin 1993; see above, p. 148). The power of the *status quo* can only be broken by the power, minute in isolation but invincible in a purposeful project, of transformed interaction between educator and educated.

Such transformation is no easy matter, and may meet with resistance from various sources, not least the students themselves, as Ira Shor illustrates in a recent book, where he recounts his experiences as a young college teacher. He wished to implement a 'critical teaching' and 'dialogic pedagogy' that posed problems from student experience for class enquiry (1992: 2), and encountered a class of students who initially resisted his efforts, expecting their teacher to 'do education to them', and to be 'one more talking head who would shellack them with grammar and knowledge' (*ibid.*). For Shor, as for others who wish to transform education, dialog is crucial to the creation of a participatory process (1992: 84), leading to empowerment, critical thinking, and democratic education. However, not all dialog is the same, as we shall see below.

As a counterweight to such institutional domination and resistance to dialog, here is an example of talk-as-liberation, from a child's perspective of communication with the adult world, taken from a recent book by Richard Restak:

> 'Guess what,' a three-year-old boy who lives nearby says at the start of each of his sentences. His mother, of course, responds, 'What?' At that instant a warm smile breaks out on the child's face. Even at age three he recognizes that his presence has been confirmed, love asserted, connectedness and communication reaffirmed. 'Guess what' is often a meaningless phrase in a particular context, but the feelings evoked are far from meaningless. Many social rituals ('How are you?' 'I am fine, thank you. How are you?' 'I am fine, too.') exist not so much for the communication of information as for emotional sharing: we experience a kind of warmth not unrelated to what's experienced by the little boy when his mother responds with wide-eyed interest, 'What?' Being denied that shared warmth can be extremely traumatizing. (Restak 1991: 134–5)

Restak's example points to the power of conversation, in terms of connectedness, co-construction of meaning, affirmation of communication, and emotional sharing.

> As suggested in note 6, it is important for my argument for the centrality of interaction to note that conversation can be *power-creating*. Whereas in Bourdieu's conception of language speakers have a contextually determined amount of *linguistic capital* which various institutions endow them with, we can propose conversation as a weapon to counteract this power and increase one's 'capital'. Manipulating interaction, in this way, is like changing the rules of the language game. If the rules that are changed are fundamental ones, the game is transformed into a different game; if they are trivial rules, then the game stays the same. In soccer, changing, say, the off-side rule, would affect the game only in minor ways, but allowing players to pick up the ball and run with it would create a totally different game. Deliberately manipulating and changing interactional structures in the classroom would, I have no doubt, change the rules of the pedagogical game in fundamental ways.

The qualities of connectedness, affirmation, and emotional sharing illustrated in Restak's 'Guess what?' quote are undeniably of great importance in education, especially where the students' motivation cannot be taken as a given. Furthermore, and this is even more crucial, the importance of conversational engagement signaled by Restak relates closely to Vygotsky's ZPD (see chapter 3), which could not exist without the intersubjectivity established through conversation.[7] The ZPD, as we shall see in the next chapter, is the key to establishing pedagogical scaffolding strategies.

For the moment we will concentrate on the interactional dichotomy put before us by the two quotes: institutional determinism (or reproduction, in Bourdieu's own terms) on the one hand, and interactional engagement (and self-determination) on the other, legislation versus empowerment, as it were. Using these two extremes as signposts can be quite instructive when evaluating particular educational models and instructional recommendations, a few of which will be discussed in the next section. I will elaborate on the misgivings about the IRF noted earlier in this chapter, and show what other options might be available.

Recitation and responsive teaching

In his recent book, *The enlightened eye*, Elliott Eisner reports two critical analyses of a videotaped history lesson (on Madison's Federalist Papers) taught by the former Secretary of Education William Bennett in a high school near Washington, DC. The first analysis is by Roger Shuy of Georgetown University, the second by Eisner himself.

Shuy examines Mr Bennett's performance in terms of a distinction (first made by Gallimore & Tharp 1983) between *recitation teaching* and *responsive teaching* (see also Bowers & Flinders 1990, Wood 1988). Recitation heavily uses the IRF exchange, or the 'Question – Response – Evaluation model,' as Mehan called it (1979).[8] Responsive teaching, Shuy explains, uses *contingency* questioning rather than *evaluation* questioning, and is

> closer to conversational dialogue, a two-way communication mode with both parties initiating topics, changing the direction of the lesson, and relating it to their own lives. (Shuy, in Eisner 1991: 147)

Shuy argues (following Gallimore & Tharp 1983) that a response model of teaching is necessary in order to 'lead the student to higher levels of development in a self-generated fashion' (*ibid*.:139). By contrast, recitation teaching (which uses IRF as a basic structure) basically just draws out what students already know.[9] This argument reflects the distinction we made in the last section between Bourdieu's description of control and determinism, and the engagement and self-determination illustrated in the 'Guess what?' example. Before examining Eisner and Shuy's analyses further, a brief digression on this argument is necessary.

The argument is similar to those made by other researchers. Wertsch (1985), for example, studies interaction in the zone of proximal development (Vygotsky 1986), and notes that adult and child (or, in more general terms, we might say, expert and novice) are faced with the task of creating states of *intersubjectivity* (defined by Rommetveit [1974] as shared situation definition), so that meaningful participation by the child becomes possible and learning can take place. Intersubjectivity means that participants are jointly focused on the activity and its goals, and they draw each other's attention into a common direction. In Rommetveit's terms, intersubjectivity means 'a constant oscillation between one's own role as an actor . . . and the role of one's counterpart in interaction' (Marková 1982: 150).

When one partner is more knowledgeable than another or others, as is the case in the teacher–student relationship, this process often involves the creation of shared background knowledge out of incomplete clues, an extrapolation, as it were, from shared words (and acts) to shared worlds. Rommetveit uses the term *prolepsis* to refer to such creation of shared background knowledge, contrasting this term with *ellipsis*. Ellipsis occurs in sentences or texts when information is left out because it is considered redundant, and the listener or reader is supposed to be able to fill in the missing pieces. So, for example, in the sentence 'Mary likes garlic but Pete doesn't,' the words 'like garlic' are left out of (ellipted from) the second clause (after *doesn't*), but the listener automatically fills in the missing information. The essence of ellipsis is thus that the information left out is unproblematically recoverable, that is, it is already known and shared.

Prolepsis, in the original conception by Rommetveit, also consists of leaving things out, but in this case the assumption is that the hearer does not yet have the requisite knowledge to fill in the missing pieces; rather, the proleptic clues are so designed that the hearer is invited to step into an enlarged common pragmatic space, and shared background knowledge is thereby *created*, rather than *assumed*. The idea is that prolepsis, by the very nature of its minimal clues, suggests and encourages *rapprochement* or intimacy, where explicitness, spelling out every detail, would have meant maintaining or increasing distance, or condescension.

Rommetveit gives as an example a man who says to a colleague that 'Yes, we went to see that movie; I liked it very much , but Mary Ann did not,' trusting that his interlocutor will be able to figure out (given the situation) that Mary Ann is the speaker's wife, and the interlocutor is thereby drawn into a circle of first-name familiarity with the speaker and his family. As Rommetveit puts it, 'the listener is made an insider of a tacitly expanded here-and-now' (1974: 88).

This subtle and complex notion of prolepsis has made its way into the educational literature as 'proleptic instruction' (Rogoff & Gardner 1984). As elaborated by Rogoff and Gardner, proleptic instruction 'integrates explanation and demonstration with an emphasis on the learner's participation in the instructional activity' (1984: 102). Defined in this way, the concept falls well within the scope of the IRF exchange, since in any series of exchanges the students participate with their responses in the instruction planned by the teacher and unfolded in the series of elicitations and feedback moves within which the students' answers find their predictable place. Indeed, in a study designed to show the merits of proleptic instruction, Donato and Adair-Hauck (1992) include as examples of it teacher–student exchanges such as the following (C is the teacher):

C   Yesterday, today, next year ((on board)). What are these?
S1 Time expressions
C   Yes, temporal expressions. What is the date today?
S2 April 16
C   And yesterday?
S   April 15

(Donato & Adair-Hauck 1992: 81)

Eventually, the students 'correctly assume the teacher's perspective on the task goal' (1992: 82). In other words, the students find out what it is that the teacher wants, and we are dangerously close to the recitational practices Young has identified as 'WDPK,' or 'What Do Pupils Know,' and 'GWTT,' or 'Guess What Teacher Thinks' (Young 1992).

We cannot assume that recitation is a form of proleptic teaching, merely because it is dialogic (pseudo–dialogic would be more accurate) in character and involves participation. While it seems reasonable to prefer recitation to monologic lecturing or reading prepared speeches, or a teaching style which consists of orders and instructions, there is clearly far more to responsive teaching than recitation alone. We are still left, therefore, with the necessity of evaluating recitation and the IRF exchange, and possibly other types of teacher-led interaction, in terms of their pedagogical value. Similar to my recommendation in chapter 6 (p. 131) concerning teacher talk, *either* rejecting *or* embracing recitation is less productive than investigating carefully when, how often, and how recitation might have a useful place in an overall educational program based on sound principles such as the AAA proposed in this book.

Returning to Secretary Bennett's lesson, we note that it is characterized by recitation teaching, although, according to Eisner, a quite advanced version of it:

> Bennett asks an open-ended question, one that requires recollection of the material read and an interpretive understanding of it. Students respond with an answer designed to satisfy the question. Bennett then responds by asking for elaboration or clarification. (Eisner 1991: 132)

Eisner recognizes the limitations of the teaching style, admitting that it could be accused of being 'a lecture disguised as a discussion,' that it is directed by the teacher and there is no student-to-student talk, that it might be called a 'pingpong approach to teaching' (1991: 135). However, he defends it for the skill, thoroughness, and enthusiasm with which it is conducted and the efficiency with which it gets students to focus on important issues.

Shuy agrees that Bennett 'utilized the recitation model of teaching about as well as it could be done' (Eisner 1991: 142). However, as we already saw above, Shuy regards recitation teaching as being more limited in scope than responsive teaching, particularly when, in the terminology of Vygotsky, we want to push the students' zone of proximal development outwards and systematically foster autonomy. Shuy then suggests that a teacher might move from a recitation mode to a responsive mode when the students appear to be ready to extend themselves and be challenged to higher levels of thinking. The relationship between recitation and responsive teaching would then be one of preliminary/ subsequent, or easier / more advanced.

When Shuy suggests that the recitation model 'would have worked better . . . with a less intelligent, less motivated, less prepared group of students' (1991: 147), he appears to reserve the responsive mode for exceptional students ready for a superior challenge, and the simpler, more regimented recitation style for the average, less motivated student. In my following discussion I will advance the exact opposite view: responsive teaching, or in general any pedagogical interaction which is contingent, is especially important for less motivated, culturally disenfranchised, and other at-risk groups. The bigger the gap between students' backgrounds, ideals, and aspirations (if any), and the school's institutionalized norms and purposes, the more crucial a responsive or contingent form of interaction will be, if we are to assist the students in their development. This does not mean that responsive teaching would not benefit Bennett's students as well, but it is probably less crucial for them given their educational starting capital.

The instructional conversation

Shuy's *responsive teaching*, discussed above with reference to a demonstration lesson taught by William Bennett, is based on work by Tharp, Gallimore and associates, and has come to be known by the name *instructional conversation* (Tharp & Gallimore, 1988; see also Bowers & Flinders 1990). The concept is derived from Vygotsky's zone of proximal development, and it regards teaching as basically assisted development and assisted performance. Tharp and Gallimore frequently employ the metaphor of weaving. Comprehension, for example, is 'the weaving of new information into existing mental structures' (1988: 108). Discourse '[weaves] together spoken and written language with previous understanding' (1988: 111). This notion of language as connecting different entities together in interaction is important in their conception of the instructional conversation (see also Halliday's concept of *texture*, e.g., 1989).

Tharp and Gallimore, as we saw earlier (see the quote on p. 142), note the contradiction we illustrated by way of Bourdieu's lecturer and Restak's child's 'Guess what?' and suggest that the task of teaching is to resolve the paradox between instruction and conversation. Interestingly, Tharp and Gallimore do not link recitation to the IRF exchange in the way that I have been doing here. In fact, many of the instructional conversations they quote – as positive examples – in their book fit the IRF mold quite well, as the following excerpt shows (1988: p. 157):

T	Tell us more about that. Who told them to go to a private school?
Jamie:	((inaudible)) Kicked them out and expelled them.
T	Who did that to them? According to what you read in the story, who did that?
Students:	((Chorus)) Teachers. Parents. Courts.
T	I got teachers, parents, courts. . . . Did everybody read the same story here? Pensie?
Pensie:	From the school . . .
T	A school. Pensie was correct. I think she was looking for . . .

We can clearly see the Initiation – Response – Feedback elements of the IRF exchange structure in this extract, as in most other extracts quoted by Tharp and Gallimore. Furthermore, the fact that the teacher has a planned agenda is clearly illustrated in their transcripts by remarks such as 'I think you're on the trail here,' 'Is everybody with me,' and 'You're pushing us forward here' (p. 157).

Yet, Tharp and Gallimore quite sharply condemn 'the pertinacious recitation script' (p.188). They describe it as follows:

> It consists of a series of unrelated teacher questions that require convergent factual answers and student display of (presumably) known information.

Recitation questioning seeks predictable, correct answers. It includes up to 20 % yes/no questions. Only rarely in recitation are teacher questions responsive to student productions. Only rarely are they used to assist students to develop more complete or elaborated ideas. (Tharp & Gallimore 1988: 14)

For all their professed abhorrence of the recitation script, Tharp and Gallimore quite happily embrace the structural format in which it typically occurs: the IRF exchange, where a student response is called forth by a teacher initiation, and vetted by a teacher feedback move. Interaction remains teacher-centered and teacher-controlled rather than becoming learner-centered and learner-controlled. As I will suggest in the following sections, true conversational teaching must at some point break out of the IRF mould if it is to allow students to develop their own voice, to explore and invest in their own agenda, and to learn to choose and plan their own trains of thought and action.

What may happen on the rare occasions when students break out of the recitation script (and, I would argue, out of the IRF exchange mould), is illustrated in a fascinating transcript in Sinclair & Coulthard (1975: 63–89), where students regularly offer spontaneous information, thus interrupting the usual neat IRF format. At one point, a student says: 'Miss, the er London Bridge they're transporting that to America.' After positively acknowledging the contribution, the teacher says (referring to a name in the text they have in front of them) 'Have a word about this chap we don't seem to have finished do we?' (p. 88). Clearly, the teacher maintains the right to cut off any contribution by the student that does not fit into the predetermined patterns or the mandated text, and orders a return to the 'safe' IRF format. The lesson in question in Sinclair & Coulthard is an excellent illustration of the struggle between control and initiative, between IRF and conversation, that may occur in a classroom context. I do not believe that Tharp and Gallimore's instructional conversation can resolve that conflict unless it is willing to engage in some 'interactional engineering' to manipulate canonized interactional structures such as the IRF. In order to understand how interaction may be brought under the shared control of all participating parties, it is necessary to look at *general conversation*, which we will do in the next section.

Dialog and conversation

In the foregoing I have used dialog and conversation without systematically distinguishing between the two words. It is now time to introduce some more precision, define terms, and locate essential properties.

The word dialog may, along with consciousness and motivation, join the list of constructs treated in this book that cannot be pushed into a single definition and into unified employment. I would like to distinguish at least three realms of use:

(a) general
(b) critical
(c) textual

Taking the general definition first, dialog can be defined as language use which is not monologic, or as any talk to which two or more people contribute. Therefore, all verbal interaction is in this sense dialogic. This very broad definition clearly includes recitation (and the IRF exchange), questioning, interrogation, commanding, as well as more symmetrical forms of talk-sharing, such as ordinary conversation. It is neutral in terms of equality, power, control, and educational value. Some sociologists, including Goffman (cf. 1981: 14), use the term *conversation* in this general sense, though for our purposes it is preferable to reserve that word for its more specific, everyday sense, where it is marked by an orientation towards symmetry (see also Luckmann 1990; Drew and Heritage [1992: 4] prefer the term 'talk-in-interaction' for this general sense of dialog).

For the second definition we can consult the work of Paulo Freire (1972), where the term dialog is anything but neutral. In critical pedagogy, dialog is essentially an instrument of liberation. In Freire's words, 'dialogue is the encounter between men, mediated by the world, in order to name the world' (1972: 76). It cannot consist of one person dominating or controlling another, rather, the only domination is that of the world by the dialogers. It is premised upon love, faith, humility, and mutual trust (1972: 79–80). For Freire, dialog is impossible without authenticity, and in authenticity reality is transformed, and one's actions coincide with one's words. This is thus a profoundly ideological and moral definition, one which seeks to allow people to find their own voice, and which struggles against inequality. Dialog in this sense is indispensable for education: 'Without dialogue there is no communication, and without communication there can be no true education' (1972: 81).

The third definition takes us to the work of Bakhtin, for whom dialog, or 'dialogicality' was the essence of language, and meaning is constructed through 'dialogic interanimation' (Wertsch 1991: 54). Utterances mean what they mean through an interplay between one's own and others' intentions, for as Bakhtin puts it, 'the word in language is half someone else's' (Wertsch 1991: 59). Viewed in this way, language is not primarily a vehicle for the transmission of information between a speaker and a listener, rather, it embodies a variety of 'voices,' one's own and those of others. This definition is textual in the sense that it stresses the contingent interrelatedness of words and utterances with other (and others') words and utterances.

We now turn our attention to *conversation* as one particular subtype of dialog. Conversation is a type of dialog which is characterized by a high degree of orientation towards *communicative symmetry* (Luckmann 1990, Linell & Luckman 1991, Markovà 1991). As Luckman puts it, conversation is

> characterized by a tendency toward intrinsic (communicative) equality of the participants – typically under conditions of relatively weak social-structural (institutionalized) constraints upon the communicative situation (unless, exceptionally, communicative equality itself is institutionalized), as well as by multimodality and polyfunctionality of the communicative process. (Luckman 1990: 58)

Three things are important here, particularly as far as our exploration of conversation-for-education is concerned: first, a tendency towards communicative equality, second, a relative dissociation of conversation from institutional constraints, and third, multimodality and multifunctionality. We do well to note right away that all three characteristics go against the grain of traditional education:

(a) Relations in education are inherently unequal between administrators and teachers, and between teachers and students.
(b) The very existence of the institution of education, the school, demands that educational processes are constrained by its rules, purposes, and procedures.
(c) The success of institutionalized education is measured by goals and objectives, ways and means of achieving them, enshrined in curricula, syllabuses, and textbooks, and evaluation procedures designed to establish and maintain standardized norms. In such a climate, efficiency, linearity and singularity of modality and function are likely to be valued over plurality and multifunctionality.

The employment of conversation – that is, a type of dialog which strives towards symmetry – as a form of pedagogical action, is thus a potentially subversive act which cannot be expected to be easy or uncontroversial. The reader may remember that I recommended *interactional* change (in effect, a kind of 'interactional engineering') as a promising avenue for *educational* change, drawing support from complexity theory (e.g. pp. 148, 158). To try this out and monitor its effects requires a clear understanding of what conversation is, and how it is distinguished from other kinds of interaction, such as the IRF exchange or recitation.

Conversation is generally regarded as the central and most basic form of language use in social life. Thus, Levelt (1989: 29) calls it 'the most primordial and universal setting for speech . . . the canonical setting for speech in all human societies.' In a similar vein, Heritage and Atkinson, echoing the ethnomethodologists Sacks, Schegloff and Jefferson (1974), accord to conversation a 'bedrock' status in relation to other types of speech, and call it 'the most pervasively used mode of interaction in social life and the form within which . . . language is first acquired, . . . also it consists of the fullest matrix of socially organized communicative practices and procedures' (Heritage and Atkinson 1984: 12–13).

Vygotsky provides some clues as to why conversation might have such a preferential status among types of interaction:

> In conversation, every sentence is prompted by a motive. Desire or need lead to request, question to answer, bewilderment to explanation. The changing motives of the interlocutors determine at every moment the turn oral speech will take. It does not have to be consciously directed – the dynamic situation takes care of that. (Vygotsky 1986: 99)

In this quote, we note how utterances are interconnected, how conversation is intrinsically motivated (compare Sacks *et al.*'s observation [1974: 43] that conversation provides 'an intrinsic motivation for listening'), how conversations are locally assembled rather than planned in advance, and how a conversation has a dynamism all its own. The importance of the intersubjectivity of conversation, including the affective factors noted in connection with Restak's 'Guess what?' example, is highlighted by Merleau-Ponty as follows:

> In the experience of a conversation . . . my thoughts and his make up a single tissue, my words and his are called out by the phase of the discussion, they insert themselves in a common operation of which neither of us is the sole creator. A double-being comes about, and neither is the other one for me a simple behavior . . . nor am I that for him, we are, one for the other, collaborators in a perfect reciprocity, our perspectives glide one into the other. (Merleau-Ponty 1945: 407; quoted in Marcus & Zajonc 1985: 210)

Such observations make it clear why conversation should be important in our social life or in learning.

Against this enumeration of the advantages of conversation must be set the everyday opinion that conversing is almost synonymous with 'doing nothing.' We converse when we are relaxing, when we have a break, before we get down to serious business, and so on. Conversation would therefore seem to be very much a frivolous, relaxation-oriented sort of activity, something done in between important things. This perception certainly pertains in classrooms, where conversations may happen in spite of lessons plans, but hardly ever because of them (since, by definition, conversations are not planned). Therefore, upon witnessing a conversation in a lesson, a supervisor or principal observing (say, for contract renewal) might well regard this as a digression from the academic business at hand, or as a lack of management skill. The claim that conversation has pedagogical value must therefore be carefully substantiated and eloquently promoted.

In an earlier paper (van Lier 1989) I proposed the following basic characteristics of conversation:

1. face-to-face interaction (which means that telephone conversations, computer forum conversations, and so on, are derived forms, with their own specific structural characteristics)
2. local assembly, i.e. not planned in advance (however, it can, and often does, contain planned elements, such as a request, or a proposal)
3. unpredictability of sequence and outcome
4. potentially equal distribution of rights and duties in talk
5. reactive and mutual contingency (see Jones & Gerard 1967)

My current view is that the essential dynamism of conversation (the sorts of things captured in Vygotsky's statement quoted above) depends on various kinds of contingency that operate in the interaction. Specifically, the notion of contingency collapses points 2–5 above into one phenomenon, leaving point 1 as a range of factors relating principally to perceptual access (cf. Goffman's [1981] *system constraints*).

A detailed analysis of conversation, and an adaptation of conversational interaction for pedagogical purposes, thus involves an examination of the phenomenon of contingency. My claim is that contingency lies at the core of the Vygotskyan sociocognitive interface, and, furthermore, that contingency is closely linked to the structure of language, through such processes as thematization, indexing, topicalization, and focusing. Indeed, I would claim that grammaticalization itself (see Rutherford 1987, Dittmar 1992) can only take place in contexts of contingent interaction .

Contingency

The word *contingency* is a janus-faced one, just like the words *sanction* and *host*, harboring meanings which appear contradictory to one another. Dictionaries define contingent as likely (but not certain) to happen, and as dependent on (or linked to) something else. For example:

Our trip is contingent upon the weather (= depends on)
We must be prepared for any contingencies (= unpredictable occurrences)

The two key features are *dependency* and *uncertainty*, and the concept thus combines elements of predictability (known-ness, the familiar) and unpredictability (new-ness, the unexpected). This dual aspect of contingency is related closely to such linguistic phenomena as indexicality (Peirce, in Büchler 1955), the given–new contract, topic–comment structure, and focusing (see Brown & Yule 1983a). Further, if speech involves the creation of relevance (Sperber & Wilson 1986), then interaction can be seen as contingency management, in the sense that key tasks in interaction involve relating and projecting speech actions through signaling and interpreting intentions. Conversation itself, since it is often embedded in other forms of talk and action, and conversely, often has other forms of talk and interaction embedded in it, can be seen as 'contingency work' that we do in order to relate actions and events to one another and to the world.

> We can trace contingency back to C.S. Peirce, whose concept of indexicality expresses the relatedness aspect of contingency. Indices, on Peirce's account, focus the attention, and connect one thing to another thing. In interaction, words are connected to intentions, utterances forge relations between speaker's mind and hearer's mind, and text is connected to context (C.S. Peirce, in Büchler 1955: 98–119). Two contingently related utterances are unintelligible except in terms of their relation to one another, like two moving hands in a handshake.
>
> We can further build on Parsons' theory of action, in which *intersubjectivity* is established by means of a doubly contingent process of reaching understanding between two free actors (Parsons 1937, Habermas 1987, Rommetveit 1974). Both Peirce's notion of indexicality and Parsons' notion of intersubjectivity are part of the foundation of ethnomethodology (see, e.g., Garfinkel's [1967] 'common understandings,' Garfinkel & Sacks's [1970] 'practical actions,' and Schegloff's [1972] 'conditional relevance'). Conversation analysis, as one branch of ethnomethodology, is instrumental in revealing the contingent properties of everyday talk (see Atkinson & Heritage 1984 for some clear examples; it is worth noting that their title, *Structures of social action*, overtly points to Parsons' similarly titled book).
>
> A contingent view of language and of language education negates the causal determination of both, but is compatible with a view of development as chaos-with-feedback, and a view of organisms as not self-contained but complemented by other organisms, in the way that genetic information is distributed across different genes which complement one another (Dawkins 1976). This is important, because it means that we can neither claim that learning is caused by environmental stimuli (the behaviorist position) nor that it is genetically determined (the innatist position). Rather, learning is the result of complex (and contingent) interactions between individual and environment (once again, the *ecological* metaphor comes to mind – see p. 52).
>
> Contingency can also be related to control or competence, or a feeling of being in charge. Weiss & Cameron (1985) define it as the degree to which a target event can be controlled (i.e. causally influenced in an intended direction) by variations in people's behavior or attributes. Here contingency relates to the Vygotskyan concept of self-regulation, and the availability of choices.

In order to learn, a person must be active, and the activity must be partly familiar and partly new, so that attention can be focused on useful changes and knowledge can be increased. The reader may recall that, in our discussions of awareness (chapters 3 and 4), we said that neither the totally familiar nor the totally new are likely to be noticed. Learning takes place when the new is embedded in the familiar, so that risks and security are in balance (Murray & Trevarthen 1985; see also p. 52).

Conversation, or any language use which plays with contingencies (storytelling, for example), can therefore be expected to be the most stimulating environment for learning. Conversational interaction naturally links the known to the new. It creates its own expectancies and its own context, and offers choices to the participants. In a conversation, we must continually make decisions on the basis of what other people mean. We therefore have to listen very carefully (Sacks *et al.* note that conversation provides 'an intrinsic motivation for listening,' 1974: 43), and we also have to take great care in constructing our contributions so that we can be understood. As Wittgenstein puts it:

> In a conversation: One person throws a ball; the other does not know: whether he is supposed to throw it back, or throw it to a third person, or leave it on the ground, or pick it up and put it in his pocket, etc. (Wittgenstein 1980b:74e)

It is often assumed that in interaction new linguistic items serve as input and are, once noticed, transferred from the more proficient to the less proficient person. I have argued against such an input–output view in chapter 3 (see p. 50), and want to suggest at this stage that it is far more profitable (in research as in teaching) to focus on the various ways in which contingencies can be created in interaction, since it is in its contingent employment that language provides affordances that engage learners.

Contingency in discourse analysis

In the last section I have proposed that contingency is the quality of language use that can most directly be associated with engagement and learning. At this point, this argument is merely a plausible hypothesis, based on analysis of social theory and learning theory, corroborated by informal analysis of classroom data at my disposal. There is no doubt that sustained and systematic research must be undertaken to substantiate and specify the crucial importance of contingency. For that to be possible, the construct must be made amenable to observation, description, and analysis.

Contingency is what gives language first an element of surprise, then allows us to connect utterance to utterance, text to context, word to world. The conditions for a contingent language act are set up by alluding to the familiar, the given, the shared, then a surprise is sprung in the form of the new, the unexpected, and then joint interpretive work is undertaken which simultaneously connects the new to what is known, and sets up expectations for what is to happen next. This process is analogous to a parent hugging his child prior to bouncing her up into the air, and catching her again safely, while giving indications that further surprises may follow (see Murray & Trevarthen 1985).

The signaling of departures and connections is achieved at many different levels and in many different ways. It occurs at the interface between the individual and the social, the internal and the external, the word and the world. The appropriate way to study contingency is through detailed discourse analysis, that is, the analysis of language use in context. Discourse analysis looks at the coherence of language use from two perspectives: the cognitive or internal perspective, and the social or external perspective, and it charts relations between those two perspectives. The contingent utterance manifests itself in discourse first of all by its new-ness or known-ness, then by its various connections both to the world around the speakers and listeners, and to the thoughts, beliefs, and intentions of the participants. Ideally, discourse analysis should tell us about intensities and kinds of contingency, that is, what instances of language use are more contingent or less so, and how they differ in the types of connections and expectations they embody.

As I mentioned, contingent utterances connect the individual to the social, the internal to the external, the word to the world. At the same time they surprise and bring news, about internal or external things. Discourse analysis shows how such connections and surprises are created by the use of language. In Figure 19 I show how intersubjectivity is the interface between the internal (I) and the external (E), and I place some of the most relevant discourse-analytical concepts within this framework. Discourse-analysis is the study of language use in context, and many of its central concepts show how speakers use language to create their world and place themsleves and each other in it. Discourse analytical concepts range from those dealing with social and cultural concepts (the external end) to those dealing with personal and mental phenomena (the internal end), with intersubjectivity as a dynamic interface between the external and the internal worlds. Though the fluidity of all these contingencies is invisible in the diagram, it may help the reader to form an idea of the resources out of which contingencies are created. I will briefly gloss the concepts from top to bottom.

At the external end of our existence, it is clear that many *conventions* and social rules tell us what to do and how to do it much of the time.

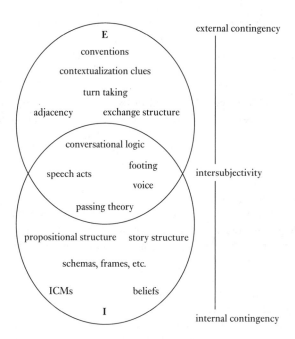

Figure 19 Contingencies

This is part of our culture. *Contextualization clues* (Gumperz 1982, 1992; Auer 1991) anchor our utterances in the real world and also give clues as to the way in which we want to be understood. We *take turns* and manage topics in highly regular ways, ensuring that an appropriate balance is maintained, whereby all participants have equal rights and duties in talking (Sacks, Schegloff & Jefferson 1974). As part of interaction, we expect our utterances to alternate with other people's utterances, in ways which reflect our sensitivity to reciprocity and initiative. This alternation of utterances, and the ways in which utterances are paired and grouped, have been studied using concepts such as *adjacency pairs* (greeting – greeting, question – answer, etc.; see Sacks, Schegloff & Jefferson 1974) and *exchange structure* (of which the IRF discussed earlier in this chapter is a prime example; see Sinclair & Coulthard 1975). The discourse notions mentioned so far mostly fall under the clusters of phenomena Goffman calls ritual and system constraints (1981: 14–16), and are at the external end of the contingency continuum.

Moving more directly into the intersubjective sphere, Grice's *conversational logic*, with its cooperative principle and maxims of quality, quantity, relation, and manner (see Grice 1989), give speakers and hearers a set of groundrules to which they orient themselves when they interact. Goffman's notion of *footing* (1981: 123–59) refers to 'the alignment we take up to ourselves and the others present as expressed in the way we manage the production or reception of an utterance' (1981: 128). Bakhtin's concept of *voice* (or heteroglossia; Bakhtin 1981; Wertsch 1991) is closely related, at one end of its manifestations, to Goffman's footing, but it also points to the ways in which the voice of others can be embedded in our own (Maybin 1994). The study of *speech acts* (Searle 1969, Levinson 1983), and particularly the illocutions (intentions) they signal and effects they bring about (perlocutions), and the interpretations hearers arrive at, can bring into view the central quality of relevance of contingent talk (Sperber & Wilson 1986). Davidson's (1986) view of language as *passing theory* focuses attention on the temporal quality of language production and interpretation, where meanings are constructed ongoingly rather than by drawing items from a ready-made language system or set of reference materials.

Finally, we turn to the mental or internal aspects of contingency signaling in discourse. A large number of categories and units have been proposed Lakoff (1987: chapter 4), while introducing his concept of *idealized cognitive model* (ICM), a sort of prototype mental structure, lists schemas, frames, scripts, and others. We may add such common concepts as thoughts, ideas, propositions, stories, beliefs, sensations, and so on, to illustrate the rich variety of mental life that has been studied by psychologists and philosophers (Ryle 1949, Humphrey 1992, Chafe 1994). It is notoriously difficult to tease apart the linguistic from the mental, and I will not go into detail here (H. Gardner 1985 and Churchland 1988 are helpful overviews). From the perspective of contingency it is sufficient to say that speakers, in their use, give evidence of the mental life behind their utterances, by using words such as 'I believe that . . .,' 'it's like x,' 'that reminds me of . . .,' as well as in a myriad of more covert and subtle ways. It should therefore be possible to capture the richness of contingency in detailed microsociolinguistic descriptions, as a precursor to understanding its role in the construction of learning, work, and social life in general.

The list of discoursal phenomena in Figure 19 offers a set of tools that can be used to examine the many ways in which contingencies are created in interaction. Contingency can be seen as a web of connecting threads between an utterance and other utterances, and between utterances and the world. This web can be sparse and flimsy, as in the case of recitation, or it can be thick and strong, as in the case of conversation. Contingencies draw upon what we know and connect this to what is new. It is thus part of the essence of learning.

In the next section we will look briefly at the potential occurrences of contingency in classroom interaction (the next chapter will give some further examples).

Contingency in classroom interaction

It is probably wishful thinking to expect that classroom interaction (which is institutionally mandated interaction) could ever be entirely conversational. Nor is it at all certain that this would be a good thing in terms of pedagogical efficiency. As we saw above, the relationship between teacher and learner is an inherently unequal one, and all parties engaged in the educational enterprise expect this and in most cases demand it: the teacher is an expert in ensuring that students learn.

This does not mean that conversational interaction is at all times impossible. Even the highly regimented lessons recorded by Sinclair and Coulthard have episodes (usually student-initiated) in which conversation momentarily replaces the more common recitation patterns. Many lessons include such spontaneous moments of conversation, perhaps in the way that any work context can also be interspersed with chat. However, as I pointed out above, such chat is usually regarded as light relief rather than part of the work, and the same tends to be true in lessons (except that, in language lessons, it might be more justifiable than elsewhere to consider conversation an integral part of the work).

Piaget once said that 'discussion is possible only among equals' (1932: 390).[10] It is quite common to assume the same of conversation in general, so that teacher–learner conversation would be intrinsically impossible. However, we can resolve this problem by making a clear and systematic distinction between *equality* and *symmetry* (as I suggested in our discussion of authenticity in chapter 6; see also Luckmann 1990; Linell & Luckmann 1991). Equality refers to factors extrinsic to the talk, such as status, age, role, and other social and societal factors that decide one person has more power, is 'more important' (or more knowledgeable, wiser, richer, and so on) than another. Symmetry refers purely to matters relating to the talk and the interaction itself. In terms of the characteristics of conversation I listed above, symmetry refers to equal distribution of right and duties *in talk*. More precisely, interaction is conversational to the extent that it is *oriented* towards symmetrical contributions. As Luckmann (1990) rightly points out, complete symmetry is never possible. Indeed, whenever one person is speaking another person has to wait, and in that sense there is constant asymmetry. But conversation tries to balance and equalize those asymmetries.

Conversational teaching, or pedagogical interaction characterized by contingency (including, presumably, Shuy's responsive teaching and Tharp and Gallimore's instructional conversation) depends on the possibility of achieving interactional symmetry among unequal participants. The following classroom extracts provide some examples of greater or lesser degrees of contingency (see also the examples provided in chapter 3, pp. 62–4, and chapter 6, pp. 140–2).

1. *(author's data)*

   An ESL class. Making a list of countable/uncountable nouns on the blackboard.

   1 T Countable and uncountable, very good. Nouns. All of them are nouns . . . Okay. We need one person to help. Uh, Y? Can you help me? You come right here . . . you'll be the writer . . . the chief writer. Please . . . think of some things that go on each side . . . countable and uncountable nouns . . . that you remember . . . K, can you give us an example?
   2 L Uh, countable . . . tea . . .
   3 T Okay, tea, good. Write it down.
   4 L Wine.
   5 T What did you say? I'm sorry, I didn't hear you.
   6 L Wine
   7 T Wine. Okay. Some more things. R, can you think of one? On this side maybe?
   8 L Students.
   9 T Students. Very good. Okay . . .

2. (van Lier 1988: 153)

   L 2 is male, L6 is female; throughout the lesson they engage in much mutual joking.

   1 L2 'Which' – a person or things
   2 T   yes .. yea which dog is yours . . . okay? which baby is yours . . . okay?
   3/4 LL [yes/ya   [m:
   5 L2 I don't have baby
   6 LL ((loud laughter))
   7 T   Are you sure?
   8 LL ((loud laughter))
   9 L6 I don't know ((teasingly))
   10 LL ((laughter))
   11 L2 o:::h ((mock consternation))

3. *(author's data)*

   1 L1 Can you fo- can you follow any conversation? Any people?
   2 L2 Sometime yes but ah. . . many times I can't
   3 L1   [hm::
   4 L1 And what about you?
   5 L3 The same but depend of (who) the conversation, no?
   6 L2 Yah
   7 L3 Or the point, because sometimes is point very very easy, but the::: depend of the theme

```
 8  L1   [si:m]
 9  L3   Theme
10  L1   [si:m]
11  L2   The topic
12  L1   [si:m] ah! [si:m] ah yes [si:m] . . . yeah yes=
13  L2              [ ((chuckle)) ((unint)) topic
         = yes [si:m] tee- aitch- ((spells)) . . . theme . . . theme
14  L3                                           [ yes
15  L2                                                   [ yeah
16  L3   Yeah theme
17  L2   Okay . . . next thing
```

In the first extract it is clear who is the teacher, and dominates the interaction, in other words, who is 'in charge.' The inequality between teacher and students is matched by various kinds of asymmetry (in turn taking, amount of talk, questioning, and so on), and the result is a reduced contingency between utterances. This is particularly noticeable in the student responses which do not include verbal links to preceding or following utterances, but merely fill slots prepared by the teacher and determined by the design of the activity.

The second extract begins in a similar way, with a student offering a rule for a relative pronoun, and the teacher accepting it and giving examples. Then, however, the class breaks out of the recitation format (conversation 'erupts,' we might say), and an example by the teacher is exploited for some banter among the students. It is interesting to consider the possibility (we shall never know for sure, of course, but we may suspect) that the teacher 'planted' the example of the baby to get the students going, to encourage a conversational episode. Indeed, the lesson in question (see also Allwright 1988) contains frequent examples of such switching between more formal 'lesson talk' to highly informal conversation. It is easy to see how, from turn 3 onwards, progression is fast, unpredictable, and turns are tightly interwoven, each one firmly anchored to the preceding one and holding out expectations (creating possibilities, raising exciting options) for the next one. Looking back to our discussion of attention, focusing and vigilance in chapter 3, it should be clear that partaking in such a conversational interchange requires conversational vigilance to a degree not possible in the more plodding and stodgy format of extract 1.

It is not easy to find examples of conversational interaction between teacher and students which yet appears to be oriented towards learning and teaching (we'll explore this further in the next chapter), and it is no coincidence that my third example is taken from a group discussion among language learners. We see in this extract a high degree of contingency between all turns while students struggle to express their opinions and understand those of their peers. Note that the extract includes a teaching sequence, but also note how this is seamlessly integrated in the discussion. L3 and L2 'teach' L1 the word theme at the behest of L1 (they do not *offer* to teach, but are *invited* to teach, a distinction we will return to in the next chapter), without disturbing the symmetry of the discussion.

At this stage the reader may wish to study the various extracts presented (including those in chapters 3 and 6) and reflect on their pedagogical value (or potential to provide opportunities for learning). The AAA principles do not rule in or out any particular way of interacting in classrooms, although they are quite explicit in the responsibility of education to permit learners to find their own voice and become autonomous (self-directed) learners as well as understand the value of striving towards autonomy. Further, the classroom should reduce, not increase, any gaps that might exist between learners' cultures and experiences and academic goals and procedures, not by brainwashing the learner or by forced assimilation, but by respecting and valuing the learner's primary world.

Education is not a matter of choosing, then imposing one way of interacting, a single mode of discourse (whether conversational or recitational), but rather a continuous studying and monitoring of the entire array of ways of talking and interacting, and finding effective and enabling ways to speak to the right person at the right time for the right reasons (where 'right' is defined by our basic principles and values, such as the AAA). In the following section I attempt to present an integrated and dynamic overview of the primary modes of discourse available in education.

From transmission to transformation

To address the varieties of social interaction for the purpose of examining their learning power, I invite the reader to examine Figure 20 and to keep its various distinctions and continua in mind in the following discussion. I broadly distinguish four types of pedagogical interaction, as follows:

1. *Transmission*: the delivery of information or directives from one person (the knower) to another or others, in a one-way, monologic format. Typical exponents are lectures, sermons, recipes in a cook book, drills and commands. In classrooms, this is the typical monologic lecture format, and the prototypical 'banking model' described by Freire (1972).

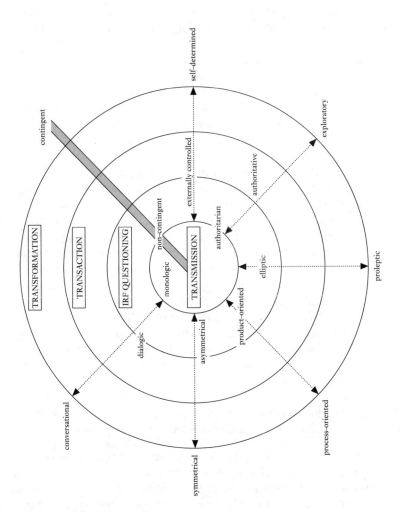

Figure 20 Types of pedagogical interaction

2. *IRF questioning*: here a distinction must be made between recitation proper, oriented towards display/assessment, and a number of other types of IRF questioning, as illustrated in Figure 17. Recitation is the elicitation of displays of performance or information (usually using the IRF format), by means of questions and answers, where all the questions are asked by one person (the knower), and all the answers are given by the others (e.g. students). Commonly, the plan and the direction of the discourse are determined by, and familiar to, the questioner rather than the questioned. Students are 'led' in a certain direction by the questioner. In Socratic and other variants, an argument is constructed by the 'expert' using questions and answers as stepping stones, or students are prodded by questions to articulate their thoughts, back up opinions, and so on. All IRF-based dialogs share the basic feature that the roles of questioner and answerer are rigidly separated.

3. *Transaction*: information exchange by means of a two-way process, where the direction of the discourse, and the relevance of contributions, the timetable of events, etc., are jointly determined by all participants. Group discussions, business negotiations, and information exchange tasks are typical examples. In classrooms, most cooperative learning falls in this category since, even though talk tends to be contingent, symmetrical, and at times conversational, there is usually an externally imposed structure and agenda, which group members are not free to transform.

4. *Transformation*: jointly managed talk that has the potential to change learning situations, role relationships, educational purposes and procedures. Here it is no longer the case that one person, the teacher, has the agenda, and the students have no option but to follow it. Rather, the agenda is shaped by all participants, and educational reality may be transformed. Participants' contributions are self-determined or produced in response to others' requests. At this level it is appropriate to speak of true *co-construction* of meanings and events.

The model presented here, with its four levels of pedagogical action, and range of continua, borrows elements from several descriptions of critical pedagogy, e.g. Leithwood's curriculum orientations (1986), and Berlak and Berlak's dilemmas (1981). I must emphasize, however, that this is not intended as a clear-cut or neat category system, rather, it serves as a map of pedagogical options. Nor am I suggesting that only one level of action, say transformation, is sufficient to propel an educational enterprise. I would expect that there is need for all four levels, at different times, and for different purposes. However, I do think (and see Shor

1992 for a similar perspective) that level 4 is crucial and has hitherto been neglected.

A further caveat against taking the four pedagogical modalities as discrete action types is the consideration that many pedagogical activities will turn out to be *hybrid* ones, in which aspects of different modalities are dynamically interwoven in the discourse. In many cases such hybrid interaction types, much like Bakhtin's *double-voiced dialog* (Bakhtin 1981), will prove to be the most powerful and creative ones. One may think of the pedagogical power of, e.g., *storytelling* and *playing games*.

In Figure 20 I have highlighted the non-contingent–contingent cline, suggesting that levels of contingency increase as interaction moves outwards in a centripetal fashion, away from the closed center of the spectrum. At the same time, other features of interaction also begin to be more prominent, and I will briefly gloss these below, so as to place contingency in its proper context:

(a) *monologic* ·········▶ *dialogic* ·········▶ *conversational*

From lecture talk, or one-directional information flow in the transmission mode, the IRF mode shifts to dialogic talk (in the general sense indicated on p. 166), where speakership alternates, though it remains under the control of the knower, or the 'questioner.' Moving from transactional to transformational interaction (including Brown and Yule's [1983b] *interactional function*, though potentially much more than that) the talk becomes increasingly conversational, exhibiting features such as local assembly, unpredictability of sequence and outcome, and so on (see above), as well as more superficial markers such as the 'ah!'s and hesitations one can note in extract (3) above, and back channels, turn overlaps, etc.

(b) *asymmetrical* ·········▶ *symmetrical*

Talk is asymmetrical when rights and duties *of speaking* are unequally distributed. I emphasize *of speaking*, since we must not confuse symmetry with equality. One participant can be more powerful than the others, perhaps because of greater knowledge (such as L2 and L3 in extract [3] above), age, or wisdom, without necessarily making the talk asymmetrical. All other things being equal, however, talk is likely to become more symmetrical as we move away from the center. In the outer circle, two or more persons can have a symmetrical interaction, i.e. one in which rights and duties of speaking are equally shared, even if one of them is a teacher, a parent, a genius, or whatever, and the other is a student, a child, etc.

(c) *product-oriented* ·········► *process-oriented*

Education that is based on a specification of subject matter, on performance in tests, and on measurements of outcomes of one kind or another, is product-oriented. Such education can work quite well for highly motivated students with strong, supportive home backgrounds, in other words, the elites which have traditionally done well in school and for whom the school system was originally designed. In such an environment, top-down transmission can be effective, since there is no gap between institutional and student expectations. However, in a system in which all children have the right to be educated, and in which there is great diversity of cultures and languages, a process-oriented approach is needed to engage the students and allow them to grow academically. A process-oriented approach of necessity must be conversational in character.

(d) *elliptic* ·········► *proleptic*

Ellipsis occurs in sentences or texts when information is left out because it is considered redundant, and the listener (or reader) is supposed to be able to fill in the missing pieces. However, the speaker (or writer) who uses ellipsis does not explicitly check or facilitate the listener's interpretive processes, or invite the listener into a shared intersubjective space. As I explained above, when Rommetveit (1974) proposed the notion of prolepsis, he was thinking of a speaker who gives the hearer clues for the enlargement of common ground without spelling out every detail. Proleptic discourse therefore is aware of gaps in understanding and invites the less-competent into sharing with the more-competent. Whereas ellipsis can be dismissive (or at best indifferent), prolepsis is always invitational and generous.

(e) authoritarian ·········► authoritative ·········► exploratory

The person who commands, and who tells people things without paying much heed to feedback, uses language in an authoritarian way. A person can be authoritative, however, without being authoritarian, as L3 illustrates in extract (3). In education the distinction between these two concepts is extremely important, since a teacher may not want to be authoritarian, but the students will continue to expect him or her to be authoritative. In ideal circumstances, discourse may become, in Bakhtin's terms, 'simultaneously authoritative and internally persuasive' (1981: 342).[11] At the outer end of the continuum participants are equal in all relevant respects, and interaction becomes truly exploratory. Such discourse is also responsive in Shuy's terms (although authoritative discourse can also be responsive), and learning is reciprocal.

(f) *externally controlled* ·······▶ *self-determined*

When the students' actions are externally controlled, by the teacher, by a prespecified curriculum, by an educational institution, by a test-driven policy, and so on, pedagogical communication is likely to remain in the inner circles of our chart, and the student will not have the opportunity to become an autonomous person, in charge of his or her own learning. In a conversation, one's motivation, attention, and participation are self-determined. For the development of critical thinking, self-regulated action, and intrinsically motivated learning, a focus on transactional and transformational modes of pedagogical action are necessary.

(g) *non-contingent* ·······▶ *contingent*

Finally we reach the phenomenon of contingency, which is the focus of my discussion. Non-contingent discourse is not anchored within the experiential world (including the here-and-now context) of all participants, nor does it set up expectancies for what is to happen next. Perhaps one person follows an agenda which the others are unfamiliar with, or what comes next is either totally unpredictable or totally predictable to one or more of the participants. As interaction moves towards the outer realms, sharedness of perspectives increases, and expectancies are effectively created and exploited. When that happens, we can speak of contingent interaction, and this will mean that a number of the other polarities mentioned above will be 'pulled' outwards, opening up and enriching the discourse. The predictability of the IRF exchange will be loosened, ellipsis might be replaced by prolepsis, authoritarianism yields to authority, creating the potential for joint exploration, and so on.

As Figure 20 shows, classroom interaction can vary along a number of dimensions. It is not my purpose here to prescribe or proscribe particular forms of classroom talk, but by unfolding the many aspects of social interaction, it should be possible to make more informed choices and strategic plans than would otherwise be the case. Presenting varieties of pedagogical discourse in the form of concentric circles allows us to highlight the dynamic struggle between centrifugal and centripetal forces (i.e. those pulling outwards, towards diversification, and those pulling inward, towards unification of perspectives, voices, and meanings) in language. As Bakhtin has noted, 'this struggle constitutes the energizing principle of all linguistic life' (Morris 1994: 15).

I have suggested that, in this dynamic tension between diversity and homogeneity, between many voices and one voice, between autonomy and external control, between conversation and monolog, and so on, the

phenomenon of contingency plays a crucial role. By noticing the ties that
we create between our utterances and those of others, and between our
words and the world, we can basically determine the direction (centripetal or centrifugal) we wish to go at any point in time, and to the extent
that all participants share this meta-interactional awareness, this direction can be negotiated and rationally controlled. I suggest that
contingencies are creatable, controllable and noticeable in our own and
others' utterances, and that therefore contingency is the key that unlocks
all varieties of social interaction and, in doing so, simultaneously unlocks
our students' learning potential.

Although I agree with Bakhtin that both forces – centrifugal and centripetal – are necessary, I argue for a strong push towards more
contingent forms of classroom interaction, especially since education has
for so long been limited to the central confines of the circle, and when it
has moved outwards for the sake of reform or innovation, it has often
done so in erratic and unbalanced ways, and these efforts have subsequently backfired.

In general, as classroom interaction becomes more contingent, several
benefits become available to students in terms of increased learning
opportunities and increased depth of learning. These benefits are
directly related to the dynamic nature of contingency. Recall that there
are two sides to this: a contextual anchoring which relates that which is
said to what is known, including that which has been said before, and an
expectancy which encourages students to reach higher levels of functioning. The anchoring, or indexing, allows students to relate and connect,
and to build understanding, and the expectancy is a built-in motivator.
Contingent utterances, then, do a number of valuable things, among
them:

1. They relate new material to known material.
2. They set up expectancies for what may come next.
3. They validate (value, respect) both preceding and next utterance.
4. They are never entirely predictable, nor entirely unpredictable.
5. They promote intersubjectivity.
6. They ensure continued attention.

Conclusion

We have examined a range of ways of speaking that may take place
between teacher and learner. We have noted that the IRF exchange and
the related pedagogical discourse mode of recitation are common in
classroom interaction and present a number of advantages in terms of
control, efficiency of delivery of predetermined material, and so on.

However, we also saw how this efficiency comes at the cost of reduced student participation, less expressive language use, a loss of contingency, and severe limitations on the students' employment of initiative and self-determination.

When a teacher asks, 'What are three major character traits of Hamlet, Ingrid?,' he is not only making Ingrid speak, but also specifying to a large extent the content of her utterance. As a result, Ingrid is not focusing on the play as a work of art, or Hamlet as a person, but rather on the play as a source of information to tell the teacher what he wants to hear. She is not trying to formulate her own expressions of appreciation or her understanding of the story, but complying with a demand. When someone else asks her later what she thinks of Hamlet she may not be able to do better than 'Hamlet was a jerk' or 'Hamlet sucks.' Perhaps we should not be surprised at such poverty of expression, if it turns out that students are not encouraged to find sources of speaking, their own voice, within themselves, and with each other, developing expressivity through contingent interaction.

Developing voice through contingent interaction requires also a change in our definition of achievement: it is not primarily the number of answers marked 'correct' by a teacher or a testing agency, and a resultant numerical label such as '500 on the TOEFL', or 'B+ for classroom participation', but rather an inner (and shared) sense of self-determination (the autotelic person of Csikszentmihalyi 1990, 1993), a consciously experienced sense of progress in the direction of competence, relatedness, and autonomy (Deci *et al.* 1991; see also above, p. 108), in accordance with goals personally and collaboratively articulated.

Although it is clear that the principles of awareness, autonomy, and authenticity demand a focus on contingent interaction, since this focuses attention, stimulates intrinsic motivation, and develops authenticity of expression, this does not mean that non-contingent or less-contingent ways of speaking, including recitation, IRF questioning, chorus repetition, and many other ways, are useless. As I have recommended, careful reflection on and monitoring of how we interact with our students should assist us in developing ways of tactful teaching (van Manen 1991), that is, 'the ability to act quickly, surely, confidently, and appropriately in complex or delicate circumstances' (1991: 125). As van Manen points out, tact cannot be planned, rather, it is 'a mindfulness that permits us to act thoughtfully with children and young people' (1991: 128). This is not something we can just learn and then apply, like some technique or task type. It has to become part of our way of working. In the next chapter we look at some options for contingent and thoughtful pedagogy.

Notes

1 See Farr 1990 for an interesting discussion of the prefix 'inter,' in which he shows how 'self,' mind, and consciousness emerge out of social interaction.

2 There are, however, significant structural differences between Socratic questioning and the classroom IRF exchanges illustrated, which are particularly visible in the third turn; in the former case, the third turn continues the argument, in the latter case, it evaluates – or otherwise comments on – the second turn. More on different IRF types below.

3 Exceptions, discussed below, are Eisner's comments on Bennett's lesson, and several studies which see the IRF as interaction in the ZPD; on the other hand, Sinclair & Coulthard (1975) and Wells (1993) basically take a neutral position.

4 This example is adapted from a larger extract which you will find on p. 203.

5 An exception (perhaps the only exception) is 'ordinary conversation,' which may be basically the same wherever it occurs. Since we will discuss conversation in detail below, we will ignore it for the moment.

6 It may be argued (see, e.g., Fairclough 1992b) that talk isn't that powerful. However, when carefully and deliberately used for specific ends, I believe that talk holds enormous power, for good or for evil. Politicians, speech writers, propagandists of various kinds, and many others engaged in the manufacture of public opinion would seem to attest to the power of language. Usually, it is clear, such examples illustrate strategic (in league with dramaturgical) action in Habermas's terms, so it remains to be seen if communicative action as proposed by the AAA curriculum can be similarly powerful, but in liberating rather than indoctrinating ways.

7 And note how this engagement is not a natural feature of the IRF exchange, as illustrated earlier in the chapter.

8 Recitation is never clearly defined, but it seems safe to assume that it refers primarily to the display/assessment orientation in Figure 17, with a preponderance of repetition/regurgitation. It is possible that Eisner's interpretation includes also the lower-right types on my diagram, and this difference might explain the differing evaluations by Shuy and Eisner.

9 This is not necessarily always the case. Skilled questioning, perhaps along Socratic lines, may make students think hard and critically. However, even Socrates claimed only to get his respondents to make explicit some knowledge they already had, as is cleverly illustrated in dialogs such as the *Meno*. Moreover, as I pointed out in note 2, Socrates did not evaluate his interlocutors' responses, but used them as stepping stones in the argument. The Socratic structure is a chaining of adjacency pairs, rather than a succession of IRF exchanges, as the following example, from *Meno*, illustrates:

    S   Does not this line from one corner to the other cut each of these figures in two?

    M   Yes

    S   So these are four equal lines which enclose this figure?

    M   They are

    S   Consider now . . . (etc.)

10 Piaget felt that cognitive restructuring (equilibration) was not possible for children in discussion with adults, because of the inherently unequal power relationship and asymmetrical interaction (see Rogoff 1990). Adults can, in

the view of Piaget, only overcome this by effacing themselves and becoming equal rather than superior to the child. Here the adult's pedagogical role is in my view misconstrued because of Piaget's failure to distinguish equality and symmetry.

11 For Bakhtin, internally persuasive discourse is tightly interwoven with 'one's own word' (1981: 345). He explains:

> In the everyday rounds of our consciousness, the internally persuasive word is half-ours and half-someone else's. Its creativity and productiveness consist precisely in the fact that such a word awakens new and independent words, that it organizes masses of our words from within, and does not remain in an isolated and static condition . . . The semantic structure of an internally persuasive discourse is not finite, it is open; in each of the new contexts that dialogize it, this discourse is able to reveal ever newer ways to mean. (1981: 345–6)

8   The curriculum as interaction

Introduction

In the last chapter we looked at the different options we might have in terms of interacting with students in the classroom. We saw how the educational institution, the school, may favour certain types of interaction over others, but also how an awareness of the options available might allow the teacher to exercise control over the interaction and therefore the educational process.

In this chapter we will look at some of the strategies the teacher has available to create a curriculum driven by social interaction and founded on well-articulated principles such as the AAA outlined in this book. It tends to be accepted, without much question or doubt, that the way we teach is determined by a particular method or approach, such as the communicative approach, the content-based approach, whole-language teaching, phonics, or whatever. Similarly, the direction in which our syllabus moves, including its speed and measurement, is often determined by lists of objectives, a standard test somewhere on the horizon, or some sort of 'exit mechanism'.

In view of what we have said about intrinsic motivation, and in view of the centrality of interaction in learning, it is clearly appropriate to ask if the central determining factors of our curriculum, and of the specific syllabus for a class, should not be our basic educational ideals and beliefs, coupled with practical actions which most clearly promote learning. To suggest how this might be done is the topic of this chapter.

It should be emphasized from the start that this way of working is neither easy nor uncontroversial. For one thing, there are the institutional constraints we noted, following Bourdieu and Passeron 1977, in chapter 7. For another, it would be foolish to deny the power of mandated tests to wreak havoc with innovations, and our duty as teachers to ensure that our students perform well on exams that are important for them. Further, well-laid-out objectives and materials give a predictability to the syllabus and a stability to the lessons which are very important for most students. These – and other – considerations should warn us against undue zeal in our innovatory attempts, or naive expectations of immediate success. The cautious canon 'think small,' fortified by the tenet of complexity theory that small changes may have powerful consequences, may once again be useful (see also chapters 4, 7).

Principles, strategies, action

The central question, from a practical point of view, that faces us is the following: In the absence of a clearly defined and detailed teaching method or syllabus, how can a consistent and methodical way of teaching be elaborated which focuses on the pedagogical process (or even the pedagogical moment) as the primary locus of learning?

Figure 21 shows how a curriculum can be designed which proceeds from principles to strategies, and from strategies to pedagogical action.

John Dewey, as far back as 1904, spoke of a dual perspective or dual vision as a central characteristic of a good teacher. What he meant by this was that teachers need a long-range vision of where they want to take the students. Such a clear view of the long-term purpose of education, which teachers keep in mind at all times, ensures that the teaching maintains a sense of purpose and direction that guides overall educational decision-making.

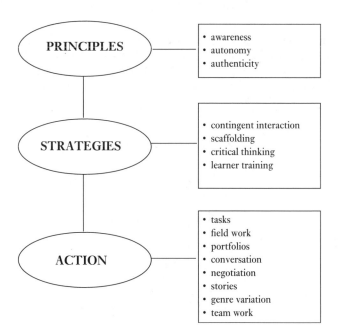

Figure 21   Curriculum design

At the same time teachers also need a short-range vision of the immediate circumstances of educational activities and encounters with students so as to be able to make the moment-to-moment decisions that are necessary in the classroom (the sorts of things van Manen [1991] refers to as *pedagogical tact*).

In Dewey's discussion, both types of vision were equally necessary: a long-range vision on its own would lead to a neglect of daily tasks and the power of the moment. Conversely, an excessive preoccupation with the short-term details of teaching without a long-term perspective would lead to a clutter of detail with no sense of direction.

The ZPD and interaction

The reader may recall that at several points in the book we have spoken about Vygotsky's developmental psychology, particularly the '*zone of proximal development*,' and Bruner's related notion of scaffolding (1983; see p. 46 for a definition of the ZPD). Figure 22 illustrates the ZPD in a simple way. At any given point in time, there are things a person can do confidently on his or her own. This we might call the area of self-regulated action. Beyond that there is a range of knowledge and skills which the person can only access with someone's assistance. In the case of the performance of some complex action, then the person can perform the action if someone more capable is available to help. In the case of some piece of knowledge, this becomes available because it can be linked to existing knowledge or experiences, again, perhaps with someone else's guidance. This material, which one might say is within reach, constitutes

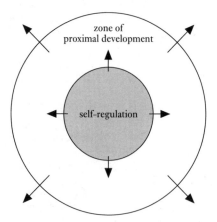

Figure 22   Zone of proximal development

the ZPD. Anything outside the circle of proximal development is simply beyond reach and not (yet) available for learning.

According to Vygotsky, any learning is of necessity in advance of development. This means that it is somehow one step ahead of the innate schedule of growth, the genetically coded program of the person's development. How do we, as caretakers or educators, ensure that our teaching actions are located within the ZPD, especially if we do not really have any precise idea of the innate timetable of every learner? In answer to this question, researchers in the Vygotskyan mould propose that social interaction, by virtue of its orientation towards mutual engagement and intersubjectivity, is likely to home in on the ZPD and stay within it.

It is customary in the literature on the ZPD (and the related pedagogical notion, scaffolding) to speak of 'the' ZPD, as if there were only one zone of a uniform nature for every learner. However, Vygotsky emphasizes that 'for each discipline and each student the interacting curves of learning and development need to be plotted individually' (Kozulin 1990: 171). It is also customary to assume that progress across the ZPD occurs as a result of assistance from a more capable person, e.g. a teacher, or a more capable peer (Vygotsky 1978,Tharp & Gallimore 1988). This assumption is also far too simplistic, and if we look a little further afield, a much more complex picture emerges.

Newman, Griffin and Cole, who call the ZPD the 'construction zone,' define it as 'changes that take place in socially mediated interactions' (1989: 2). As they explain, 'when people with different goals, roles, and resources interact, the differences in interpretation provide occasions for the construction of new knowledge' (*ibid.*). This view is close to the Piagetian idea of the process of *disequilibration* as providing the impetus to new knowledge. Different perspectives, knowledge, and strategies create cognitive conflict in the participants, and in the resolution of such conflict, in the context of social interaction, new perspectives, knowledge, and strategies are created.[1] But in which direction will the changes occur? Will they automatically be *better* perspectives, etc.? In addition to mere *change*, we have to account for change in a *desirable direction*, towards set goals (in other words, *achievement*).

A number of studies have been conducted to try to find answers to these questions, so far with conflicting results. Glachan and Light (1982) report a number of studies involving children doing Piagetian conservation tasks, paired with more capable, less capable, or equal peers. In such tasks children are asked to judge if liquids change in volume when they are poured into containers of different shapes and sizes. Given sufficient opportunities to discuss possible solutions and engage in practical actions, children can reach higher levels even when both members initially used inferior strategies for solving problems. 'Interaction between inferior strategies can lead to superior strategies or, in other words, two wrongs can make a right,' they conclude (1982: 258).

A strikingly different result was obtained by Tudge (1990), who asked children to solve problems relating to weights placed on balance beams (another well-known Piagetian task). In this case, only children who were paired with more capable peers improved, whereas many others actually regressed. Tudge isolates two positive factors that were of importance in predicting whether or not a child improved: a partner's *confidence* in making predictions and an ability to support these predictions with higher-level *reasoning*. In a second set of experiments Tudge found an additional, more powerful factor: the provision of *feedback* (in the first set the beams of the balance had been fixed, so that the children got no feedback on the accuracy or their predictions). When feedback was provided (the beams of the balance were loosened), all children had a roughly even chance of improving, whether they were paired with a higher, and equal, or a lower peer, or even if they worked on their own. In other words, the feedback provided by the apparatus 'overshadowed any effects of discussion with a partner' (1990: 167).

I have spent some time discussing these experiments in order to show how complex these issues are. Simply to provide students with a problem and some guidance in the form of peer interaction or expert assistance, does not mean that one is working in the ZPD, and it is no guarantee at all that any progress will be achieved. I mentioned in the last chapter that some researchers mistakenly regard IRF interaction as being a good example of interaction in the ZPD (see above, p. 152). As Tudge rightly points out, the ZPD cannot be separated from the overall theoretical context in which it was developed. He continues:

> In fact, failure to see the connections between the zone and the theory as a whole means that it is difficult to differentiate Vygotsky's concept from any instructional technique that systematically leads children, with the help of an adult, through a number of steps in the process of learning some set of skills. The difference for Vygotsky is that the *context* in which the interaction occurs is of crucial importance. (Tudge 1990: 156)

I now return to interaction in the ZPD for language education. Clearly, the tasks, procedures, and challenges here are quite different from problem-solving in physics and mechanics. For example, it is theoretically quite possible that language development might occur in equal measure through discussion about a Piagetian problem, whether or not that problem is satisfactorily resolved. It is even possible (though more difficult to imagine, at least for me) that language development might occur regardless of the amount of interaction that occurred in the solution of a task.

I have argued in earlier chapters that language education is enhanced by such things as engagement, intrinsic motivation, and self-determination, and that these conditions are promoted by certain kinds of social interaction. In the last chapter I argued that a crucial element in the interaction is contingency, which is easiest to achieve when interactants are oriented towards symmetry. This means that conversational interaction among language learners of roughly equal ability might be particularly useful, perhaps more so, in certain circumstances, than interaction with more capable peers or with native speakers. This is exactly what van Lier & Matsuo (n.d.) suggest, after comparing conversations of an adult language learner with other learners of various levels of proficiency. In that study we also suggest that it may be beneficial for language students to interact with learners who have a lower level of proficiency, since this encourages the creation of different kinds of contingencies and discourse management strategies.

Adding one more ingredient to the mix of elements in the ZPD, the notion of a capable adult guiding a learner through the ZPD is most appealing in the case of young children and their caretakers. However, in the case of adolescents or adults learning a second language or participating in adult literacy classes, this metaphor may be less convincing. Clearly, learners of all ages need (or can benefit from) expert guidance, but in addition to that, older children and adults increasingly have *inner resources* on which they can rely to provide guidance and support to themselves, as the success of self-study programs and the accomplishments of auto-didactic adults demonstrates.

To summarize, productive work in the ZPD can be accomplished by learners using a variety of different resources, including:

(a) assistance from more capable peers or adults
(b) interaction with equal peers
(c) interaction with less capable peers (in accordance with the Roman dictum *Docendo discimus* – (we learn by teaching))
(d) inner resources.

These resources for construction in the ZPD are shown in Figure 23, an adaptation of the ZPD illustration in Figure 22. According to this view, a learner's zone of self-regulated action can be expanded in a number of different ways, not only through the assistance of teachers or other experts. This suggests the value of a rich menu of activities, which include teacher-led work, interaction with peers who are of equal proficiency, activities such as peer teaching (e.g. reciprocal teaching, see Palincsar & Brown 1984), and individual study. The desired mix and balance of these activities will depend on characteristics of the learner,

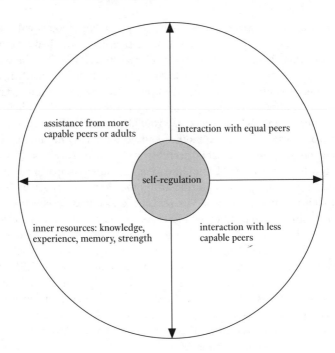

Figure 23   Multiple zones of proximal development

the situation, and the linguistic skill or subject matter to be learned. Once again, therefore, my argument goes in the direction of variety and balance, pinpointing the need for a rich (or 'thick') curriculum, and for developing a theory of practice which allows teachers to monitor and judge their professional activities.

The ZPD and scaffolding

If we agree with Vygotsky that the ZPD is a powerful concept in our conceptualization of the learning process, we then must think about how we, as teachers, can promote work that falls within the ZPD and that extends the students' area of self-regulation outwards by pulling them into challenging but attainable areas of work. For this, the work of the American developmental psychologist Jerome Bruner provides interesting guidelines through his notion of scaffolding. This idea, which has since gained much popularity in educational circles, is based on Bruner's work on the social interaction between mothers and very young children, particularly the universal game of 'peekaboo' (Bruner 1983). In this game, the adult will disappear and reappear before the baby, making appropriate noises such as 'peep' or 'boo,' to the considerable excitement (caused by a delicate balance between consternation and delight, of course) of the infant. Gradually, over the years, the infant takes an ever more active role in this game, and many others like it, and the adult 'hands over' pieces of the action, including vocal and verbal action, as the infant shows signs that he or she is ready for it. In Bruner's own words, scaffolding is defined as

> a process of 'setting up' the situation to make the child's entry easy and successful and then gradually pulling back and handing the role to the child as he becomes skilled enough to manage it. (Bruner 1983: 60)

In other words:

> One sets the game, provides a scaffold to assure that the child's ineptitudes can be rescued or rectified by appropriate intervention, and then removes the scaffold part by part as the reciprocal structure can stand on its own. (Bruner 1983: 60)

The notion of scaffolding, then, gives us an idea of the dynamism of working within the ZPD, as characterized, in general terms, by a number of features such as the following:

1. There are repeated occurrences, often over a protracted period of time, of a complex of actions, characterized by a mixture of ritual repetition and variations (the principle of *continuity*).
2. The activity is structured so as to create a safe (but somewhat challenging, see also p. 52) environment within which the participation of the child is encouraged without being forced, and within which errors are tolerated if not expected (the principle of *contextual support*).
3. Throughout the activity the emphasis is on mutual engagement and 'intersubjectivity of attention' (Wells 1985; the principle of *intersubjectivity*).
4. Elements in the activity event can be changed, deleted, or repeated, depending on actions and reactions of each of the participants, in other words, all actions are contingent (the *contingency* principle).
5. The child (or to speak in more general terms, the learner) is observed closely as the parent (or teacher) watches for opportunities to hand over parts of the action as soon as the child shows signs of being ready for them (the *handover* principle).
6. Actions of participants are jointly orchestrated, or synchronized, in rhythmic terms, so that the interaction flows in a natural way (the *flow* principle).

As indicated above, it cannot be assumed without further study that scaffolded activities, conforming to the principles outlined, apply to adult learning contexts (what is called androgogy by Knowles 1984) or academic instruction in general, even if we can agree that they are a central feature of learning in children. After all, we learn different things in different ways, and we learn things differently at different times in our life. However, it is clear that as educators it is to our advantage to study ways in which the power of scaffolding can be brought into the classroom, particularly in areas of learning in which social interaction clearly plays a central role, such as in language learning.

In the preceding chapter I already made an argument that the notion of contingency is central in interaction, and that, if interaction is important in language learning, then it is the feature of contingency which makes interaction an efficient learning context. In the following section I shall explore some ways in which the principles of scaffolding can be brought into the classroom, so that their effect on language learning can be monitored and understood.

Pedagogical scaffolding

In the past, the application of scaffolding to classroom work has generally concentrated on one-on-one interactions between a teacher and a student (e.g. Cazden 1988). At best, small-group activities are illustrated, such as in reciprocal teaching (Palincsar & Brown 1984). Such ideal circumstances are of course the exception rather than the rule, since in most cases one teacher will have to handle 30 or more students, with educated parent volunteers being in decidedly short supply. Therefore, it is important to explore the use of scaffolding and related support structures in large classes, in the less than ideal circumstances in which most teachers have to work.

Studies discussing interaction in larger groups or whole-class activities have, as I demonstrated in the preceding chapter, insufficiently distinguished teacher-led questioning (along IRF lines) from other, more contingent types of interaction (Tharp and Gallimore's [1988] *instructional conversation* is a case in point). Useful though such descriptive studies are (see also Edwards & Mercer 1987, Rogoff 1990, Rudduck 1991), a more precise analysis is required for teachers who wish to conduct their own research in their own context.

The following extract illustrates an activity I expressly designed with pedagogical scaffolding in mind during the action-research experiment I referred to in chapter 1 (see also van Lier 1991a). Rather than setting up the OHP before class the way a well-organized teacher is supposed to do, I adapted an activity in Willis 1981, which suggested that setting up the

OHP itself might be turned into an activity. By repeating the activity (with some minor variations, sometimes including 'setting up the VCR' or 'setting up the cassette recorder' in the same format) over a number of lessons, I tried to see if this could bring out the central principles of scaffolded activities in a systematic manner.

At first I accompanied the ritual of setting up the OHP by a monolog, in which I asked myself questions such as 'Let's see, what should I do next?,' answering them myself: 'Ah, switch it on.' Gradually, in line with the principles of scaffolding, I tried to pause longer to see if students were ready to take a more active part in the activity. The extract below is about midway through the series, where one of the students is setting up the OHP in accordance with instructions and prompts by me as their teacher. There is still quite a lot of teacher control, though student participation is much greater than in the early lessons. Here is the extract:

Setting

The setting is an ESL grammar class with about ten students, all Asian. The teacher (myself, indicated here as 'T') wants to use the overhead projector (OHP), which is standing, disconnected, on a little table in a corner, and is enlisting the help of a student, S2, as well as asking other students to give directions. A broad grammar focus is practicing phrasal verbs, which has been a recurrent focus in a number of lessons.

Extract

1	T	. . . S2 . . . can you help me? . . . . . . who wants to tell S2 what to do? remember the verbs we practised last time? you all want to help him? . . . and give him some instructions? . . . . .
2	S1	((softly)) (plak it in) . . .
3	T	say it again?
4	S1	plug it in
5	T	((unintelligible)) . ahah, plug it in. okay, we'll plug it in . . . . . . plug it in. and now?.
6	S3	turn it on
7	T	turn it on .. ((to S2:)) you just do what you're told, okay, just do what they tell you . . . nonononono .. ((to S3:)) what did you tell him?
8	S3	turn it on . . . . . . turn it on
9		((click))
10	T	turn it on. okay. next?
11	S5	around
12	S3	[turn around
13	SS	[turn around//around//((unintelligible))
14	T	pardon?
15	S5	turn around
16	T	turn-..
17	S5	[around
18	T	[IT. . . around

```
19 SS                                    ((unintelligible))
20 T    turn it around
21 SS   ((unintelligible))
22      ((noise of OHP being turned around))
23 T    o:::hkay .. ya .. has he finished? is that every- what else does he have
        to do?
24 S1   focus . . .
25 S              [focus
26 T    pardon?
27 S1   focus
28 T    focus. okay. focus . . .
```

The activity illustrated here shows three different levels of scaffolding, ranging from global to local, or from 'macro' to 'micro'. It is therefore in line with Dewey's dual vision, though 'multiple vision' might be a more appropriate term. Beginning at the global level, the long-term aim is to encourage students to use a variety of phrasal verbs in instructions about how to conduct a complex activity. No specific time limit is set for this aim, rather, like the peekaboo game, the intent is to repeat it as often as seems feasible, with variations as seems advisable, with increasing student participation and control as this becomes possible. The aim is to 'pull' (without forcing) the students into an ever-expanding zone of proximal development, so that they gradually become more confident and independent language users in accordance with their growing proficiency.

Once the activity as such is conceptualized, it need not be planned every time: it illustrates a process syllabus, in that it is self-regulating, and controlled by the students' developing abilities to use the language. In the lesson plan, the only thing that needs to be done is to put in a time slot for it – 'OHP activity, 5 minutes' – or something like that. If it seems to be getting a bit stale, it can be varied by using the VCR, a tape recorder, a video camera, a computer, or any other piece of equipment that seems appropriate and that is close at hand. However, it should not be assumed that students want to have 'something different' all the time. If they are asked, they are likely to indicate that they appreciate regularity and a bit of ritual, a point I will come back to below.

The second level of scaffolding is at the level of the activity itself. During the five or so minutes that it takes, there are a number of steps that need to be gone through, especially if we want to get as much mileage out of it as possible in terms of practice (in this case, practice of phrasal verbs). The sequence of these steps can be plotted to obtain some sort of script, not unlike a script for going to a restaurant, or applying for a driving license, etc. In the case of setting up an OHP, such a script might contain the following steps:

1. Put the OHP on the table.
2. Carry or wheel it in front of the screen.
3. Pull down the screen.
4. Plug in the OHP.
5. Switch it on.
6. Put the transparency on it.
7. Focus the OHP.
8. Turn the transparency over.
9. Turn it around.

That such a script is in the mind of the teacher is clearly seen in turn 7, where I stop the student (S2) from completing actions ahead of the other students' instructions, or out of the projected sequence. After all, if S2 does not 'play the game,' the other students' opportunities for language-using will be diminished.

Finally, the activity is also scaffolded at a third, a local, interactional level. At this level the teacher decides, from moment to moment, when to prompt, help, pause, correct, and in other ways try to encourage the students' participation. This interactional scaffolding cannot be planned or scripted beforehand, since it relies on on-the-spot decision-making in reaction to often unexpected student utterances. Here the teacher tries to ensure that the activity is neither too difficult nor too easy for the students, and is intent on keeping them intersubjectively engaged. Even though it does not show up in lesson plans or syllabuses, this local or interactional scaffolding may well be the driving force behind good peda-gogy, the hallmark of a good teacher (see van Manen 1991 on *pedagogical tact*).

Pedagogical scaffolding, as illustrated here, is thus a multilayered (or at least three-layered) teaching strategy consisting of episodes, sequences of actions, and interactions which are partly planned and partly impro-vised. At every level the focus of the scaffolded activity is on an understanding of, indeed a continuous scrutinizing of, what is difficult and what is easy for the students. It allows the teacher to keep in mind, at all times, a long-term sense of direction and continuity, a local plan of action, and a moment-to-moment interactional decision-making. It is thus very much in the spirit of Dewey's vision (1904), and it is clearly an example of a focus on process rather than product.

Can everything we do in classes be conceptualized in this way? The answer most likely is no, since I believe we should see the classroom as a place where many different kinds of work and interaction need to occur (see also the previous chapter). The well-balanced lesson can, and prob-ably often should, contain a range of ways of working with language.

The balanced lesson

I mentioned above that a lesson contains both planned and improvised elements. The exact ingredients, and the precise mix of them, cannot be legislated. Every teacher needs to work them out anew in every situation, and in this resides much of what can be called the teacher's theory of practice. Seeing the classroom as a complex system (or complex adaptive system – CAS, see Stites 1994, Abraham 1994) leads us to adopt an ecological approach (J.J. Gibson 1979; see also Bowers & Flinders 1990, Best 1994).[2]

The term 'balanced' suggests that in most cases a lesson which is so tightly planned (and implemented) that there is no room at all for improvisation, and conversely, a lesson which is not planned at all and therefore entirely improvised, would generally be considered unbalanced and perhaps not terribly effective (though one must be very careful, of course, not to generalize unduly). Within each lesson, however, there might well be events or episodes (or activities, tasks, etc.) which are tightly planned or wholly improvised. Or, as in the case of the OHP task above, activities which require some planning, but also leave room for improvisation.

The issue of balance is an important one. Teachers are often evaluated on the basis of lesson plans and the implementation (according to plan) of the lessons. When things happen that are not in the plan, an evaluator might see this as a negative point: 'the lesson got out of hand,' or 'you didn't stick to the plan.' At the same time, as I have argued throughout the book, and particularly in the last chapter, social interaction, especially more contingent kinds, cannot be planned but rather must be constructed locally. On the other side of the coin, planned, recurring activities lend a certain reassuring predictability to lessons, an element of ritual which is an essential part of any culture (or subculture, if we wish to define the classroom that way). A teacher who, for the sake of spontaneity and variation, looks for new things to do all the time, and just lets things happen, may be forgetting that most students also need points of stability in lessons, and these are achieved by recycling tasks, planning certain sequences of activities in predictable ways, ritual beginnings, endings, and transitions, and so on.

For this reason it might be a good idea to design syllabuses and lessons as if they formed a small organic culture (or an ecosystem) in themselves, where participants strive to combine the expected and the unexpected, the known and the new, the planned and the improvised, in harmonious ways. Within such a flexible arrangement, there might be fertile ground for 'finding' innovations and improving one's own practices.

In Figure 24, I attempt to relate the parameter of planning and improvisation to another parameter, that of routine versus innovation. It is important to realize that both planning and improvisation can become routine, and, likewise, both can be oriented towards innovation (which can be defined as change for the better). We can plan innovation on the basis of reflection about our practice, or because of input from other sources, such as books, workshops, conversations with colleagues, and so on. On the other hand, innovation can also come about on the basis of monitored improvisation which is subsequently reflected on or talked about. Then, what started as improvisation may come under the control of planned action, thus adding to our professional stock. Routinely planned, or routine improvised behavior, however, may not be available for professional improvement, unless our awareness about what we are doing is raised in some way.

To summarize, when conceptualizing good lessons, it may be useful to strive for balance between ritual and new elements, and between planned and improvised actions. Points of stability, created by recurring activities or sequences, can give students a sense of security, and these predictable elements can become points of departure for new and unexpected activities. Recall the quote from Trevarthen & Marwick 1986 (see above, p. 52), where engagement between caretaker and child hinges on an exciting challenge departing from within a safe environment.

Form and meaning

On several occasions in this book I have commented on the tension between form and meaning, or structure and function. We came across

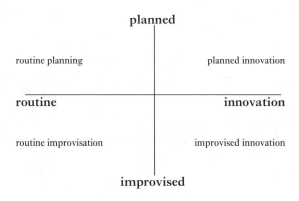

Figure 24   Planning and improvisation

this problem in chapter 3 when we briefly discussed the issue of practice (and 'malpractice'), and again in chapter 4 when we talked about meta-linguistic awareness and knowledge about language.

In practice, one of the perennial problems a teacher faces is when to address the formal properties of language, and how to do this. Most teachers have felt caught up in the periodic pendulum swings from emphasis on form to emphasis on meaning, and back again. Although in reality most proponents of communicative language teaching, for example, emphasize the need for some form of grammar teaching (see, e.g., Johnson & Morrow 1981, Savignon 1983, Littlewood 1981), their opponents often accuse them of neglecting formal features and assuming that they will take care of themselves in a context of meaningful language use (Higgs & Clifford 1982). To a certain extent this is probably true: social interaction in and of itself can probably lead to significant levels of grammaticalization (Rutherford 1987, Dittmar 1992), an assumption which is also behind the task-based work in the Bangalore project, reported by Prabhu (1987). However, we should not assume that such grammaticalization occurs by some magic force that emanates from language input.

A similar discussion takes place in the context of initial literacy between educators who are in favor of the whole-language approach (Goodman 1986) and those who favor explicit work on phoneme discrimination, e.g. the phonics approach to literacy (see chapter 4).

Finally, in the context of the National Curriculum in Great Britain, many educators discuss the need for teaching metalinguistic terminology (terms of grammar, morphology, etc.). It is difficult to see, however, what sense such discussions make in the absence of clear goals for the use of such terminology: why would it be useful, for what purpose, in order to achieve what goals? It is possible that in some cases the rationale, implicitly or explicitly, may be that such knowledge is more easily assessed, and is closely related to more traditional forms of grammar teaching with which many educators are familiar. In general, formal knowledge is easier to handle, since it is more tangible, more unequivocally assessable (in exams), and unambiguously expressible (in answers to questions).

Functional knowledge, on the other hand, is always to a certain extent intangible, translates into personal and interpersonal riches, and is manifested in contextual performance. It is therefore quite difficult to discuss, in separation from administrative criteria, the precise value of formal knowledge for an individual's language development. When discussing the sorts of things that count as *achievement*, therefore, we have to be clear about the form–meaning issue, both linguistically and politically.

I have suggested (chapters 3 and 4) that we should not let ourselves be trapped inside a dichotomy between *focus on form* and *focus on meaning*, but rather use the term *focus on language* to indicate our different attempts, as teachers and students, to look at language for the purposes of awareness-raising, practicing, appreciation, field work, and so on. The contexts, purposes, and needs of learners will decide where and how perceptual, interactional, emotional, and cognitive energies will be directed. When focusing on meaningful tasks that engage the students, we can see in many cases that in practice it becomes impossible to separate form and function neatly in the interactional work that is being carried out. Instead, all and any aspects of situated language can come under the scrutiny of learners, if this is needed to carry out the work at hand. The following extract is a good example of such focusing on language.[3] The situation is a class of civil engineering students, who are working in small groups with a diagram of a central heating system, and discussing how to write a description of the system.

	T	. . .wrote water heating, so obviously I am suggesting that water is heated should be written instead. The question is why? What's the difference? Is there a difference in meaning? If so what is the difference?
350	S6	yes.
	S8	I never heard- the first
	T	Water is heating?
	S8	I never heard about it. I never [seen such a sentence
	S10	It's a right sentence here
355	S4	It doesn't make sense anyway.
	S10	No here. Yes here it does, here.
	S6	Water is heating.
	S10	Yes
	S4	No but not here [points at the board]
360	S10	I mean not in the text but on the board it's all right. It's all right here [turns to S2]
	S6	He said he never seen.
	T	Does that make sense to you S4?
	S4	Yes.
365	S8	If you put the-[
	T	Water is heating the radiators.
	S4	But we can say water <u>heats</u> the radiators.
	S6	Yes.
	T	OK, but I- if I'm talking about right now, OK. What's the water
370		doing now? The water is heating the radiators.
	S4	Present.
	T	(You) could. I mean it's a little artificial but you could, OK?
	S8	Water is heating, it it's the one who's heating.
	T	Aha, can you explain that in a little more detail?
375	S8	Water is heating. It means water is already hot, it's giving the heat to another object. The second one it means another object is hot and that object is giving, heating water.

T   OK , so the first one, water is heating, water is actually doing
     something, here it's actually doing something to something
380 else. Ok, if you're boiling an egg, water is heating an egg for
     example.
S6   Water is heating an egg.
T   In this case we can always say here something else is
     transferring the heat.

This episode merits close study, though I cannot go into full detail here. Note, however, how the teacher begins the episode by drawing learners' attention to a problem that had surfaced in one of the groups: a disagreement about whether to write *water is heating* or *water is heated*. He is not providing an answer, but rather asking the students to clarify the problem and decide on a solution collaboratively. The result is a truly joint construction, with the teacher providing some (non-controlling) guidance and feedback, but the students arriving at a conclusion by themselves (see especially S8 in line 373). It should be clear at a glance how far this kind of interaction is removed from the IRF examples we looked at in the last chapter.

Designing and doing tasks

Designing a syllabus based on the AAA curriculum must take into account the balance between *planned* and *improvised* elements, and between *stability* and *variety*, that we noted above. A syllabus is often visually represented as a series of steps, a ladder, a spiral or series of cycles, or other metaphors indicating progression and sequence. It is essential for a syllabus based on AAA principles that it is driven by *learning* and *interaction*, in other words, that it be a true *process* syllabus (cf. Breen & Candlin 1980). How can such a syllabus be planned at all, especially if we add the requirement of learner autonomy and self-determination?[4]

In golf, as W.C. Fields told us, we have to 'keep our eye on the ball,' but the golfer of course also needs to have a pretty good idea of the destination of the ball. Dewey's dual vision, similarly, also scrutinizes here-and-now activities while at the same time keeping an eye on the long-term goal. The heart of the syllabus, following this analogy, is the moment-to-moment pedagogical interaction, but the valuing of this interaction, and the decision-making that every pedagogical moment requires, is informed by the goal that is kept firmly in mind, though perhaps at the back of the mind. These goals must be accessible to the student as well as to the teacher, indeed, they must be jointly constructed and agreed upon. If such a pedagogical infrastructure can be created, the syllabus can be constructed (co-constructed by teacher and learners) from lesson to lesson, but it will be possible to ensure that, like the building of a park or a highway, the construction proceeds according to plan. A suitable metaphor for such a syllabus is Wittgenstein's rope:

> What ties the ship to the wharf is a rope, and the rope consists of fibres, but it does not get its strength from any fibre that runs through it from one end to the other, but from the fact that there is a vast number of fibres overlapping.
> (Wittgenstein 1958a: 87)

We let go of the idea that the syllabus is designed beforehand and brought whole before the students on the first day of class. Rather, like the ropemaker, we know what we want, but at the beginning we only have a pile of raw material and no rope at all: only the knowledge that we need to make such and such a rope, and an idea of how to do it. Does this mean that we do not have to 'prepare' any more, but just go in and start doing whatever comes to mind? No, the ropemaker is well-prepared, and so should the teacher be. But it is a different kind of preparedness. Instead of being prepared with what Krashen called a 'macho syllabus' (1990; see also p. 137), the teacher comes to class with a pedagogical vision, as much pedagogical tact as possible, backed up with ample resources, and so on. The teacher should have a very 'thick' curriculum available, but perhaps only a very 'thin' syllabus.

To work in this way, nothing is ruled out, except perhaps the kinds of activities I called in chapter 3 'malpractice.' Traditional dictations, stories, chorus repetitions, role plays, all these can be resources for potential use. However, two organizational strategies stand out as being most useful for providing material for 'strands' in the 'rope': task-based and content-based language learning, and I will discuss them briefly to give some concrete suggestions for constructing the process syllabus.

Task-based (Candlin & Murphy 1987; Nunan 1989) and *content-based* (Mohan 1986, Brinton, Snow & Wesche 1989) language learning are currently popular ways of organizing the language curriculum. The former focuses on the construction, sequencing, and evaluation of particular goal-related action complexes that learners carry out either by themselves (as in Prabhu's [1987] model) or jointly (for a variety of definitions of task, see Kumaravadivelu 1993). The latter aims to integrate the teaching of content and language. This content may be subject matter that is part of an academic program, such as math or history, or it may be chosen for its interest level or perceived relevance (e.g. culture, video production, environmental issues, etc.).

Task-based and content-based language teaching really go hand in hand, since a progression of tasks without some continuity or systematicity in terms of content progression (or coherence) would lead to a very disjointed, 'scattergun' syllabus. Conversely, content-based teaching in which little or no thought has been given to the design and sequencing of tasks will be a transmission, most likely in lecture or IRF form, of lesson material (see Swain 1991 for a good discussion about this). Therefore, task and content should be seen as a unity.

There is little point in designing a syllabus around tasks unless these tasks will engage students, challenge them, and allow for contingent interaction. Ideally they should produce the kind of flow experiences studied by Csikszentmihalyi and associates. According to Csikszentmihalyi, activities with the following characteristics are likely to produce flow experiences:

1. They have concrete goals and manageable rules.
2. They make it possible to adjust opportunities for action to our capacities.
3. They provide clear information about how well we are doing.
4. They screen out distractions and make concentration possible. (Csikszentmihalyi 1993: xiv)

These features, particularly the first three: *clarity*, *flexibility*, and *feedback*, are clearly important for the design of all tasks. The fourth feature is probably in most cases a product of setting, engagement, and the learner's powers of concentration, although there may well be a number of things teachers and students can do to facilitate concentration.

Candlin (1987) suggests that tasks place three kinds of demands on learners: *learning* demands, *content* demands, and *action* demands. All three kinds of demands constrain the design and execution of tasks, and these constraints have to be matched by resources that can be marshaled from different quarters, by the students themselves, or with the help of their teacher. Recall that in Csikszentmihalyi's model (see Figure 11), the occurrence of flow requires a balance between challenges and skills. If the challenges outweigh the skills, anxiety and frustration result. If, on the other hand, the skills are ahead of the challenges, boredom will result. Effective tasks therefore do at least two things: they carefully balance the demands between learning, content and action (so that, if the demands for learning are high, familiar content may be chosen, or demands for action may be decreased, and so on for different configurations of demands), and they also build in flexibility for action, so that the performance required can be adjusted in accordance with the resources that are available.

There are many different ways in which this can be done. In teacher-led activities, such as the OHP task illustrated above, it is done by encouraging, but not forcing, participation, and by adjusting the demands placed on the learners in accordance with their own demonstrations of readiness to act. In group tasks involving interaction and negotiation, the self-regulating powers of conversation can be exploited, though we must be watchful in case excessive asymmetry destroys the flexibility that characterizes contingent interaction. In individual tasks, choices must be built in so that every student has realistic chances of success as well as appropriate challenges. By providing a variety of tasks, some teacher-led, some conducted in groups, and some individual, flexibility can to some extent be built into the syllabus. Moreover, there are many tasks (and especially also extended projects) which may involve some group work, some individual work, and even an amount of planning to decide the best way in which certain outcomes are to be pursued.

There is thus no easy answer to the need for adjusting the complexity level of tasks to learners' abilities. The more students can participate in the design, and the more they can feel in charge, experience ownership, have a sense of being in control of their own actions, the more likely it is that students will be engaged, that they will be intrinsically motivated, and that they will make choices that are in the best interest of their language development.

The complexity and selection of tasks, and the design of options for different students, depend to a large extent on how well the teacher understands the students. This is another reason why pedagogical scaffolding is beneficial for teachers: it requires constant watching and monitoring of student activity, and therefore fosters an understanding of the student's interests and abilities. However, in addition to design and selection, careful thought must be give to the *sequencing* and *progression* of tasks over the life of a course. The organizing principle of a course may be a well-specified goal, such as the establishment of a recycling program (of cans, bottles, and paper) at the school, or it may be content-related as in the case of literature, engineering, or culture. It may be long-term or short-term, or somewhere in between.

The most consistent and innovative example of sequencing tasks is probably Candlin *et al.*'s set of ELT materials called *Challenges*, which was first published in the early 1980s (Candlin & Edelhoff 1982; for some discussion, see Nunan 1989). In these materials, which include films as well as printed materials and tapes, tasks are related into *chains*, and each chain consists of several *steps*, which are tasks in themselves. Students have a large measure of choice as to how they chart their course through these chains and steps, which generally present different ways of looking at the issues presented in the films. Giving students choices and thus fostering self-determination does therefore not necessarily mean giving up all planning. On the contrary, designing a syllabus with choices is far more complex than designing one without them, but the extra effort pays off in terms of increased student commitment (see Legutke & Thomas1991 for excellent advice and detailed examples).

Materials and textbooks

Most teachers I know have a rather ambivalent attitude to language textbooks. On the one hand, it is hard to do without them (in many cases of course, you have to use them whether you like to or not, because the authorities tell you to). On the other hand, textbooks tend to severely hamper your ability to engage in innovative, exploratory teaching. For students, textbooks can provide the points of stability that, as we have seen, are an important feature of a balanced classroom. For teachers, textbooks are an objective sequencing device which, like a handrail on a steep climb, provides support and shows the way.

In the ESL course I mentioned earlier (see chapter 1, chapter 3) it had been my original intention to work without a textbook, using only scaffolded tasks and student-generated questions and problems, backed up by a small set of reference and source materials. However, it took less than a week to realize that students would be more comfortable with some sort of textbook which allowed them to do exercises in class and for homework and have a sense of progress. Reluctant to choose a full-blown ESL text series for fear that it might not allow me to explore innovative practices, I instead opted for a small, straightforward grammar practice book, the aim being to set aside a segment of class time every lesson for traditional grammar practice, but leaving enough time to do other things as well. I was hoping to emulate the teacher in extract 2 on p. 176, and use the dry grammar examples as jumping off points for conversational asides, jokes, and so on.

In this configuration, the textbook was only one strand among a number of other strands in the course. However, most full-blown textbooks aim to be the heart of the sort of all-encompassing syllabus Krashen called the 'macho syllabus' (1990; see also p. 137). In such textbooks, which exist in all subject-matter areas, not just ESL, all the material that is supposed to be 'covered' during a specific period of time is included. Modern textbooks aim to be not just comprehensive but also interesting, varied, inviting, and so on. They are full of photographs and drawings, and allusions to the types of things the authors imagine the target audience is interested in. At the same time, to be commercially viable, they must appeal to as broad a population as possible, and this requirement tends to lead to a certain blandness, and, in certain cases, to the uncritical presentation of an 'official' point of view. Thus, a major high school textbook in the US, Magruder's *American Government* (McClenaghan 1987) sets out to show how Marx was wrong when he said that, under capitalism, 'the rich would become richer and the poor, poorer.' Magruder proudly proclaims that in fact the contrary has happened: 'The economic gap between workers and owners has narrowed almost to the point of extinction, especially in the United States . . . The poor have not become poorer. They have, in fact, become much, much richer' (p.22; see also van Lier 1995a: 113).

In addition, at the school level, publishers have to ensure that their textbooks contain nothing controversial, or else particular constituencies are bound to complain and demand that the books be banned (examples of this kind of public censorship abound in the US, where even books such as *Alice in Wonderland* and *Catcher in the rye* are banned in some school districts). This often results in arcane demands and peculiar restrictions on authors, making the publication of truly interesting textbooks virtually impossible. For the development of a critical and autonomous language user, such textbooks fall therefore far short of the mark.

Where textbooks are less constrained by various political considerations, such as in the international market of EFL materials (English as a Foreign Language), it is in principle possible to produce more variety and more food for critical thought, speech, and action. However, even in such cases the various types of authenticity mentioned in chapter 6 – *curricular*, *pragmatic*, and *personal*, with their various subtypes such as *finder* and *user* authenticity – may make authentication by teachers and learners problematic. An example from a recent textbook should make this clear.

The activity shown in Figure 25 is from book 3 of the textbook series *Interchange* (Richards, Hull and Proctor, 1991: 61). Most students will find this an interesting exercise. Some choice is involved, and students can use their prior knowledge. However, the overall structure and options are laid down in the textbook. One could adapt such an exercise for the purpose of enhancing the students' engagement with the topic, of promoting critical thought and discussion, and of increasing opportunities for authentication. One could, for example, collect (or ask students to collect) information about 'celebrities' who are in the news at a given time, and for what reasons. Useful sources here are tabloids, popular magazines, TV talk shows, and so on. Students might be interested in surveying the popularity of different people according to categories such as sports, movies, music, politics, literature, and so on. They could then produce brief case-studies (or poster or multimedia presentations) of two famous people of their choice, or perhaps discuss the concept of 'fame' and its advantages and disadvantages. Perhaps students in groups can

5. Famous people

1. *Group work*   Choose two famous people from the box below. Give as much information about them as you can. One student takes notes.

Paula Abdul	Jane Fonda	Bruce Lee
Corazon Aquino	Martha Graham	Nelson Mandela
Simón Bolívar	Mikhail Gorbachev	Marcello Mastroianni
		and so on . . . another 21 names

2. *Class activity*   Groups compare information. Which group knows most about each person?

Figure 25   Activity from 'Interchange'

map out their own little investigation and report about a chosen subtopic, collecting further information from a variety of sources.

In this way (or a variety of other ways), a topic such as 'famous people' can be a source of investment and critical engagement for students. Unless topics are fleshed out in some way, the textbook encourages a superficial hopping from one interesting tidbit to the next, rather than the 'deep learning' recommended in this book (see also Stevick 1976). Further, lessons should include opportunities for students to tell each other things that are of genuine interest. When all students have seen or read exactly the same text or task, reporting on it probably lacks the freshness and enthusiasm of reporting on something students themselves have found or created.

To summarize, the AAA curriculum will require the support of textbooks (and a host of other resources), whether of the 'thin', grammar practice kind, or the 'thick' comprehensive kind, but the place of such textbooks will be less prominent and less central than in many other types of curriculum. The textbook will be merely one strand among several in the 'rope' we are weaving.

Achievement, assessment, and accountability

In their seminal paper on the communicative curriculum, Breen and Candlin (1980) argue that evaluation in such a curriculum is continuous, and built into the very procedures for carrying out communicative tasks. We can relate this view to Csikszentmihalyi's point (1990) that one of the requirements for flow activities is that they should provide clear information about how well we are doing. Communicative language use in a sense naturally does this, since we might say that if the other person hears us the way we want to be heard, or reads us the way we want to be read, then we have passed the test. In this sense, effective (and creative) language use is its own reward. In contingent interaction, its evaluation will be instantaneous, since it will be validated by the next speaker. In an ideal world, therefore, additional assessment should be superfluous.

However, we clearly do not live in an ideal world. All stakeholders in an educational enterprise have insecurities and want to be reassured that things are going OK. A learner's sense of achievement will be derived to a variable (individually and culturally variable) extent from a comparison with other learners, and in many cultures we have come to expect that this comparison be expressed in numerical terms. If such public and comparative assessments are important to the learners (and, possibly, to employers, educational administrators in charge of placement, etc.), our teaching will have to reflect this importance. If our students want to do well on the TOEFL, then we, as teachers, do not do them a service by pretending that the TOEFL does not exist. However, we may find a way to simultaneously give students a sense of communicative and creative achievement, inherently through contingent interaction, through criterion-referenced assessments of various kinds (e.g. portfolios), and through self-assessment procedures (see Brindley 1989 for a clear and highly practical discussion of various options).

The third concept in this triad is accountability. This is the other side of the coin to responsibility, since one cannot be held accountable for something one is not responsible for. The teacher (and the students as well) must be able to defend their actions against criticism. Learning to do this is part of the project of being a teacher or learner. What are the kinds of things that teachers and learners are held accountable for? In general they are physically and quantitatively measurable things, such as attendance, scores on tests, evaluations by students (of their teacher), grades given to students (by their teacher), and so on. We might prefer to be held accountable for the quality of our classroom experiences, and for the memorable occasions created there, but accountability deals in tangibles rather than intangibles.

This means that there is likely to be a conflict between the values expressed in the AAA curriculum, and the values expressed in the mechanisms by which society holds teachers and learners accountable. This conflict is a crucial part of the problems posed and addressed by the theory of practice. It takes the field of operations out of the narrow confines of the classroom, and links that classroom to the institution and the society in which it is situated. At this point, the theory of practice may well have to become a political struggle, but that would take us to a different discussion which is beyond the scope of this book.

Conclusion

In this chapter we have looked at some practical considerations of the AAA curriculum. Given the central place that interaction occupies in it, I have raised a number of questions about the kinds of interaction that may be fostered in the classroom. We do not know, at this time, what kinds of interaction are most beneficial for learning. My basic claim is that, whatever else is important, contingency is a crucial property of any interaction that has learning value. Beyond that, the relative merits of interaction among equals versus interaction between a more competent person and a less competent one (say, a teacher and a student) are unclear. In the absence of clear evidence one way or another, I recommend the heuristic strategy of aiming for a balance between various participation formats (see also van Lier 1988), while focusing on the optimization of contingency.

When a teacher sets out to design activities in the ZPD, a range of strategies that can be collectively called pedagogical scaffolding are required. In the literature, scaffolding has primarily been illustrated in one-on-one or small-group activities, but the reality of education today is such that it is necessary to find ways of scaffolding in large classes. I gave an example of a task that can be recycled indefinitely and that, like Bruner's 'peekaboo' game (1983), automatically adjusts to the level of the students' abilities. In this way the curriculum is driven by the learners' learning processes, rather than by an externally determined body of subject matter brought into the classroom to be unveiled and consumed.

In language education, a dichotomy is perennially created between *structure* and *function*, or *form* and *meaning*. Prevailing methodologies often force a choice e.g. between *phonics* and *whole language*, between *accuracy* and *fluency*, or between *correctness* and *creativity*. Using a task-based and content-based approach (these two approaches should be inseparable), and fostering contingent interaction, it becomes clear that it is unnecessary to accept this dichotomy. When students carry out tasks that have meaning for them, they will focus on language (*both* form *and* meaning) when such focusing is meaningful for them, in the context of the work in hand.

Tasks are very much in vogue these days, whether as part of a communicative curriculum in foreign language teaching, or as part of cooperative learning. Important elements to consider are appropriate *selection* (i.e. chosen from the perspective of an understanding of the students, their levels, their interests, their needs), and *continuity*. Gradually, students must learn to make choices about how to plan and conduct tasks (including field work, investigations, reports, presentations, etc.), since only then will they develop the sense of self-determination that fosters intrinsic motivation.

Finally I discussed textbooks, suggesting that there is certainly a place for them in the AAA curriculum, but that they are just one 'strand' in the 'rope' that is being woven. Lessons, as well as the syllabus as a whole, consist of a mix of planned and improvised elements. Whereas the curriculum should be 'thick,' the most useful syllabus is probably rather 'thin,' providing points of stability (ritual, predictability, and continuity), but leaving sufficient opportunities for contingent action.

Teaching from the AAA perspective (or any perspective embodying clear foundational principles) is a *project* rather than a job consisting of circumscribable skills. This means that its outcomes cannot be predicted, its constituent actions cannot be cataloged, and its assessment cannot be piecemeal.

Notes

1 For an excellent overview of Piagetian, neo–Piagetian, and social-cognitive research, see Forrester 1992, especially chapter 2.
2 J.J. Gibson 1979 is a highly influential ecological approach to visual perception. Bowers & Flinders 1990 suggest an ecological approach to teaching. Best 1994 draws on the ecological metaphor to discuss phonological development in children. See also Forrester 1992.
3 This is an extract from data collected by graduate students in English for Specific Purposes classes at the University of Lancaster (in the Institute for English Language Education) in 1981 or 1982. My files unfortunately do not contain information as to which individuals should be credited for participating in, collecting, or transcribing the data.
4 I have often been told by teachers that a process syllabus won't work because students don't know from one moment to the next what to expect: there is insufficient structure, no sense of direction, and so on. Ironically, a process syllabus which fosters self-determination will, on the contrary, be much clearer, because the students have themselves taken part in its construction, and are therefore likely to be much more aware of where they are going than if they were exposed to an externally controlled syllabus, where quite often the only person who knows where it all leads is the teacher.

9   The profession of teaching: development and research

Introduction

In this final chapter I will discuss some of the implications of working towards a curriculum like the AAA illustrated in this book. As a reminder, here are the main features of the AAA curriculum:

1. It is based on foundational principles which articulate and clarify *knowledge* and *values*.
2. It treats the language curriculum as a *theory of practice*.
3. It *integrates* insights from three sources:
   a) theory of learning
   b) theory of pedagogical interaction
   c) theory of instruction
4. It *critically* examines *resources* and *constraints* in the learning environment.
5. It regards learning as *jointly constructed* by all participants in the process, i.e. as a collaborative achievement.
6. It regards *contingent interaction* as crucial in achieving the transformations which characterize all true learning.

New pedagogical trends abound. Browsing through the pages of a handful of issues of *Educational Leadership* I come across proposed innovatory practices with names such as OBE (Outcomes-Based Education), TQM (Total Quality Management), Responsive Teaching, FCU (Fostering a Community of Learners), TFU (Teaching for Understanding), and there are a great many more. While in many cases there may be less that is unique and new in these innovations than their proponents wish to suggest, all such efforts contain much that is laudable and useful. My concern is that they end up looking *inward* rather than *outward*, attract a core of proponents and a group of devotees, develop their own small world of discourse (starting with the acronyms their names engender), and cease to grow. I fervently hope that the AAA curriculum does not join this procession, but that it promotes a way of thinking and acting that is free and autonomous, that it encourages teachers to think for themselves (rather than being told what is 'the right way' to think) and reject pigeon-holes as well as fashion trends. In this final chapter I want to look for ways in which teachers can be aware, autonomous, and authentic through development and research.

Laboratories and apprentices

John Dewey argued in 1904 that there are two sides to teacher development, one which stresses practical work, the tools of the profession, techniques of instruction, management skills, and another which stresses that practical work is based on solid knowledge (and 'intellectual control,' [1904: 144]) of subject matter and an understanding of educational principles. The former he termed the *apprenticeship* approach, the latter the *laboratory* approach. Too much and too early a focus on apprenticeship puts, in Dewey's opinion, 'the attention of the student-teacher in the wrong place. and tends to fix it in the wrong direction' (1904: 147). Dewey's argument is best summed up in his own words:

> There is a technique of teaching, just as there is a technique of piano-playing. The technique, if it is to be educationally effective, is dependent upon principles. But it is possible for a student to acquire outward form of method without capacity to put it to genuinely educative use. As every teacher knows, children have an inner and an outer attention. The inner attention is the giving of the mind without reserve or qualification to the subject in hand. As such, it is a fundamental condition of mental growth . . . It means insight into soul action, ability to discriminate the genuine from the sham, and capacity to further one and discourage the other.
>
> External attention, on the other hand, is that given to the book and the teacher as an independent object. It is manifested in certain conventional postures and physical attitudes rather than in the movement of thought . . . Now the teacher who is plunged prematurely into the pressing and practical problem of keeping order in the schoolroom has almost of necessity to make supreme the matter of external attention. (Dewey 1904: 148–9)

It takes time to develop the ability to do 'two or three distinct things simultaneously':

> – skill to see the room as a whole while hearing one individual in one class recite, of keeping the program of the day and, yes, of the week and the month in the fringe of consciousness while the work of the hour is in its center. (Dewey 1904: 148)

The AAA curriculum aims to make the inherent tension between apprenticeship and laboratory (or, to use terms more relevant in our time, between *technical* and *critical* concerns) part of an ongoing research process in a theory of practice. Edmund Sullivan offers a useful model to express the 'dialectical tension between socialization and transformation' (1990: 62). It is important to point out that this tension should not be one that we aim to dissolve (since that would be both impossible and useless), but rather one that we should *nurture* (Sullivan speaks of 'dialectical integration,' [1990: 61]; see also Bakhtin's struggle between centrifugal and centripetal forces in discourse, discussed in chapter 7). In diagram form, Sullivan puts the central questions as shown in Figure 26.[1]

To see the curriculum (and one's theory of practice) as a *project*, rather than as an objective body of knowledge that determines how practical syllabuses are drawn up, allows us as teachers to shift the focus away from an exclusive or excessive concern with the technical aspects of teaching, and towards a perspective in which the critical context of our work becomes central (without, of course, neglecting the technical side). In making this shift, teaching must acquire a research dimension in the sense advocated by Stenhouse (1975), and the implicit theories that we all have must be made explicit (Widdowson 1990), so that they can be examined and developed.

Habitus	Project
How does culture reproduce itself? Another way of putting the question is to ask: How does the personal world become integrated into a larger cultural world so as to reproduce (socialize) that world in the new generation?	How does culture transform or change itself? Another way of putting the question is to ask: How is the personal world changed by new interactions that move away from the past so as to change the culture (transform) in some essential characteristics?

Within this basic distinction, Sullivan identifies seven polarities (p. 61) which a theory of practice seeks to integrate dialectically:

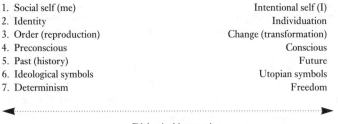

1. Social self (me)	Intentional self (I)
2. Identity	Individuation
3. Order (reproduction)	Change (transformation)
4. Preconscious	Conscious
5. Past (history)	Future
6. Ideological symbols	Utopian symbols
7. Determinism	Freedom

Dialectical integration

Figure 26 Habitus and project

Research and reflection

It is useful to place teacher research in the context of educational research in general. We may ask questions such as WHO? WHAT? HOW LONG? WHERE? and WHY? In terms of the WHO? question, we can distinguish basically between three types of research: that done by academics alone (perhaps on-site, with passive collaboration – as subjects – of teachers and students), research that is done by academics and teachers in active collaboration, and research done by teachers on their own (or together with other teachers or students). We may further specify a type of research that is done by teachers, either on their own or in collaboration with academics or other teachers, called *action research*. Finally, we can discuss the less obvious status (as research) of reflection, as an integral part of professional practice. These various types of research modalities are shown in Figure 27. The continuum from reflection to research is one of increasing systematicity and sharpening of questions, as well as documentation and diffusion. Reflection (Zeichner 1983) or pedagogical thoughtfulness (van Manen 1991) is part of every teacher's professional activity. The daily demands of teaching are such that it is difficult to step back and think about what is going on or why certain things happened. It is easy to feel that one is 'missing in action', to adapt a phrase of Lee Shulman (1987), a condition that is conducive neither to purposeful action nor to peace of mind (the opposite condition, being 'lost in thought', may provide more peace of mind, but it may come at the expense of efficient practice).

There are two problematic aspects of reflection which make it difficult to adopt a reflective stance in one's teaching, and to teach such a stance to beginning teachers: the *time* for reflection, and the *content* of reflection. In some situations, teachers are given time for planning (e.g. the

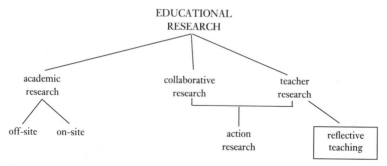

Figure 27 Educational research

'prep period' in the US), but nowhere is time officially set aside for reflection. Further, staff development (or INSET – inservice training) sessions are occasions where new information and strategies are discussed, rather than occasions for reflecting with colleagues about the practice and meanings of pedagogical experiences (van Manen 1991: 99). One of the major challenges in education is to create spaces and opportunities for reflection. Otherwise it will be an activity which only the most inquiring minds among teachers will persistently engage in, while driving home from work or doing the dishes, not perhaps the most congenial of arrangements.

The next question concerns the *content* of the reflecting, or what it is that the reflective teacher is advised to reflect *about*, and why. A basic distinction that can be made, parallel to the technical/critical distinction above, is between practical classroom experiences on the one hand, and the wider institutional or sociopolitical context on the other. I argued earlier (see chapter 2) that, within the AAA curriculum, classroom research must have a critical dimension, if only because it is impossible, in most circumstances, to separate what goes on in class from what goes on elsewhere in the world of students and teachers. There are many different constraints operating in the teaching context, both inside and outside the class, and in order to systematically explore the resources that may be available, these constraints, and the connections between them, must be investigated thoroughly. Figure 28 gives a few simple examples of how such connections might operate.

Van Manen describes four different types of reflection that address different concerns:

1. *Anticipatory reflection*: deliberating about possible alternatives, planning and preparing for future action.
2. *Active* or *interactive reflection* (reflection-in-action): 'stop-and-think' reflection allowing us to make moment-to-moment decisions; thinking 'on your feet'.

	Constraints	Resources
Classroom (micro) technical, managerial	• class size • discipline	• cooperative learning • intrinsic motivation
Social (macro) critical, political, economic	• administrative control • budget cuts	• support groups • networking • grants

Figure 28   Constraints and Resources in research

3. *Mindfulness*: a level of action (similar to Csikszentmihalyi's flow experience) which distinguishes the tactful pedagogue from mere technically proficient action.
4. *Recollective reflection*: making sense of past experiences. (van Manen 1991: 101)

Action research and politics

I mentioned above that one of the types of educational research conducted by teachers is action research. On p. 31 I briefly introduced action research in relation to classroom research, saying that such research may address either practical issues or the critical context of educational work. As I pointed out, research that starts out to address a circumscribed problem that appears to have no wider implications, may yet require critical investigation if continuing questions are asked. This is an important point, since the movement from technical to critical concerns may require a conscious step across a threshold that may seem more like a leap into the abyss to some, and many teacher researchers may shy away from going beyond the solution of superficial classroom problems. Teachers may feel that they shouldn't mess with politics or administrative issues, they may feel that they shouldn't 'make waves' (as one teacher told me who decided to quit on a project she had started a year before). Professionalism may be defined narrowly as having to do only with issues of classroom teaching and syllabus implementation, rather than with issues of educational infrastructure and policy. On the other hand, if professionalism is defined more broadly to include these latter issues, then stepping across the threshold from technical to critical research is inevitable.

This same point is made by Stenhouse, who argues that 'a limited role and limited autonomy [is not] a satisfactory basis for educational advance' (1975: 144). Similarly, McNiff warns the action researcher that 'politics will intrude,' and elaborates:

> Action research is political, in that it is to do with change. Often an individual researcher will find himself at odds with the established system . . . This is a cautionary note: that opposition will come the way of the action researcher who goes public. People are usually afraid of change and will often resist it by whatever means they have available. Action research needs teachers of courage. (McNiff 1988: 72)

One dichotomy the action researcher has to deal with is thus the *technical/non-political* versus *critical/political* one. Another dichotomy which intersects with the first is the dichotomy of *practice/improvement* versus *theory/knowledge*. John Elliott, who otherwise fully endorses the critical dimension of action research, remarks that 'the fundamental aim of action research is to improve practice rather than to produce knowledge' (1991: 49).[2] Clearly, my proposals for seeing the AAA curriculum as a theory of practice (see chapter 2) will not accept a separation of territories or domains of action between practice and knowledge (or theory). The production of knowledge and the improvement of practice are not separate goals between which a researcher needs to choose. To use an analogy, when we play a game with friends, say, soccer or tennis, we do not have to choose between the objectives of 'having fun' or 'getting some exercise'. These (and potentially other) goals are both addressed, inseparably and organically, in the activity of playing the game. In the theory of practice, one cannot improve practice without critical knowledge, and one cannot increase knowledge without critical practice. An assumption of separability of practice from knowledge is part of the dominant view of what scientific activity is (or *should be*), and of how its component activities must be selectively distributed among various constituencies with resulting differentials in power distribution. As I have repeatedly stressed, it is precisely this orthodox view that must be challenged.

Action research (or teacher research in general) can thus be visualized as occurring at the cross-section of two dichotomies between which the research mediates: the practice/theory dichotomy, and the technical/critical dichotomy.[3]

Comments from teachers engaged in action research clearly show how practice and theory, improvement and knowledge, are an organic unity in teacher research. A few relevant quotes follow.

> Experienced teacher-researchers stated that their research brought them many personal and professional benefits, including increased collegiality, a sense of empowerment, and increased self-esteem. Teacher-researchers viewed themselves as being more open to change, more reflective, and better informed than they had been when they began their research. They now saw themselves as experts in their field who were better problem solvers and more effective teachers with fresher attitudes toward education. They also saw strong connections between theory and practice. (Bennett 1993: 69)

> Teacher research again had led to new knowledge, changed instructional practice, involved students in reflecting on their own learning, and encouraged colleagues to learn from one another. (Johnson 1993: 68)

> Another unforeseen aspect of my job exchange was the opportunity for reflection. Unlike at schools, where teachers have no common office space, the consultants' offices encouraged collegial reflection. As I read something that excited me, I often popped next door to get input from my peers, who were often able to shed new light on the topic. From these experiences, my knowledge also deepened. (Lier & Bufe 1993: 27)

The main thing wrong with the world of education is that there's this one group of people who do it – and then there's another group who think they know about it – the researchers . . . Teachers are the ones who do it and, therefore, are the ones who know about it. (Meek 1991: 34)

As anyone who has tried working with language and gender – or any gender issue – will verify, such work can be difficult and sensitive. On several occasions students have been quite hostile to the idea of discussing the issue, and such hostility is as likely to come from girls as from boys . . . If we want to remove some of the barriers that exist, the language we use is a powerful tool. (Jacqueline Barnfield, in Bain *et al.* 1992: 54)

I have achieved a greater awareness of what is going on in my own classroom. I am now less concerned about the potential hazards of the still political debate on knowledge about language. (Karen Hill, in Bain *et al.* 1992: 29)

Some examples of teacher research

In this section I will enumerate and describe very briefly a few projects that are loosely based on personal experience, conversations at conferences, reports in the literature, and so on. Good sources of first-hand examples are Nixon 1982, Bain *et al.* 1992, and McNiff 1992.

1. Two teachers decide to observe each other's classes on a regular basis, using some form of a peer-coaching 'contract', where they agree beforehand what to focus on, and subsequently discuss their observations and reactions. As they proceed they find that new questions emerge, and old questions are sharpened, leading to the design of new projects.

2. A consultant (for a local education authority) and a teacher switch jobs for a year and document their experiences. Both find that their new role adds enormous insight to their regular job.

3. A group of foreign language teachers obtain a grant to communicate with each other over E-mail about innovations they start in their classrooms in listening comprehension, reading and writing instruction. They wish to document how they can generate and exchange ideas and thereby enhance professional development through interaction. One idea leads to another and they soon find that their communications create a momentum and a climate of innovation. Their newfound familiarity with E-mail also leads them to use this technology in their classes with the students.

4. A group of ESL teachers in the rural Midwest of the US form a consortium to discuss the problems of their work: part-time jobs involving traveling from school to school, lack of resources, no classroom or space of their own, no health insurance, and so on. Their discussions address issues of pedagogical practice as well as plans to improve their working

conditions. They develop a concrete plan and present it to the School District, with positive results.

5. Two teachers in a secondary school, one who teaches Spanish as a second language, and another who teaches English as a second language, decide to combine their classes and do reciprocal teaching for part of the week, where Spanish-speaking and English-speaking students are paired to teach each other.

The results of education: achievement and assessment

There are two distinct trends in people's perceptions about what constitutes 'good' education. It is likely that these trends have coexisted for as long as there has been formal education of any sort, though the issues may be more acute and controversial now than they have been during most of history. The first trend is the familiar one of public measurement and comparison, using standardized tests that are applied across the board to the applicable population, the numerical results of which are then published to illustrate how well or badly a given group has fared by comparison with other groups before them, or other groups elsewhere. In this way, students in the US are continually faced with figures showing that they are far behind their counterparts in Japan (and most other countries). Schools are compared as well, and proposals are made to somehow link public funding for schools to their scores on tests. Some policy-makers (or politicians, newspaper columnists, and others who feel they have advice to give in these matters) also suggest from time to time that teachers receive higher or lower pay depending on their students' combined performance on the ruling generation of tests.

The key word is that everyone must be held *accountable* for their performance, i.e. for the results of their activities. However, the way these results are documented does not address the things that are of most and lasting value in education: the quality of learning experiences, habits of critical thinking, clarity of expression and creativity, personal and professional fulfillment, and the ability to continue learning for the rest of one's life. Instead, students, teachers, schools, and entire countries are evaluated on the basis of numerical scores on multiple-choice tests which measure itemized and ephemeral pieces of knowledge, items unconnected to anything but the test itself, and forgotten as soon as the test is over. In addition, they are measured, via awards for 'good citizenship', levels of discipline and good order, and absence of undesirable incidents, on their level of achieved docility. Thirdly they are measured on their ability to be employed, with little regard for the human quality of the job, or its ability to afford a decent living (it is noteworthy that, in recent years, any report of increases in jobs available is accompanied by a decrease in the average level of pay for those jobs; it is not surprising that measurements of job satisfaction have suffered a concurrent decline). The more importance policy-makers attach to such manufactured measures, and the more such measures influence subsequent social and economic benefits, the more we will see that the test will determine the teaching. Instruction becomes test-driven instruction (see Madaus & Kellaghan 1992 for insightful discussion on such 'high-stakes testing').

Measurement of results, indicators of success, and signs of progress are thus statistically manufactured to favor certain outcomes over others, outcomes determined by political forces and those interested in a perpetuation of the *status quo*. In this climate, achievement equals such things as 'an A for math' or '500 on the TOEFL,' rather than more intrinsic achievements such as a desire to learn more, increased curiosity, confidence in one's abilities, a greater awareness of values and social issues, and so on. Of course, these latter qualities are hard to measure in terms of the mechanisms to which we have become accustomed, but that should not be an excuse to perpetuate the kinds of evaluation we now have.

The second trend, then, is one which, instead of breaking down education into measurable objectives, outcomes, or competencies, attempts to document the less tangible but more basic (and long-lasting) qualities of education. This approach focuses on the students' creation of portfolios (see H. Gardner 1991, who also calls them 'process-folios'), students' project reports and presentations, narrative evaluations by teachers (instead of letter grades), and other forms of so-called 'authentic assessment' (see *Educational Leadership*, May 1992, April 1993; Darling-Hammond & Ancess 1994). In the first, the 'measurement trend', qualities such as autonomy, ethical standards, and critical thinking, are turned into *epiphenomena*, presumed byproducts of test scores, simply because they do not lend themselves to the preferred forms of mass measurement. In authentic assessment, or assessment of authentic achievement, these intangible qualities will have to become the substance of assessment, and judgments of accountability, and performance on SATs, GREs, TOEFLs, Cambridge exams, and so on, will have to be seen as no more than the trivial pursuits they really are.[4] Assessment therefore will have to be *instruction-driven*, rather than vice versa (see Madaus & Kellaghan 1992).

It is clear that in the AAA curriculum assessment should be instruction-driven. Moreover, given the insistence on intrinsic motivation and self-determination, not to speak of the fostering of an authentic person, there should ideally be no room for grades or coerced work in such a curriculum (Kohn 1993). As teachers we should be able to say to our students, as Dr Shevek said to his in Ursula Leguin's science fiction novel *The dispossessed*: 'Well of course, if you do not want to do the work, you should not do it' (1974: 103). I expect that few among us are actually able to say this quite seriously, but I think it is beneficial for all of us to *imagine* saying it and to think of the attendant conditions and consequences surrounding such a statement, as a thought experiment. Why can't we say it? What would happen if we did?

The time that we will be able to do away with mass evaluations yielding numerical scores is surely far away. However, it is important to find ways of not letting such tests dominate our teaching. Portfolio assessment, in which learners have a significant say in the content and assembly of the material presented for assessment, is certainly a step in the right direction (Darling-Hammond & Ancess 1994). It allows learners to create a dossier of their work that should be of lasting value to them, and that they can defend against critical questioning. This may be done through a presentation to a committee consisting of teachers and others, perhaps including peers, as illustrated in Darling-Hammond & Ancess 1994, who describe the portfolio system as the creation of 'a corpus of high-quality work, . . . especially conducive to the development of sustained habits of thought and work'. They continue:

> They [the portfolios] demand that students organize their time and their thoughts; commit to an in-depth process of inquiry, critique, and reflection on a variety of topics and on their own work; acknowledge and participate in standard-setting; and find their own voice in the process. (Darling-Hammond & Ancess 1994: 6)

In spite of its advantages, portfolio assessment is not a panacea: it does not substitute for a sustained process approach to language education, but it is much more in harmony with such teaching (though we should beware of 'teaching to the portfolio' just as much as we used to be of 'teaching to the test', as one teacher comments in Darling-Hammond & Ancess 1994), and it is likely to provide more of a sense of ownership in the learners than tests arriving in envelopes from far away.

Conclusion

On reaching the end of the book, I would like to return to the questions I started out with. What kinds of theoretical and practical issues are relevant in a language curriculum? How can knowledge and values be brought in balanced view? What are the true aims of education, and what role does language play?

It has been my aim to present at one and the same time a highly theoretical (and philosophical) and an eminently practical view of the AAA curriculum, with the special purpose of showing how theory and practice, and ideals and reality, do not have to be mutually exclusive. I have not traced a detailed method, or a catalog of techniques, that anyone might be able to master through diligent study and practice. Nor have I wished to suggest a new theory, model, or movement that the reader can join or reject. Rather, it was my aim to suggest that as teachers we become aware and think for ourselves, as well as interact with our peers, for the purposes of developing our own curriculum, and becoming aware, autonomous, and authentic professionals. If we are committed to doing that, then it is likely that we will also foster the same qualities in our students.

Notes

1 Habitus is a central construct in the work of Pierre Bourdieu. It is hard to define (Bourdieu would probably say that it is pointless to define it), but it refers roughly to dispositions, perceptions, attitudes, and patterns of action, that are regular but not consciously coordinated or governed by rational rules, and that are acquired through experience, and adaptable to specific situations, a 'feel for the game,' as Bourdieu often calls it (see, e.g., Bourdieu 1990).

2 Elliott's statement, in slightly edited form, would actually summarize the theory of practice quite well: 'The fundamental aim of scientific research is to improve human practices rather than to produce knowledge for its own sake.' As it is, however, it defines action research in the terminology of dominant scientific orthodoxy.

3 The micro/macro distinction would add a third dimension.

4 This would not necessarily diminish their popularity, indeed, it might enhance their attraction, if America's fascination with the 'spelling bee' is anything to go by. So far as I know, there are no 'portfolio bees' or 'critical thinking bees', even though these aspects of education are clearly far more important than the ability to spell obscure words.

References

Abraham, A. 1994 *Chaos, Gaia, Eros*. New York: Harper Collins.

Adair-Hauck, B. and Donato, R. 1994 Foreign language explanations within the zone of proximal development. The Canadian Modern Language Review/La Revue Canadienne des langues vivantes **50** (3): 533–57.

Allwright, D. 1988 *Observation in the language classroom*. London: Longman.

Allwright, D. and Bailey, K. 1991 *Focus on the language classroom*. Cambridge: Cambridge University Press.

Anderson, J. R. 1982 *Acquisition of cognitive skill*. Psychological Review, **89** (4): 369–406.

Anderson, J. R. 1983 *The architecture of cognition*. Cambridge, MA: Harvard University Press.

Apel, K-O. 1981 *Charles S. Peirce: From pragmatism to pragmaticism*. Amherst, MA: University of Massachusetts Press.

Ardener, E. 1989 *The voice of prophecy*. Oxford: Basil Blackwell.

Armstrong, D. M. and Malcolm, N. 1984 *Consciousness and causality*. Oxford: Basil Blackwell.

Arnold, M. B. 1960 *Emotion and personality, Vol. 1: Psychological aspects*. New York: Columbia University Press.

Atkinson, J. B. and Heritage, J. (eds) 1984 *Structures of social action*. Cambridge: Cambridge University Press.

Auer, P. 1991 Introduction: John Gumperz' approach to contextualization. In Auer, P. and di Luzio, A. (eds) *The contextualization of language*: 1–37. Amsterdam: John Benjamins.

Austin, J. L. 1962 *How to do things with words*. Oxford: Oxford University Press.

Bailey, K. M. 1983 Competitiveness and anxiety in adult second language learning: Looking *at* and *through* the diary studies. In Seliger, H. W. and Long, M. H. (eds) *Classroom-oriented research in second language acquisition*.: 67-102. Rowley, MA: Newbury House.

Bain, R., Fitzgerald, B. and Taylor, M. (eds) 1992 *Looking into language: Classroom approaches to knowledge about language*. London: Hodder & Stoughton.

Bakhtin, M. M. 1981 *The dialogical imagination*. Austin: The University of Texas Press.

Barnes, D. 1976 *From communication to curriculum*. Harmondsworth: Penguin.

Bateson, G. 1972 *Steps to an ecology of mind*. London: Granada.

Beebe, L. 1988 Five sociolinguistic approaches to second language acquisition. In L. Beebe (ed), *Issues in second language acquisition*. Rowley, MA: Newbury House.

Bell, A. 1984 Language style as audience design. *Language in society*, 13, 145-204.

Bellack, A. A., Kliebard, H. M., Hyman, R. T. and Smith, F. I. 1966 *The language of the classroom*. New York: Teachers' College Press.

Bem, D. 1972 Self-perception theory. In Berkowitz, L. (ed) *Advances in experimental social psychology*. Vol. 6: 1–62. New York: Academic Press.

Bennett, C. K. 1993 Teacher-researchers: All dressed up and no place to go? *Educational Leadership* 51, 2, 69–70.

Berlak, A. and Berlak, H. 1981 *Dilemmas of schooling*. London: Methuen

Berlyne, D. E. 1950 Novelty and curiosity as determinants of perceptual curiosity in the rat. *Journal of Comparative and Physiological Psychology* 48: 238-46.

Best, C. T. 1994 The emergence of native-language phonological influences in infants: A perceptual assimilation model. In Goodman, J. C. and Nusbaum, H. C. (eds) *The development of speech perception: The transition from speech sounds to spoken words*: 167–224. Cambridge, MA: MIT.

Bialystok, E. 1990 *Communication strategies: A psychological analysis of second-language use*. Oxford: Basil Blackwell.

Birdsong, D. 1989 *Metalinguistic performance and interlinguistic competence*. Berlin: Springer-Verlag.

Bolinger, D. 1980 *Language: The loaded weapon*. London: Longman.

Bourdieu, P. 1990 *The logic of practice*. Stanford: Stanford University Press.

Bourdieu, P. 1991 *Language and symbolic power*. Cambridge, MA: Harvard University Press.

Bourdieu, P. and Passeron, J. C. 1977 *Reproduction in education, society and culture*. London: Sage.

Bowers, C. A. and Flinders, D. J. 1990 *Responsive teaching: An ecological approach to classroom patterns of language, culture, and thought*. New York: Teachers College Press.

Breen, M. 1985 Authenticity in the language classroom. *Applied Linguistics*, 6 (1): 60–70.

Breen, M. and Candlin, C. N. 1980 The essentials of a communicative curriculum in language teaching. *Applied Linguistics*, 1 (1): 89–112.

Brindley, G. 1989 Assessing achievement in the learner-centered curriculum. Sydney: NCELTR, Macquarie University.

Brinton, D. M., Snow, M. A. and Wesche, M. B. 1989 *Content-based second language instruction*. New York: Newbury House.

Brown, A. 1987 Metacognition, executive control, self-regulation, and other mysterious mechanisms. In Weinert, F. E. and Kluwe, R. H. (eds) *Metacognition, motivation, and understanding*: 65–116. Hillsdale, NJ: Lawrence Erlbaum Associates.

Brown, G. and Yule, G. 1983a *Discourse analysis*. Cambridge: Cambridge University Press.

Brown, G. and Yule, G. 1983b *Teaching the spoken language*. Cambridge: Cambridge University Press.

Bruce, B. 1991 The discourses of inquiry: Pedagogical challenges and responses. Paper presented at the conference: *Literacy, Identity, and Mind*, University of Michigan, Ann Arbor, October 1991.

Brumfit, C. 1991 Language awareness in teacher education. In James, C. and Garrett, P. (eds), *Language awareness in the classroom*: 24–39 London: Longman.

Bruner, J. 1963 *The process of education*. New York: Vintage Books.

Bruner, J. 1983 *Child's talk: Learning to use language*. New York: Norton.

Bruner, J. 1986 *Actual minds, possible worlds*. Cambridge, MA: Harvard University Press.

Bruner, J. 1990 *Acts of meaning*. Cambridge, MA: Harvard University Press.

Bruner, J. and Haste, H. 1987 *Making sense: The child's construction of the world*. London: Methuen.

Büchler, J. 1955 *Philosophical writings of Peirce*. New York: Dover Books.

Burrell, K. 1991 *Knowledge about language*. Walton-on-Thames: Nelson.

Butzkamm, W. 1980 Verbal play and pattern practice. In Felix, S. (ed) *Second language development: Trends and issues*: 233–48. Tübingen: Günther Narr.

Candlin, C. N. 1987 Towards task-based language learning. In Candlin, C. N. and Murphy, D. F. (eds) *Language learning tasks*: 5–22. Lancaster Practical Papers in English Language Education, Vol.7. Englewood Cliffs, NJ: Prentice-Hall.

Candlin, C. N. 1993 Probelmatising authenticity: Whose texts for whom?. Paper presented at the TESOL Convention 1993, Atlanta.

Candlin, C. N., Burton, J. and Coleman, H. 1980 Dentist-patient communication. University of Lancaster Department of Linguistics and Modern English Language/Institute for English Language Education: Report for The General Dental Council.

Candlin, C. N. and Edelhoff, C. 1982 *Challenges: Teacher's guide*. London: Longman.

Candlin, C. N. and Murphy, D. (eds) 1987 *Language learning tasks*. Lancaster Practical Papers in English Language Education, Vol.7. Englewood Cliffs, NJ: Prentice-Hall.

Carroll, L. 1991. *The complete Sylvie and Bruno*. San Francisco: Mercury House. (First published 1889 and 1893)

Carter, R. (ed) 1982. *Linguistics and the teacher*. London: Routledge & Kegan Paul.

Carter, R. A. (ed) 1990. *Knowledge about language and the curriculum: The LINC reader*. London: Hodder and Stoughton.

Carter, R. 1992. Language in the National Curriculum. Presentation at Thames Valley University, Ealing, London.

Carter, R. and McCarthy, M. 1994 *Language as discourse*. London: Longman.

Cathcart, R. L. 1989 Authentic discourse and the survival English curriculum. *TESOL Quarterly*, **23** (1), 105–26.

Cazden, C. B. 1976 Play with language and metalinguistic awareness: One dimension of language experience. In Bruner, J. S., Jolly, A. and Sylva, K. (eds), *Play: Its role in development and evolution*. Harmondsworth: Penguin.

Cazden, C. B. 1988 *Classroom discourse: The language of teaching and learning*. Portsmouth, NH: Heinemann.

Cazden, C. B. 1992 *Whole language plus: Essays on literacy in the United States and New Zealand*. New York: Teachers College Press.

Chafe, W. 1994 *Discourse, consciousness, and time*. Chicago: University of Chicago Press.

Chaudron, C. 1988 *Second language classrooms: Research on teaching and learning*. Cambridge: Cambridge University Press.

Chomsky, N. 1988 *Language and problems of knowledge*. Cambridge, MA: MIT.

Churchland, P. M. 1988 *Matter and consciousness* (revised edition). Cambridge, MA: MIT.

Cizek, G. J. 1993 On the disapearance of standards. *Education Week*, **XIII**, 10, Nov. 10, 1993, p.24.

Clarke, M. 1983 The scope of approach, the importance of method, and the nature of techniques. In Alatis, J. E., Stern, H. H. and Strevens, P. (eds) *Georgetown University Round Table on Languages and Linguistics*: 106–115. Washington, DC: Georgetown University Press.

Cohen, L. and Manion, L. 1985 *Research methods in education*. London: Croom Helm.

Cole, M. 1990 Cultural psychology: A once and furture discipline? In Berman, J. J. (ed) *Cross-cultural perspectives*. Nebraska Symposium on Motivation, 1989: 280–335. Lincoln, Nebraska: University of Nebraska Press.

Corder, S. Pit 1981 *Error analysis and interlanguage*. Oxford: Oxford University Press.

Corson, D. 1990 *Language policy across the curriculum*. Clevedon: Multilingual Matters.

Crookes, G. 1993 Action research for second language teachers – It's not just teacher research. *Applied Linguistics* **14** (2): 130–144.

Crookes, G. and Schmidt, R. 1991. Motivation: Reopening the research agenda. *Language Learning*. 41: 469–512.

Csikszentmihalyi, M. 1985 Emergent motivation and the evolution of the self. In Kleiber, D. A. and Maehr, M. L. (eds) *Motivation and adulthood. Advances in motivation and achievement, Vol 4*: 93–120. Greenwich, Conn.: LAI Press Inc.

Csikszentmihalyi, M. 1990 *Flow: The psychology of optimal experience*. New York: Harper & Row.

Csikszentmihalyi, M. 1993 *The evolving self: A psychology for the third millennium*. New York: Harper Collins.

Csikszentmihalyi, M. and Rathunde 1993 In Jacobs, J. E. (ed) *Developmental perspectives on motivation*. Nebraska Symposium on Motivation, 1992: 57–97. Volume 40. Lincoln, Nebraska: University of Nebraska Press.

Cummins, J. 1989 *Empowering minority students*. Sacramento, CA: California Association for Bilingual Education.

Damasio, A. 1994 *Descartes' error: Emotion, reason, and the human brain*. New York: The Putnam Publishing Group.

Darling-Hammond, L. and Ancess, J. 1994 *Graduation by portfolio at Central Park East Secondary School*. New York: The National Center for Restructuring Education, Schools, and Teaching (NCREST).

Davidson, D. 1986 A nice derangement of epitaphs. In LePore, E. (ed) *Truth and interpretation: Perspectives on the philosophy of Donald Davidson*: 433–46. Oxford: Basil Blackwell.

Dawkins, R. 1976 *The selfish gene*. Oxford: Oxford University Press.

Deci, E. L. 1971 Effects of externally motivated rewards on intrinsic motivation. *Journal of Personality and Social Psychology*, 18, 105–15.

Deci, E. L. and Ryan, R. M. 1985 *Intrinsic motivation and self-determination in human behavior*. New York: Plenum Press.

Deci, E. L. and Ryan, R. M. 1991. A motivational approach to self: Integration in personality. In Dienstbier, R. A. (ed) *Perspectives on motivation*. Nebraska Symposium on Motivation, 1990. Vol 38. Lincoln: University of Nebraska Press. pp.237–88.

Deci, E. L and Ryan, R. M. 1992 The initiation and regulation of intrinsically motivated learning and achievement. In Boggiano, A. K. and Pittman, T. S. (eds) *Achievement and motivation: A social-developmental perspective*. Cambridge: Cambridge University Press. pp. 9–36.

Deci, E. L., Vallerand, R. J., Pelletier, L. G. and Ryan, R. M. 1991 Motivation and education: The self-determination perspective. *Educational Psychologist*, **26**, (3 and 4), 325–46.

Dennett, D. 1991 *Consciousness explained*. London: Allen Lane.

Department of Education and Science 1975 *A language for life (The Bullock Report)*. London: HMSO.
Department of Education and Science 1988 *The Kingman report* . London: HMSO.
Dewey, J. 1904 The relation of theory to practice in education. *Third Yearbook*, Part 1 (pp. 9–30). Bloomington, Il: National Society for the Study of Education.
Dewey, J. 1938 *Experience and education*. London: Collier Books.
Dittmar, N. 1992 Grammaticalization in second language acquisition: Introduction. *Studies in Second Language Acquisition* 14, (3): 249–57.
Donato, R. and Adair-Hauck, B. 1992 Discourse perspectives on formal instruction. *Language Awareness* 1, (2): 73–89.
Donmall, B. G. (ed) 1985 *Language awareness*: NCLE Reports and Papers. London: CILT.
Dörnyei, Z. 1994 Motivation and motivating in the foreign language classroom. *The Modern Language Journal* (78)(iii): 273–84.
Drew, P. and Heritage, J. (eds) 1992 *Talk at work: Interaction in institutional settings*. Cambridge: Cambridge University Press.
Duff, A. 1989 *Translation*. Oxford: Oxford University Press.
Educational Leadership, May 1992 *Using performance assessment*. Alexandria, VA: ASCD.
Educational Leadership, April 1993 *Authentic learning*. Alexandria, VA: ASCD.
Edwards, D. and Mercer, N. 1987 *Common knowledge: The development of understanding in the classroom*. London: Routledge.
Eisner, E. 1991 *The enlightened eye: Qualitative inquiry and the enhancement of educational practice*. New York: Macmillan.
Elliott, J. 1991 *Action research for educational change*. Milton Keynes: Open University Press.
Ellis, R. 1985 *Understanding second language acquisition*. Oxford: Oxford University Press.
Ellis, R. 1988 The role of practice in classroom language learning. *Revue de l'AILA/AILA Review* 5: 20–39.
Ellis, R. 1992 On the relationship between formal practice and second language acquisition. *Die Neueren Sprachen* 91: 131–47.
Ellis, R. 1994 *The study of second language acquisition*. Oxford: Oxford University Press.
Fairclough, N. 1989 *Language and power*. London: Longman.
Fairclough, N. (ed)1992a *Critical language awareness*. London: Longman.
Fairclough, N. 1992b *Discourse and social change*. Cambridge: Polity Press.
Farr, R. 1990 The social psychology of the prefix 'inter': A prologue to the study of dialogue. In Marková, I. and Foppa, K. (eds) *The dynamics of dialogue*: 25–44. New York: Harvester Wheatsheaf.
Feyerabend, P. 1987 *Farewell to reason*. London: Verso.
Fisher, C. D. 1978 The effects of personal control, competence, and extrinsic reward systems on intrinsic motivation. *Organizational Behavior and Human Performance*, 21, 273–88.
Flanagan, O. 1992 *Consciousness reconsidered*. Cambridge, MA: MIT.
Flesch, R. 1951 *The art of clear thinking*. New York: Barnes & Noble.
Ford, M. E. 1992 *Motivating humans: Goals, emotions, and personal agency beliefs*. Newbury Park, CA: Sage Publications.

Forrester, M. A. 1992 *The development of young children's social-cognitive skills.* Hove: Lawrence Erlbaum Associates.

Foucault, M. 1972 *The archeology of knowledge.* New York: Pantheon.

Foucault, M. 1977 *Discipline and punish: The birth of the prison.* New York: Pantheon.

Freire, P. 1972 *Pedagogy of the Oppressed* New York: Herder & Herder.

Fries, C. 1952 *The structure of English.* London: Longman.

Gallimore, R. and Tharp, R. G. 1983 *The regulatory effect of teacher questions: A microanalysis of reading comprehension lessons* (Report No. 109). Honolulu: Center for the Development of Early Education: The Kamehameha schools.

Gallimore, R. and Tharp, R. G. 1990 Teaching mind in society: Teaching, schooling, and literate discourse. In Moll, Luis C. (ed) *Vygotsky and education: Instructional implications and applications of sociohistorical psychology*: 175–205. Cambridge: Cambridge University Press.

Gardner, H. 1985 *The mind's new science.* New York: Basic Books.

Gardner, H. 1991 *The unschooled mind.* New York: Basic Books.

Gardner, R. C. 1985 *Social psychology and language learning: The role of attitudes and motivation.* London: Edward Arnold.

Gardner, R. C. 1991 Second-language learning in adults: Correlates of proficiency. *Applied Language Learning,* 2 (1), 1–28.

Gardner, R. C. and Lambert, W. E. 1972 Attitudes and motivation in second language learning. Rowley, MA: Newbury House.

Gardner, R. C. and Tremblay, P. F. 1994 On motivation, research agendas, and theoretical frameworks. *The Modern Language Journal* 78 (iii): 359–68.

Garfinkel, H. 1967 *Studies in ethnomethodology.* Englewood Cliffs: Prentice-Hall.

Garfinkel, H. and Sacks, H. 1970 On formal structures of practical actions. In McKinney, J. C. and Tiryakian, E. A. (eds) *Theoretical sociology*: 338–66. New York: Appleton Century Crofts.

Gass, S. M. 1991 Grammar instruction, selective attention and learning processes. In R. Phillipson, E. Kellerman, L. Selinker, M. Sharwood Smith, and M. Swain (eds), *Foreign/second language pedagogy research: A commemorative volume for Claus Faerch*: 134–41 Clevedon: Multilingual Matters.

Gass, S. and Madden, C. (eds) 1985 *Input in second language acquisition.* Rowley, MA: Newbury House.

Gee, J. 1991. What is applied linguistics? Presentation at *Second Language Research Forum,* Los Angeles, March 1991.

Geertz, C. 1973. *The interpretation of cultures.* New York: Basic Books.

Gibson, E. J. 1991 *An odyssey in learning and perception.* Cambridge, MA: MIT Press.

Gibson, J. J. 1979 *The ecological approach to visual perception.* Boston: Houghton Mifflin.

Giddens, A. 1984. *The constitution of society.* Berkeley: University of California Press.

Giddens, A. 1991 *Modernity and self-identity: Self and society in the late modern age.* Stanford, CA: Stanford University Press.

Glachan, M. and Light, P. 1982 Peer interaction and learning: Can two wrongs make a right? In Butterworth, G. and Light, P (eds) *Social Cognition.* Brighton: Harvester Press.

Gleick, J. 1987 *Chaos: Making a new science.* New York: Penguin Books.

Goffman, E. 1981 *Forms of talk.* Oxford: Basil Blackwell.

Gombert, J. E. 1992 *Metalinguistic development*. New York: Harvester Wheatsheaf.

Goodman, K. 1986 *What's whole in whole language?* Portsmouth, NH: Heinemann.

Goodwin C. and Duranti, A. 1992 Rethinking context: An introduction. In Duranti, A. and Goodwin, C. (eds) *Rethinking context. Language as an interactive phenomenon*. Cambridge: Cambridge University Press. pp. 1–42.

Gould, S. J. 1993 *Eight little piggies: Reflections in natural history*. New York: W.W. Norton & Company.

Graddol, D, Maybin, J. and Stierer, B. (eds) 1994 *Researching language and literacy in social context*. Clevedon: Multilingual Matters.

Graman, T. 1990 Authentic vs. pseudodialogue in the second language classroom. *Hands On Language*, 2, 9–16.

Graumann, C. F. 1990 Perspectival structure and dynamics in dialogue. In Marková and Foppa (eds) *The dynamics of dialogue*. 105–26. New York: Harvester Wheatsheaf.

Greenleaf, C. and Freedman, S. W. 1993 Linking classroom discourse and classroom content: Following the trail of intellectual work in a writing lesson. *Discourse Processes* 16: 465–505.

Grice, P. 1989 *Studies in the way of words*. Cambridge, MA: Harvard University Press.

Gumperz, J. 1982 *Discourse strategies*. Cambridge: Cambridge University Press.

Gumperz, J. 1992 Contextualization and understanding. In Duranti, A. and Goodwin, C. (eds) *Rethinking context: Language as an interactive phenomenon*. Cambridge: Cambridge University Press. 229–52.

Habermas, J. 1984 *The theory of communicative action*, Vol.1. Boston: Beacon Press.

Habermas, J. 1987 *The theory of communicative action*, Vol.2. Boston: Beacon Press.

Halliday, M. A. K. 1973 A rich and adaptable instrument.' In Allen, J. P. B. and Corder, S. (eds) *Readings for Appied Linguistics*: 58–65. The Edinburgh Course in Applied Linguistics, Vol.1. Oxford: Oxford University Press.

Halliday, M. A. K. 1982 Linguistics in teacher education. In Carter, R. (ed) *Linguistics and the teacher*. London: Routledge & Kegan Paul. pp. 10–15.

Halliday, M. A. K. 1989 *Spoken and written language*. Oxford: Oxford University Press.

Halliday, M. A. K. and Hasan, R. 1989 *Language, context, and text: Aspects of language in a social-semiotic perspective*. Oxford: Oxford University Press.

Harlow, H. F. 1950 Learning and satiation of response in intrinsically motivated complex puzzle performance by monkeys. *Journal of Comparative and Physiological Psychology*, 43: 289–94.

Harmer, J. 1983. *The practice of English language teaching*. London: Longman.

Harris, M. 1992. *Language experience and early language development*. Hove: Lawrence Erlbaum Associates.

Harris, R. and Savitsky, F-F. (eds) 1988. *My personal language history*. London: New Beacon Books Ltd.

Harter, S. 1993 Visions of the self: Beyond the me in the mirror. In Jacobs, J. E. (ed) *Developmental perspectives on motivation*. 99–144. Nebraska Symposium on Motivation, Vol. 40, 1992. Lincoln, NE: University of Nebraska Press.

Hawkins, E. 1987a *Awareness of language: An introduction*. Cambridge: Cambridge University Press.

Hawkins, E. 1987b *Modern languages in the curriculum*. Cambridge: Cambridge University Press.

Hawkins, E. 1992 Awareness of language/knowledge about language in the curriculum in England and Wales: An historical note on twenty years of curricular debate. *Language Awareness*, 1(1): 5–13.

Hebb, D. O. 1955 Drives and the CNS (Conceptual Nervous System) *Psychological Review*, **62**, 244–7, 250–4.

Heckhausen, H. 1987 Causal attribution patterns for achievement outcomes: Individual differences, possible types and their origins. In Weinert, F. E. and Kluwe, R. H. (eds) *Metacognition, motivation, and understanding*: 143–84. Hillsdale, NJ: Lawrence Erlbaum Associates.

Heritage, J. and Atkinson, J. M. 1984 Introduction, in Atkinson, J. and Heritage, J. (eds) *Structures of social action*. 1–15. Cambridge: Cambridge University Press.

Higgs, T. V. and Clifford, R. 1982 The push toward communnciation. In Higgs, T. V. (ed) *Curriculum, competence, and the foreign language teacher*. 51–79 Lincolnwood, Il: National Textbook.

Hubbard, P., Jones, H., Thornton, B. and Wheeler, R. 1983. *A training course for TEFL*. Oxford: Oxford University Press.

Hull, C. L. 1943 *Principles of behavior: An introduction to behavior theory*. New York: Appleton-Century-Crofts.

Humphrey, N. 1992 *A history of the mind*. London: Vintage Books.

Hunt, J. McV. 1971 Using intrinsic motivation to teach young children. In *Personality growth and learning*, A Sourcebook prepared by the Personality growth and Learning Course Team: 223–9. London: Longman.

Jacobson, R. 1990 Allocating two languages as a key feature of a bilingual methodology. In Jacobson, R. and Faltis, C. (eds) *Language distribution issues in bilingual schooling*: 3–17. Clevedon: Multilingual Matters.

James, C., and Garrett, P. 1991a The scope of language awareness. In James, C. and Garrett, P. (eds), *Language awareness in the classroom:* 3–20. London: Longman.

James, C., and Garrett, P. (eds) 1991b *Language awareness in the classroom*. London: Longman.

Jarvis, G. A. 1981 Action research versus needed research for the 1980s. In Lange, D. L. (ed) *Proceedings of the National Conference on Professional Priorities*. Hastings-on-Hudson, NY: ACTFL Materials Center.

Johnson, K. and Morrow, K. (eds) 1981 *Communication in the classroom*. London: Longman.

Johnson, R. W. 1993 Where can teacher research lead? One teacher's daydream. *Educational Leadership* 51 (2): 66–8.

Jones, E. E. and Gerard, H. B. 1967 *Foundations of social psychology*. New York: John Wiley & Sons.

Kant, I. 1934 *Critique of pure reason*. London: Everyman, Dent.

Keller, J. M. 1983 Motivational design of instruction. In Reigeluth, C. (ed) *Instructional design theories and models*: 386–433. Hillsdale, NJ: L. Erlbaum.

Kemmis, S. and McTaggart, R. 1982 *The action research planner*. Victoria: Deakin University Press.

Kinginger, C. 1994 Learner initiative in conversation management: An application of van Lier's pilot coding scheme. *Modern Language Journal* 78 (1): 29–40.

Klein, W. 1985 *Second language acquisition*. Cambridge: Cambridge University Press.

Knowles, M. 1984 *The adult learner: A neglected species*. Houston: Gulf Publications.

Kohl, H. 1965 *The age of complexity*. New York: Mentor Books.

Kohn, A. 1991a Group grade grubbing versus cooperative learning. *Educational Leadership*, **48** (5): 83–7.

Kohn, A. 1991b Don`t spoil the promise of cooperative learning: Response to Slavin. *Educational Leadership*, **48** (5): 93–4.

Kohn, A. 1993 *Punished by rewards: The trouble with gold stars, incentive plans, A's, praise and other bribes*. New York: Houghton Mifflin.

Kolb, D. A. 1984 *Experiential learning: Experience as the source of learning and development*. Englewood Cliffs, NJ: Prentice-Hall.

Kozulin, A. 1990 *Vygoytsky's psychology: A biography of ideas*. New York: Harvester Wheatsheaf.

Krahnke, K. 1987 *Approaches to syllabus design for foreign language teaching*. Englewood Cliffs, NJ: Prentice-Hall.

Krashen, S. 1985. *The input hypothesis: Issues and implications*. London: Longman

Krashen, S. 1990 Reading, Writing, Form, and Content. In *Georgetown University Round Table on Lanugages and Linguistics 1990*: 364–376. Washington, D.C.: Georgetown University Press.

Kuhn, T. S. 1970 *The structure of scientific revolutions*. Chicago: The University of Chicago Press.

Kumaravadivelu, B. 1993 The name of the task and the task of naming: Methodological aspects of task-based pedagogy. In Crookes, G. and Gass, S. M. (eds) *Tasks in a pedagogical context: Integrating theory and practice*: 69–89. Clevedon: Multilingual Matters.

Lakoff, G. 1987 *Women, fire, and dangerous things*. Chicago: University of Chicago Press.

Langacker, R. W. 1987 *Foundations of cognitive grammar: Volume I, Theoretical prerequisites*. Stanford: Stanford University Press.

Langer, E. 1989 *Mindfulness*. Reading, MA: Addison-Wesley.

Lantolf, J. P. and Appel, G. (eds) 1994 *Vygotskyan approaches to second language research*. Norwood, NJ: Ablex Publishing Corporation.

Larsen-Freeman, D. 1986 *Techniques and Principles*. Oxford: Oxford University Press.

Lee, M. 1988 Language, perception and the world. In Hawkins, J. A. (ed) Explaining language universals: 211–46. Oxford: Basil Blackwell.

Leguin, U. 1974 *The dispossessed*. New York: Harper & Row.

Legutke, M. and Thomas, H. 1991 *Process and experience in the language classroom*. London: Longman.

Leithwood, K. 1986 *Planned educational change*. Toronto: OISE Press.

Leont'ev, A. A. 1977 Some problems in learning Russian as a foreign language. In Cole, M. (ed) *Soviet developmental psychology*: 457–515. White Plains, NY: M. E. Sharpe.

Levelt, W. 1989 *Speaking. From intention to articulation*. Cambridge, MA: MIT.

Levinson, S. 1983 *Pragmatics*. Cambridge: Cambridge University Press.

Lewin, R. 1993 *Complexity: Life at the edge of chaos*. London: Phoenix.

Lier, J. and Bufe, B. 1993 Quantum leap – A teacher and a consultant change jobs. *Educational Leadership* **51** (2): 26–7.

Linnell, P. and Luckmann, T. 1991 Asymmetries in dialogue: Some conceptual preliminaries. In Marková, I. and Foppa, K. (eds) *Asymmetries in dialogue*: 1–20. Hemel Hempstead: Harvester Wheatsheaf.

Literacy and Language Task Force 1990 The language of Australia: Discussion paper on an Australian Literacy and Language Policy for the 1990s. Canberra, Australia: Department of Employment, Education and Training.

Littlewood, W. 1981 *Communicative language teaching: An introduction*. Boston, MA: Heinle & Heinle.

Long, M. 1985 Input and second language acquisition theory. In Gass, S. and Madden, C. (eds) *Input in second language acquisition*: 377–93. Rowley, MA: Newbury House.

Luckmann, T. 1990 Social communication, dialogue and conversation. In Marková, I. and Foppa, K. (eds) *The dynamics of dialogue*: 45–61. New York: Harvester Wheatsheaf.

Madaus, G. F. and Kellaghan, T. 1992 Curriculum evaluation and assessment. In Jackson, P. W. (ed) *Handbook of curriculum research*: 119–56. New York: Macmillan Publishing Company.

Maehr, M. L. 1976 Continuing motivation: An analysis of a seldom considered educational outcome. *Review of Educational Research*, **46**: 443–62.

Maeroff, G. I. 1994 My ordinary career: An ordinary teacher reflects on life in the trenches. *Education Week*, **XIII**, 31, 16–21.

Marcus, H. and Zajonc, R. B. 1985 The cognitive perspective in social psychology. In Lindzey, G. and Aronson, E. (eds) *Handbook of social psychology*: 137–230. Third Edition. Volume I: Theory and method. New York: Random House.

Marková, I. 1982 *Paradigms, thought and language*. New York: Wiley.

Marková, I. 1991 Asymmetries in group conversations between a tutor and people with learning difficulties. In Marková, I. and Foppa, K. (eds) *Asymmetries in dialogue*: 221–40. Hemel Hempstead: Harvester Wheatsheaf.

Maslow, A. 1971 *The farther reaches of human nature*. Harmondsworth: Penguin.

Maybin, J. 1994 Children's voices: Talk, knowledge and identity. In Graddol, D., Maybin, J. and Stierer, B. (eds) *Researching language and literacy in social context*: 131–50. Clevedon: Multilingual Matters.

McClenaghan, W. A. 1987 *Magruder's American government*. Newton, MA: Allyn & Bacon.

McLaughlin, B. 1990 'Conscious' versus 'unconscious' learning. *TESOL Quarterly* **24**, 4: 617–34.

McNiff, J. 1988 *Action research: Principles and practice*. London: Routledge.

McNiff, J. 1992 *Teaching as learning: An action research approach*. London: Routledge.

Meek, A, 1991 On thinking about teaching: A conversation with Eleanor Duckworth. *Educational Leadership* **48**, 6, 30–4.

Mehan, H. 1979 *Learning lessons*. Cambridge, MA: Harvard University Press.

Merleau-Ponty 1945 *Phenomenology of perception*. New York: Humanities Press International.

Milk, R. D. 1985 Can foreigners do 'foreigner talk'?: A study of the linguistic input provided by non-native teachers of EFL. Paper presented at the Colloquium on Classroom-Centered Research, TESOL International Conference, New York, April 8, 1985.

Minsky, M. 1985 *The society of mind*. New York: Simon & Schuster.

Mitchell, R., and Hooper, J. 1991 Teachers' views of language knowledge. In James, C. and Garrett, P. (eds), *Language awareness in the classroom*: 40–50. London: Longman.

Mohan, B. 1986 *Language and content*. Reading, MA: Addison-Wesley.

Moll, L. (ed) 1990 *Vygotsky and education*. Cambridge: Cambridge University Press.

Monk, R. 1991 *Wittgenstein: The duty of genius*. New York: Penguin Books.

Montessori, M. 1965. *Spontaneous activity in education*. New York: Shocken. (First published in English in 1917.)

Morris, P. 1994 Introduction. In Morris, P. (ed) *The Bakhtin reader: Selected writings of Bakhtin, Medvedev, Voloshinov*: 1–24. London: Edward Arnold.

Morrow, K. 1981 Principles of communicative methodology. In Morrow, K. and Johnson, K. (eds), *Communication in the classroom*: 59–66 London: Longman.

Moskowitz, R. 1978 *Caring and sharing in the foreign language class*. Rowley, MA: Newbury House.

Murray, L. and Trevarthen, C. 1985 Emotional regulation of interactions between two-month-olds and their mothers. In Field, T. and Fox, N. (eds) *Social perception in infants*: 177–197. Norwood, NJ: Ablex.

Neisser, U. 1976 *Cognition and reality*. San Francisco: Freeman.

Newman, D., Griffin, P., and Cole, M. 1989 *The construction zone: Working for cognitive change in school*. Cambridge: Cambridge University Press.

Newmeyer, F. J. and Weinberger, S. H. 1988 The ontogenesis of the field of second language learning research. In Flynn, S. and O'Neill, W. (eds) *Linguistic theory in second language acquisition*: 34–45. Dordrecht: Kluwer Academic Publishers.

Nicholas, H. 1991 Language awareness and second language development. In James, C. and Garrett, P. (eds) *Language awareness in the classroom*: 78–95. London: Longman.

Nixon, J. (ed) 1982 *A teacher's guide to action research*. London: Grant McIntyre.

Nolasco, R. and Arthur, L. 1988 *Conversation*. Oxford: Oxford University Press.

Nunan, D. 1988 *The learner-centered curriculum*. Cambridge: Cambridge University Press.

Nunan, D. 1989 *Designing tasks for the communicative classroom*. Cambridge: Cambridge University Press.

Oller, J. 1990 Semiotic theory and language acquisition. In *Georgetown University Round Table on Lanugages and Linguistics 1990*: 65–89. Washington, DC: Georgetown University Press.

Oller, J. and Richard-Amato, P. 1983 *Methods that work*. Rowley, MA: Newbury House.

Ontario Ministry of Education. 1984 *Ontario Schools: Intermediate and Senior Divisions*. Toronto: Ministry of Education.

Oxford, R. and Shearin, J. 1994 Language learning motivation: Expanding the theoretical framework. *The Modern Language Journal* 78 (i): 12–28.

Palincsar, A. and Brown, A. 1984 Reciprocal teaching of comprehension-fostering comprehension-monitoring activities. *Cognition and Instruction*, 1 (2), 118–175.

Parsons, T. 1937 *The structure of social action*. Glencoe: Free Press.

Paulston, C. B. and Bruder, M. 1976 *Teaching English as a second language: Techniques and procedures*. Cambridge, MA: Winthrop.

Peake, M. 1950 *Gormenghast*. Harmondsworth: Penguin.

Peddiwell, J. A. 1939 *The saber-tooth curriculum*. New York: McGraw-Hill.

Peterson, C. and Seligman, M. E. P. 1987 Helplessness and attributional style in depression. In Weinert, F. E. and Kluwe, R. H. (eds) *Metacognition, motivation, and understanding*:185–215. Hillsdale, NJ: Lawrence Erlbaum Associates.

Pfaff, C. (ed) 1987 *First and second language acquisition processes*. Cambridge, MA: Newbury House.

Piaget, J. 1932 *The moral judgment of the child*. Harmondsworth: Penguin.

Piaget, J. 1971 *Biology and knowledge*. Chicago: University of Chicago Press.

Piaget, J. 1976 *The grasp of consciousness: Action and concept in the young child*. Cambridge, MA: Harvard University Press

Piaget, J. 1978 *Success and understanding*. Cambridge, MA: Harvard University Press.

Pica, T., Young, R. and Doughty, C. 1987 The impact of interaction on comprehension. *TESOL Quarterly* 21 (4):737–758.

Pinker, S. 1994 *The language instinct: How the mind creates language*. New York: Morrow.

Plato's *Meno*. 1976 translated by G. M. A. Grube. Indianapolis: Hacket Publishing Company, Inc.

Polanyi, M. 1958 *Personal knowledge*. London: Routledge & Kegan Paul.

Politzer, R. 1970 Some reflections on 'good' and 'bad' language teaching behaviors. *Language Learning* 20: 31–43.

Potter, M. C. 1990 Remembering. In Osherson, D. N. and Smith, E. E. (eds) *Thinking*. 3–32. Cambridge, MA: MIT Press.

Prabhu, N. S. 1987 *Second language pedagogy*. Oxford: Oxford University Press.

Price, H. H. 1969 *Thinking and experience*. London: Hutchinson.

Pullum, G. 1991 *The great Eskimo vocabulary hoax and other irreverent essays on the study of language*. Chicago: The University of Chicago Press.

Pylyshyn, Z. 1984 *Computation and cognition: Toward a foundation for cognitive science*. Cambridge, MA: MIT.

Rabinow, P. (ed) 1984 *The Foucault reader*. New York: Pantheon.

Rampton, B. 1987 Stylistic variability and not speaking 'normal' English: Some post-Labovian approaches and their implications for the study of internalnguage. In Ellis, R. (ed) *Second language acquisition in context*: 47–58. London: Prentice-Hall.

Restak, R. 1991 *The brain has a mind of its own*. New York: Harmony Books.

Richards, J. C., Hull, J. and Proctor, S. 1991 *Interchange. Book 3*. Cambridge: Cambridge University Press.

Richards, J. and Rodgers, T. S. 1986 *Approaches and methods in language teaching: A description and analysis*. Cambridge: Cambridge University Press.

Ringbom, H. 1987 *The role of the first language in foreign language learning*. Clevedon: Multilingual Matters.

Rivers, W. and Temperley M. 1978 *A practical guide to the teaching of English as a second or foreign language*. New York: Oxford University Press.

Rodriguez, R, 1982 *Hunger of memory*. New York: Bantam Books.

Rogoff, B. 1990 *Apprenticeship in thinking*. New York: Oxford University Press.

Rogoff, B. and Gardner, W. 1984 Adult guidance in cognitive development. In Rogoff, B. and Lave, J. (eds) *Everyday cognition: Its development in social contexts*. Cambridge, MA: Harvard University Press.

Romaine, S. 1989 *Bilingualism*. Oxford: Blackwell.

Rommetveit, R. 1974 *On message structure*. New York: Wiley.

Rost, M. 1990 *Listening in language learning*. London: Longman.

Rowe, M. B. 1974 Wait-time and rewards as instructional variables. *Journal of Research in Science Teaching*, 11: 81–94.

Royen, G. 1947 *Taalkundig inzicht voor school en leven*. Tilburg: Drukkerij van het R. K. Jongensweeshuis.

Rudduck, J. 1991 *Innovation and change*. Milton Keynes: Open University Press.

Rudduck, J. and Hopkins, D. (eds) 1985 *Resesarch as a basis for teaching: Readings from the work of Lawrence Stenhouse*. London: Heineman.

Rutherford, W. E. 1987 *Second language grammar: Learning and teaching*. London: Longman.

Ryan, R. M. and Connell, J. P. 1989 Perceived locus of causality and internalization. *Journal of Personality and Social Psychology*, 57 (5): 749–61.

Ryan, R. M., Connell, J. P. and Grolnick, W. S. 1992 When achievement is not intrinsically motivated: A theory of internalization and self-regulation in school. In Boggiano, A. K. and Pittman, T. S. (eds) *Achievement and motivation: A social-developmental perspective*: 167–88. Cambridge: Cambridge University Press. pp.167-88.

Ryff, C. 1985 Adult personality development and the motivation for personal growth. In Kleiber, D. A. and Maehr, M. L. (eds) *Motivation and adulthood. Advances in motivation and achievement, Vol. 4*: 55–92. Greenwich, Conn.: LAI Press Inc.

Ryle, G. 1949 *The concept of mind*. London: Hutchinson (reprinted by Penguin, 1963).

Sacks, H., Schegloff, E. A. and Jefferson, G. 1974. Towards a simplest systematics for the organization of turn taking for conversation. *Language* 50 (4): 698–735.

Sartre, J. P. 1957 *Being and nothingness*. London: Methuen.

Sartre, J. P. 1992 *Notebooks for an ethics*. Chicago: Univeristy of Chicago Press.

Savignon, S. 1983 *Communicativce competence: Theory and classroom practice*. Reading, MA: Addison-Wesley.

Schegloff, E. 1972 Notes on a conversational practice: Formulating place. In Sudnow, D. N. (ed) *Studies in social interaction*. New York: Free Press.

Schmidt, R. 1990 T*he role of consciousness in second language learning. Applied Linguistics* 11, 129–58.

Schmidt, R. 1994 Deconstructing consciousness in search of useful definitions for applied linguistics. *Revue de L'AILA Review* 11: pp. 11–26.

Schmidt, R. and Frota, S. N. 1986 Developing basic conversational ability in a second language: A case study of an adult learner of Portuguese. In Day, R. R. (ed) *Talking to Learn: Conversation in second language acquisition*: 237–326, Rowley, MA: Newbury House.

Schneiders, A. J. 1937 Taalbegrip. *Taal en Leven* 1 (2):33–40.

Schön, D. 1983 *The reflective practitioner*. London: Temple Smith.

Schumann, J. 1990 The role of the amygdala as a mediator of acculturation and cognition in second language acquisition. In *Georgetown University Round Table on Lanuages and Linguistics 1990*: 169–176. Washington, DC: Georgetown University Press.

Searle, J. 1969 *Speech acts*. Cambridge: Cambridge University Press.

Seligman, M. E. P. 1981 A learned helplessness point of view. In Rehm, L. P. (ed) *Behavior therapy for depression: Present status and future directions*. New York: Academic Press.

Sharwood Smith, M. 1981 Consciousness-raising and the second language learner. *Applied Linguistics* 2: 159–69.

Shor, I. 1992 *Empowering education: Critical teaching for social change*. Chicago: The University of Chicago Press.

Shulman, L. 1987 Sounding an alarm: A reply to Sockett. *Harvard Educational Review* 57 (4): 473–82.

Shuy, R. 1991 Secretary Bennett's teaching: An argument for responsive teaching. In Eisner, E. *The enlightened eye: Qualitative inquiry and the enhancement of educational practice*: 135–49. New York: Macmillan.

Shweder, R. A. 1990 Cultural psychology – what is it? In Stigler, J. W., Shweder, R. A. and Herdt, G. (eds) *Cultural psychology: The Chicago symposium on culture and human development*. Cambridge: Cambridge University Press.

Sinclair, J. M. and Coulthard, M. 1975 *Towards an anlysis of discourse*. Oxford: Oxford University Press.

Skinner, B. F. 1953 *Science and human behavior*. New York: Macmillan.

Slavin, R. E. 1991 Group rewards make groupwork work: Response to Kohn. *Educational Leadership*, 48 (5): 89–91.

Slobin, D. (ed) 1985 *The crosslinguistic study of language acquisition*. Vols. I and II. Hillsdale, NJ: Lawrence Erlbaum.

Smith, F. 1986 *Insult to intelligence: The bureaucratization of our schools*. London: Heinemann.

Smith, W. E. 1974 The effects of social and monetary rewards on intrinsic motivation. Unpublished doctoral dissertation. Cornell University.

Sorace, A. 1985 Metalinguistic knowledge and language use in acquisition-poor environments. *Applied Linguistics*, 6 (3), 239–54.

Sperber, D. and Wilson, D. 1986 *Relevance: Communication and cognition*. Cambridge: Cambridge University Press.

Stenhouse, L. 1975 *An introduction to curriculum research and development*. London: Heinemann.

Sternberg, R. J. 1990 Prototypes of competence and incompetence. In Sternberg, R. J. and Kolligian, J. (eds) *Competence considered*: 117–145. New Haven: Yale University Press.

Sternberg, R. J., Okagaki, L. and Jackson, A. S. 1990 Practical intelligence for success in school. *Educational Leadership* 48 (1): 35–39.

Stevick, E. 1976 *Memory, meaning, and method*. Newbury House.

Stevick, E. 1980 *Teaching languages: A way and ways*. Rowley: Newbury House.

Stites, J. 1994 Complexity. *Omni*, May 1994: 42–52.

Sullivan, E. 1990 *Critical psychology and pedagogy: Interpretation of the personal world*. Toronto: OISE Press.

Sullivan, M. J. L. and Conway, M. 1989 Negative affect leads to low-effort cognition: Attributional processing for observed social behavior. *Social Cognition*, 7 (4): 315–37.

Swain, M. 1991 Manipulating and complementing content teaching to maximise second language learning. In Phillipson, R., Kellerman, E., Selinker, L., Sharwood Smith, M. and Swain, M. (eds), *Foreign/second language pedagogy research: A commemorative volume for Claus Faerch*: 234–50 Clevedon: Multilingual Matters.

Tarone, E. 1988 *Variation in interlanguage*. London: Edward Arnold.

Tharp, R. and. Gallimore, R. 1988 *Rousing minds to life*. Cambridge: Cambridge University Press.

Tinkel, A. J. 1988 *Explorations in language*. Cambridge: Cambridge University Press.

Treffert, D. 1989 *Extraordinary people: Redefining the 'idiot savant.'* New York: Harper & Row.

Trevarthen, C. and Marwick, H. 1986 Signs of motivation for speech on infants, and the nature of a mother's support for development of language. In Lindblom, B. and Zetterström, R. (eds) *Precursors of early speech*: 279–308. Wenner Gren International Symposium Series, Vol. 44. New York: Stockton Press.

Trueba, H. T. 1989 *Raising silent voices: Educating linguistic minorities for the 21st Century*. New York: Newbury House.

Tucker, G. R. 1986 Developing a language-competent American society. In Tannen D. and Alatis J. E. (eds), *Georgetown University Round Table on Languages and Linguistics*: 263–74. Washington, DC: Georgetown University Press.

Tudge, J. 1990 Vygotsky, the zone of proximal development, and peer collaboration: Implications for classroom practice. In Moll, L. C. (ed) *Vygotsky and education: Instructional implications and applications of sociohistorical psychology*. Cambridge: Cambridge University Press. 155–72.

Vallerand, R. J., Blais, M. R., Brière, N. M. and Pelletier, L. G. 1989 Construction et validation de l'échelle de motivation en éducation (EME). *Canadian Journal of Behavioral Science* 21, 3, 323–49.

van der Veer, R. and Valsiner, J. 1991 *Understanding Vygotsky: A quest for synthesis*. Oxford: Basil Blackwell.

van Essen, A. 1992 Language awareness in the Netherlands. *Language Awareness*, 1,1:19–26.

van Lier, L. 1988 *The classroom and the language learner*. London: Longman.

van Lier, L. 1989 Reeling, writhing, drawling, stretching, and fainting in coils: Oral proficiency interviews as conversation.*TESOL Quarterly*, 23 (3): 489–508.

van Lier, L. 1991a. Inside the classroom: Learning processes and teaching procedures. *Applied Language Learning*. 1 (2): 29–69.

van Lier, L. 1991b Language awareness: The common ground between linguist and language teacher. *Georgetown University Round Table* 1991: 528–46. Washington, DC: Georgetown University Press.

van Lier, L. 1991c Doing applied linguistics. *Issues in Second Language Acquisition*, 2 (1): 78–81.

van Lier, L. 1992 Not the nine o'clock linguistics class: Investigating contingency grammar. *Language Awareness*, 1 (2): 91–108.

van Lier, L. 1994 Forks and hope: Pursuing understanding in different ways. *Applied Linguistics* 15 (3): 328–345.

van Lier, L. 1995a *Introducing language awareness*. London: Penguin Books.

van Lier, L. 1995b Some features of a theory of practice. *TESOL Journal* 4 (1): 6–10.

van Lier, L. and Matsuo, N. n.d. Variation in interlanguage conversations. Unpublished manuscript, Monterey Institute of International Studies.

van Manen, M. 1991 *The tact of teaching: The meaning of pedagogical thoughtfulness*. Albany: State University of New York Press.

Vygotsky, L. S. 1978 *Mind in society*. Cambridge, MA: Harvard University Press.

Vygotsky, L. S. 1986 (1962) *Thought and Language* (new edn. A. Kozulin). Cambridge, MA: MIT.

Weinert, F. E. and Kluwe, R. W. 1987 *Metacognition, motivation, and understanding*. Hillsdale, NJ: Lawrence Erlbaum Associates.

Weiss, J. R. and Cameron, A. M. 1985 Individual differences in the student's sense of control. In Ames, C. and Ames, R. (eds) *Research on motivation in education, Volume 2: The classroom milieu*: 93–140. New York: Academic Press.

Wells, G. 1985 *Language development in the preschool years*. Cambridge: Cambridge University Press.

Wells, G. 1993 Reevaluating the IRF sequence: A proposal for the articulation of theories of activity and discourse for the analysis of teaching and learning in the classroom. *Linguistics in Education* 5: 1–37.

Wertsch, J. V. 1985 *Vygotsky and the social formation of mind*. Cambridge, MA.: Harvard University Press.

Wertsch, J. V. 1991 *Voices of the mind*. Cambridge, MA: Harvard University Press.

Westbrook, R. B. 1991 *John Dewey and American democracy*. Ithaca, NY: Cornell University Press.

White, R. W. 1959 Motivation reconsidered: The concept of competence. *Psychological Review* 66: 297–333.

Widdowson, H. G. 1979 *Teaching language as communication*. Oxford: Oxford University Press.

Widdowson, H. G. 1990 *Aspects of language teaching*. Oxford: Oxford University Press.

Willing, K. 1989 *Teaching how to learn: Learning strategies in ESL*. Sydney: National Centre for English Language Teaching and Research.

Willis, J. 1981 *Teaching English through English*. London: Longman.

Willis, P. 1981 *Learning to labor: How working class kids get working class jobs*. New York: Columbia University Press.

Wittgenstein, L. 1958a *The blue and brown books*. Oxford: Basil Blackwell.

Wittgenstein, L. 1958b *Philosophical investigations*. New York: Macmillan.

Wittgenstein, L. 1980a *Remarks on the philosophy of psychology*. Chicago: The University of Chicago Press.

Wittgenstein, L. 1980b *Culture and value*. Chicago: The University of Chicago Press. (translation of *Vermischte Bemerkungen*).

Wood, D. 1988 *How children think and learn*. Oxford: Basil Blackwell.

Young, R. 1992 *Critical theory and classroom talk*. Clevedon: Multilingual Matters.

Zeichner, K. M. 1983 Alternative paradigms of teacher education. *Journal of Teacher Education* 34 (3): 3–9.

Index

Abraham, A. 38, 200
access 35, 41–2, 44, 53, 57, 77
accommodation 130
accountability 14, 16, 27, 40, 120–1, 210–11, 222, 223
achievement 3, 13–16, 19, 35, 40, 98, 117–19, 121, 135, 185, 202, 210–11, 222–4
action research 1, 2, 4, 18, 30, 31–4, 42, 106, 196, 217, 219–21
activation 51–2, 57
Adair-Hauck, B. 152, 162
affect, see emotion
affordance 12, 36, 52–3, 66, 118, 122, 171
Allwright, D. 32, 48, 105, 177
Ancess, J. 223–4
Anderson, J.R. 57, 77, 83
Apel, K.O. 135–6
Appel, G. 27
apprehension 41, 54, 56–7, 66
Armstrong, D.M. 97
Arnold, M.B. 54
Arthur, L. 97
assessment 3, 16, 27, 40, 99, 117–18, 120–1, 154, 156, 202, 210–11, 213, 222–4
self-assessment 16, 119, 211
Atkinson, J.M. 146, 168, 170
attention 2, 11, 41, 49, 51–3, 66–7, 69, 72, 75, 77, 97, 102, 105, 147, 152, 171, 181, 202, 215
audience design 129, 133, 136
audiolingualism 73
Austin, J. 157
authentication 124, 126–8, 131, 133–6, 139, 144–5, 209
authenticity 10, 13, 14, 16, 19, 20, 22, 40–2, 66, 121, 123–46, 166, 175, 209, 215, 223
existential 143–4
interactional 139–43
materials 136–8
personal 143–4, 209
authoritarian 142, 181
authority 28, 38, 141, 181
automatic, automatization 56–7, 67, 70

autonomy 10, 12–16, 19, 20, 22, 31, 40–2, 57, 67, 72, 98, 108–10, 118–21, 134, 136, 139, 144, 145, 146, 156, 163, 178, 181, 185, 204, 209, 214, 215, 219
autotelic 4, 13, 56, 121, 185
awareness 2, 10–16, 19, 20, 22, 40–2, 49, 52, 56, 67, 69, 76, 77, 133–4, 147, 171, 215
awareness raising 34, 83, 203
critical language awareness 82, 89, 117, 134, 209
language awareness 12, 18, 42, 53, 68–97, 134
learning awareness training 42, 53, 68–97, 135
axiology 3, 10, 37, 125

Bailey, K. 32, 48, 105
Bain, R. 81, 93, 221
Bakhtin, M.M. 157, 166, 174, 181, 183–4, 187, 216
Barnes, D. 151
Barnfield, J. 221
Bateson, G. 36
Beebe, L. 130
behaviorism 73, 100, 108, 115, 170
Bell, A. 129
Bellack, A.A. 149, 151
Bem, D. 119
Bennett, C.K. 29, 220
Bennett, W. 160, 162–3, 164, 186
Bergson, H. 55
Berlak, A. 180
Berlak, H. 180
Berlyne, D.E. 100, 110
Best, C.T. 200, 213
Bialystok, E. 83
bilingual 19, 45, 47, 68, 90
Birdsong, D. 74, 76–7, 83, 96
Bolinger, D. 83
Bourdieu, P. 4, 7, 24, 39, 54, 86, 157, 158, 160, 161, 164, 188, 225
Bowers, C.A. 36, 160, 164, 200, 213
Breen, M. 23, 67, 126–7, 133, 139, 204, 210
Brinton, D.M. 205